Amanda Minnie Douglas

In trust

Dr. Bertrand's household

Amanda Minnie Douglas

In trust
Dr. Bertrand's household

ISBN/EAN: 9783337150570

Printed in Europe, USA, Canada, Australia, Japan

Cover: Foto ©Andreas Hilbeck / pixelio.de

More available books at **www.hansebooks.com**

IN TRUST;

OR,

DR. BERTRAND'S HOUSEHOLD.

BY

AMANDA M. DOUGLASS.

BOSTON:
LEE AND SHEPARD, PUBLISHERS.
NEW YORK:
LEE, SHEPARD & DILLINGHAM, 49 GREENE STREET.
1872.

DEDICATION.

IN MEMORY OF DREAMS LONG CHERISHED;

IN MEMORY OF PLEASANT WALKS AND PLEASANT TALKS,

AND YEARS OF TRUEST AFFECTION,

I DEDICATE THIS BOOK TO

My Brother and my Sister.

IN TRUST;

DR. BERTRAND'S HOUSEHOLD.

CHAPTER I.

> I see thee sitting crowned with good,
>   A central warmth diffusing bliss
>   In glance and smile, and clasp and kiss,
> On all the branches of thy blood.
> TENNYSON.

> Out of the day and night
> A joy has taken its flight.
> SHELLEY.

"It's all settled, then, Richard?"

"With your approval, yes. Ada liked the plan as much as I did. She was disappointed at not going to Europe last year with her uncle."

"But she will enjoy it better, now, eh?" and Dr. Bertrand looked up with a roguish twinkle in his merry hazel eye. "Well, you must not devote all your time to love; use your eyes and ears to some purpose, and come back with increased wisdom and experience. A young man may gain many a useful hint from those London and Paris physicians. And, Dick—"

Dr. Bertrand's pause was so long that Richard turned around, and found his father's eyes fixed steadily on the carpet. Presently he began:—

"I was about to remark, Dick, that Ada's fortune has been attended to. I suppose it is all settled on herself?"

A warm color flushed the young man's face as he answered, "Yes, I insisted upon her retaining undisputed possession of it, although she thought it unnecessary."

"Right. I want no one to call Dr. Bertrand's son a fortune-hunter. I've arranged yours so there'll be no trouble. Marchand & Co. will attend to it here and at Paris. Don't give yourself a moment's uneasiness for the next two years. When you return, I shall divide my practice; it's too large for me now. I want to make a little money for the other children, and then—"

"We shall all be grown up and settled around you, striving to make you the happiest of fathers."

"A long while to look forward," Dr. Bertrand exclaimed, musingly. "In any event, Dick, you will have the consolation that you have been a dutiful son—a comfort and a blessing. You'll remember this if you should come back, and—"

"Don't," interrupted Richard, suddenly.

Dr. Bertrand laughed, raised himself to his full height, swelled out his broad chest by a deep inspiration, and brought his fat, dimpled hand down on his son's shoulder. "No," he said, laughingly; "I don't look much like 'the retired physician whose sands of life have nearly run out;' yet the Master warned us always to be ready. Twenty-six years ago! I was thinking it over just as you came in: how happy we were that night,—*she* singing those sweet old Scotch ballads until the room rang with her melody,— and how I picked her up in my arms, and carried her off to her room; yet before dawn she had kissed me for the last time, and gone home with the angels. But God has reconciled me to it through my boy's unselfish affection, and his high, unerring sense of honor. You have never cost me an hour's anxiety, Richard: you have been kind and obedient to her who took your mother's place, and a fond brother to the rest. In the new life opening before you, though you'll never forget us, another is to share your love; children will grow up around you, increasing your cares and interest; and God grant they may be as faithful to you as you have been to me."

Dr. Bertrand resumed his seat, and leaned his head on his hand, while there fell between them a deep and touching silence, broken at length by Richard, who said, in a full, tender tone, "Thank you a hundred times for your praise and your priceless love, and believe me I shall never think of you otherwise than as the best and dearest friend I ever had."

Dr. Bertrand pulled out his watch, and, with an attempt at gayety, exclaimed, "Eight o'clock, Richard; Ada will wonder if her lover means to turn truant."

He crimsoned visibly, picked up his gloves from the desk, then came back a step, and, leaning over his father, kissed the broad, white forehead that had always been his admiration. In a moment the doctor's arms were around his neck, and if in that clasp of truest love some tears came, who shall dare to call them weak? Perhaps both were wondering if they should meet and love in this same fashion, when the years with their changes had gone by. Then Dick raised his head, said in a soft whisper, "Good night," and walked gently out of the room.

His father fell into deep musing. In fancy he lived over the bright, brief past, read again the entrancing pages of that sweet first love, when he had blushed, and trembled, and feared to woo the fair girl who showed in so many ways her regard for him. And that country wedding, with its old-time music and dancing! It made his heart bound now when he heard, "Money Musk," "Irish Washerwoman," or "Miss McLeod's Reel," for it took him back to that night of all nights, and the year of bliss following. He had been a poor young doctor, not so old as Richard was now; yet poverty had no stings for them. It was like a glimpse of fairy land, until the strange, fearful night, burned by passionate grief to a depth beyond forgetfulness, when he kissed the small mouth, no longer warm and rosy, with the despairing fervor we give to the dead in the first moments of anguish, and took his little motherless boy in his arms, conscious that some golden thread of the life just gone up among the angels ran through it.

He had overlived his grief, removed to the city, prospered in his calling, and married again. Other baby faces had learned to smile on him, and the new mother never failed to care tenderly for her husband's first born. When his grand-father left Richard a small legacy, she was first to propose setting it aside until his majority. She, too, had gone to the better land, but her memory in Richard's heart was a pleasant one. He was now possessor of ten thousand dol-lars, a fine education, and a prospect before him of a good marriage, besides several years of foreign travel.

The children's voices in the room above broke up Dr. Bertrand's reverie. The gay, ringing laughs were irresisti-ble, and a moment later he was on his way up stairs to join the merriment. Opening the door, he saw his youngest, blindfolded, stretching out her dimpled arms in the vain endeavor to catch somebody; while the others, with aston-ishingly long steps, went from corner to corner, as if tread-ing on eggs, and their fingers to their lips, imploring silence in a most pathetic manner.

" O, Tessy, it's papa ! Now's your chance ; catch him ! "

Tessy stood uncertain, as if considering the whereabouts of the door, then made a sudden plunge in the opposite direction.

" What a little goose you are, Tess ! Come here, and let me feel for some feathers. She has caught every chair and table in the room, papa," exclaimed Archie.

The doctor made such a pretence of getting out of the way, they all laughed more heartily than before, and Tessy soon began to distinguish his step. Presently he marched into an unlucky corner, which she blockaded, and in another moment had him safe and fast. "Papa, papa!" she exclaimed, triumphantly, "Archie said I could not catch any one if I was blinded all night."

"We'll soon pay up Master Archie, I think," said her father, kissing her fondly.

"O, won't you all have to look out!" cried Lilian, dancing around. "There'll be lively scampering; and I do hope papa will lay violent hands on Archie the very first thing."

"Pooh!" was Master Archie's retort.

Tessy blindfolded her father, and held up her small fingers for him to count, laughing with delight when he said thirteen. Then she led him to the middle of the room, and they did indeed have to "scamper." Round and round went the doctor, his long arms reaching everywhere; yet, strange to say, they all managed to scramble off, and, when one achieved a remarkably close escape, the rest shouted with triumph. A knock at the door caused a lull in the merriment. Mabel opened it.

"If you please, doctor —"

"What is it, Martin?" and Dr. Bertrand freed his eyes.

"Mr. Bridges has just come up, and Mr. Smalley sends for you. He's had another bad turn. Will you go, sir?"

"I suppose I must," was the rather reluctant answer.

"I wouldn't stir a step. It's beginning to storm, and you'll take the journey for nothing. Next year, this time, you'll hear the same story."

"I think I had better go. Get up the horse, Martin."

"Let me drive, sir; it's a lonesome looking night."

"It is not worth while. I may have to remain some time."

Off went Martin, grumbling, "Why couldn't people die, and have done with it, when they alarmed the whole neighborhood! Mr. Smalley was good for twenty years yet, if he was an old man. There was no sense in a doctor's posting off such a night as this, unless the case was critical, or he was courting," Martin put in, as he remembered Mr. Richard.

The children lamented more loudly, but in a different strain. It was too bad to have their fun spoiled. Why wouldn't morning do as well? and they rang choruses on the key note, until Martin called out from the hall below, "Ready, doctor."

"You must be in bed and asleep before I come back; so good night," he said, kissing them all round. Mabel, nearly sixteen, tall and pretty; Lilian, wild and eager for play as a kitten, with the fine gold of thirteen summers in her clustering curls; Archie, next in order, bright and rosy-cheeked; and darling little Tessy, the household baby, who had not yet outgrown her trick of sitting in every one's lap. Now she clasped her arms around her father's neck, and declared he should not go.

"Mabel must put you to bed immediately, or to-morrow your eyes will be green, instead of blue. Come, kiss me once more, and send me off."

But he had to unclasp the little hands himself; and as he went out into the dark night, her laughing face, with its straggling rings of shining hair, seemed to light the way. How lovely and charming they all were! It was almost a pity to have them grow up men and women.

He drove rapidly through the drizzling rain, and soon reached his destination. The tidy housekeeper answered his summons, and he said, "Well?" inquiringly.

"Poor Mr. Smalley's just gone, sir. He dropped off quietly at the last. I always thought it would be sudden, but we had no such idea when Mr. Bridges left."

"When was he taken?"

"At five, sir. He was comfortable all the afternoon; then his old trouble about breathing came on. It was nearly seven when Mr. Bridges called, and he fancied he saw a change; so he said he would send you down."

"I started as soon as I received the message, but I could not have saved him, I suppose. When did he die?"

"Fifteen minutes or so ago," said the woman, lowering

her voice; for they had reached the apartment of death.
"He just breathed shorter and shorter, and did not seem to
suffer much."

Dr. Bertrand advanced to the bedside. The peculiar
pallor of the countenance told him life was extinct. A few
neighbors had gathered in consultation, but there was no
wife or children to break the silence with passionate sobbing.
How lonely the house seemed! No one to care for the dead
man with tenderest hands! Servants and strangers surrounded him; a few careless relatives would come on the
morrow, glad to inherit his wealth; but with the most it
would be, "Only an old man dead!"

Dr. Bertrand remained some time, discussing the preparations, and writing a few messages. The darkness was intense as he turned his horse homeward; but he thought of
his cheerful house and loving children, his heart rising to
God in thanksgiving for such blessings. Then the wind
brought a noisy, roistering sound of bacchanalian glee,
which caused him to start a little, listen, and hold the reins
firmly. The party was evidently nearing him; he could
hear the plunge of the horses, and the drunken oaths of the
driver, who seemed to be fiercely urging them on. There
was a sudden dash. He sat quite still, and shouted, "To
the right! keep to the right!" then a violent concussion, at
which his own horse reared; he felt himself unseated, thrown,
and striking against something with a crash that rendered
him senseless. The other party, righting themselves a little, went on their way, too far gone to even dream of the
harm they had done.

CHAPTER II.

The thread I held has slipped from out my hand;
In this dark labyrinth, without a clew,
Groping for guidance, stricken blind, I stand,
A helpless child that knows not what to do.

BAYARD TAYLOR.

"WHAT can be the matter? The doctor is driving like Jehu!" exclaimed Martin, taking up his lantern and walking to the stable. There stood the panting horse, the reins trailing, and fragments of the broken traces hanging to him. "Poor Robin, poor Robin, what has happened?" and he stroked the terrified animal, trying meanwhile to gather his wits together, as he phrased it. An accident was evident, but that the doctor might be seriously injured did not occur to him for some moments. He unharnessed the horse and led him to his stall, then considered what had better be done. To alarm the house would be folly; the only sensible suggestion seemed to be to find Mr. Richard at once; so, lantern in hand, he sallied into the street. Proceeding a few steps, he met a watchman.

"Was that Dr. Bertrand's horse?" was the quick question.

"Yes. I'm afraid the doctor's been thrown."

"The horse came racing up Broad Street. Was the carriage out, and where had the doctor been?"

"Down to old Mr. Smalley's, on the Elizabethtown road. I'm going after the young doctor. We must have a search"

"I'll send some one to help you. Mr. Smalley's, you said? I hope it's nothing serious."

Martin had a sort of obstinate faith that it was "nothing serious," but he trudged rapidly along through the rain, which had by this time become drenching. He was not long in reaching his destination. Richard obeyed the summons, and listened to Martin's brief story.

"My father! I mustgo immediately;" and with a hurried, nervous kiss he left his betrothed, to follow Martin.

"Do you think anything *can* have happened, Mr. Richard? The doctor couldn't have come home as fast as the horse, and the carriage might have been broken, but—"

"We'll hope for the best," said Richard, reassuringly. "When we reach Broad Street, you can take one side, and I the other. We *may* meet him."

The streets in the quiet city of Newark were dark and deserted; few cared to be out on such a night. When he parted from Martin a strange sense of fear stole into Richard's heart. But no, he would not believe anything fatal *could* happen; Dr. Bertrand might be injured by the fall; good care would soon restore him to health. There were many happy years yet for that kind, tender father, when his grandchildren should climb his knees, and his own sons and daughters smile proudly over his white hair. Then a chill presentiment shivered through his frame, as he thought of that evening's conversation. Terror quickened his pace. He soon overtook the watchman, and found it a relief to talk. On they went, narrowly inspecting every cart or wagon, listening to the infrequent footsteps, and pausing at the slightest sound. On, and on.

"If he's been hurt they've taken him in somewhere," said the man. "It could not have been far from Mr. Smalley's."

"We shall find the carriage, at all events," responded Richard.

The rain poured in torrents. The lantern served only to show how dark it really was. Presently they heard a call, and crossing the street, they found Martin surveying a broken vehicle.

"A pretty good smash. It's been run against by something. You're sure you know it?"

"I think I ought to," said Martin, with some contempt for the question.

Richard took up a lantern, and went on silently, a great wave of desolation rushing over his heart. He did not need to go far. Something lay beside a large stone — a dark mass, thoroughly saturated with rain. The outline bespoke it a human being. He could not look at the face, but with frantic eagerness tore open the clothing, and felt for the heart. The body was warm; that was the only sign of life to be found. The others came up, and were uttering exclamations of pity and surprise.

"Some one go for a carriage; quick! There is no time to be lost. Any person will assist in such an extremity;" and Richard lifted the body, so the head might rest on his shoulder.

A conveyance was soon procured, and, as they drove along, the fond son chafed the cold hands he held so tenderly in his. He paused once to despatch Martin for a skilful physician, and then scarcely breathed until they reached the familiar mansion, whose lights were still cheerfully shining out on the dreary night. He opened the door with his latch-key, and the men carried in their burden, depositing it on the office sofa. Richard went to summon the housekeeper, and ask for some dry clothes. Returning, a white face confronted him in the hall.

"What is the matter?" Mabel asked, fear fairly shivering in her tones. "Papa — ?"

"Has met with an accident. Go up stairs, dear; you cannot see him now."

"He is not dead! Only tell me that."

"I will tell you all by and by. Here comes Dr. D——."

She clung to his arm: "Richard, if — I *must* give him one last kiss."

"You shall. I will let you know in half an hour. Do not disturb the others;" and he put her gently away.

The poor frightened girl crept up to the room where they had been so merry two short hours before. She could not shut her eyes to that terrible, haunting fear! She heard the stir in the room below, and watched her half hour breathlessly. Then she crept out on the stairway, for she could no longer endure the torturing suspense in that apartment where his last good night seemed yet sounding. Once she stole down to the office door, but she could distinguish nothing in the confused hum of voices.

Within, medical skill was doing its utmost to recall the injured man to consciousness, if only for a few moments. Lying in the wet and cold had thoroughly chilled him; yet they did not quite despair, although their hearts were heavy. At length a sigh of returning animation rewarded them. Dr. Bertrand opened his eyes, gazed around in an uncertain manner, and then closed them. Richard threw himself beside the couch, and seizing his father's hand, pressed it to his trembling lips. As if the action recalled the feeble mind to a sense of life, he murmured faintly, —

"To the right — I told them so, but it was dark, and I couldn't see. Where am I?" and rested his wandering glance on his son.

Dr. D—— advanced, and taking his other hand, said, "You are at home, Dr. Bertrand. You were thrown from your carriage, and picked up insensible. Can you remember any of the circumstances?"

The question had the desired effect. A shade of thought passed over the pallid countenance, and with some difficulty he returned, "I think it was a drunken party. I tried to keep out of their way, but I suppose they ran into me. Am I seriously injured?" He tried to raise himself, but fell back with a gasp.

There was a solemn stillness. Richard's breath came

freighted with agony. Dr. D—— surveyed his friend a
moment, then said, in a low, distinct tone, —

"There *may* be a little hope, but we fear the worst."

The first expression of Dr. Bertrand's face was one of
intense pain, as if the summons had come too soon. Presently it vanished, and in its place came resignation, a calm,
holy peace, comforting the beholders. Sudden as the call
was, in this last dread hour he knew in whom he had trusted,
who had said, "My strength is sufficient for thee." For
some moments the ticking of the clock on the mantel-piece
was the only sound ; then, opening his eyes, he asked, faintly,
"How long ?"

Dr. D—— felt his pulse, and answered, "Two hours,
perhaps."

"Let me see them all, Richard, for the last time."

Richard went to summon the children. At the foot
of the stairs Mabel sprang into his arms. He tried to
kiss some courage into the pale, despairing face ; but the
tears that fell on her cheek told that the worst had indeed
come.

"He has asked to see you all ; " and Richard half carried,
half led her up stairs. She could frame no questions ; her
very breath seemed strangling her. They hurriedly awoke
Lilian and Archie from childhood's peaceful slumber, too
much stunned by the announcement even for tears. Then
Richard lingered a moment by Tessy's crib. Fast asleep
lay the little darling, her golden curls making a dividing line
between her fair face and the pillow ; the red lips slightly
parted, displaying the pearly teeth, and a flush of ripe crimson on her soft cheek. He caught up a shawl lying near by,
and took her in his arms, scarcely disturbing her ; only the
small mouth started into a smile as she murmured that
dearest of all words to her — "Papa." But the grief of the
others soon startled her, for when they entered the apartment of death, her lovely eyes were wide open with a child's

bewilderment ; and following out her first impulse, she
stretched forth her arms to embrace her father, then looked
terrified at the still, pale face.

It was evident he was sinking rapidly. This new grief of
parting, eager, frantic kisses from his children's lips, and
sobs of anguish, made his face more ashen than before.
Mute caresses were all he could give ; the blessing he essayed
to speak died away unuttered. But when Tessy's quick,
sharp cry of terror ran through the room, as she began to
understand the sad truth, it unnerved them all. Dr. D——,
stooping over Mabel, hurriedly whispered, " You had better remove them ; there may be some business ——"

His ear caught the sound. "Business," he murmured
faintly ; " yes, I wanted to live a little longer for their sakes ;
but you'll be kind to them, Richard — love them as I have
loved you. Don't let them miss me too much. Poor things !
— no father, no mother ; you won't desert them, Richard ? "
and he glanced up imploringly.

Richard Bertrand knelt beside his father, and clasping the
cold hands, said slowly, " God helping me, I will be a faithful brother, and love them with my whole heart."

" Give Robert my kiss and blessing. I cannot see him
now. I shall meet *her*, Richard, your mother ; and I will
tell her what the little child she loved has been to me. God
bless you again, and again. Don't leave me," and he sank
back exhausted.

The physician held a restorative to his lips, while Mabel
led away the weeping children. When he did rally again, it
was only to murmur incoherently, and gaze about with dull,
bewildered glances. They noted the minutes as they were
told off, and the hue of death that was gradually settling on
the noble face before them. Once he roused a little, and
whispered with difficulty, —

" I meant to tell you — about the house. Don't blame
him, Richard ; he was sadly unfortunate. I couldn't refuse

2 *

him — he had your mother's eyes; but I wronged the children. I meant to make it all good; yet God knew best.
You'll be a friend to them. Some time it will come back —
a Benjamin's portion for you. Read something, Richard
— the prayer. I think I am dying."

Richard opened the little prayer book that was his constant
companion, and in a choking voice read the commendatory
prayer. A look of peace overspread his father's face, comforting him in this bitter hour. The white lips murmured
part of the prayer; then followed a long silence. Afterwards
he bent over to catch the last words — "the children —
Richard, I love you — my first-born." The breath came
fainter, then gaspingly. Richard hid his face on the broad
shoulder, until the last agony was over.

Mabel had gone back to the sitting-room, and was trying
to comfort the younger ones, though she could give them
little besides tears. She listened with painfully acute senses,
and when the hall door shut, and two persons walked away,
a thrill of terror sped through every vein. Then she heard
voices in earnest consultation, and Mrs. Hall came up to her
father's room. Afterwards Richard entered, and clasped his
arms around the little group clinging so closely together,
mingling his tears with theirs.

"You had better all retire," he said, when he could trust
his voice. "We shall need some strength for to-morrow.
Henceforth I must try to fill *his* place to you; only, it can
never be *he;* but I will do my best."

"O, Richard! Richard!" What a bitter cry it was!
He kissed them tenderly, — little wet faces and quivering
lips, — and carried Tessy back to her crib. Lily crept in with
her, and Archie, wrapping himself in a blanket, lay down on
the lounge. There was no sleep for Mabel; she went quietly about, taking care of books and playthings that had been
neglected a few hours before, when all were so happy. Only
four years had elapsed since her mother's death; but she was

younger then, and had not felt the sorrow so keenly: perhaps, too, she had clung more closely to her father since that
time, and now understood the full force of the blow. Never
again to hear him speak, never to look in his genial, loving
eyes, or be kissed by the fond lips! Never to waylay him in
the hall, and ask little favors, or spring for the first embrace
as he entered the house. Never again! ah, there was the
sting.

CHAPTER III.

Through the long, weary day,
I walk o'ershadowed by vain dreams of him.
                                        MRS. HEMANS.

Even by means of our sorrows we belong to the Eternal Plan.
                                        HUMBOLDT.

DAYLIGHT came at last. Mabel had not slept at all, and
as soon as she heard Mrs. Hall astir, stole down to the
library, where she found Richard. The children had cried
themselves into heavy slumbers; so it was late when they
made their appearance at breakfast. The meal had scarcely
ended before the undertaker came, and they all went to take
a view of the dear face. How sweet and calm that last expression was! They gazed wonderingly, and without tears,
it was so like a peaceful sleep.

"I must telegraph for Robert immediately," Richard said,
when they were again in the hall; "and, Mabel, you had
better get all that you and the children will need. Let
nothing be put off until the last day."

"And that will be —"

"Saturday afternoon, I think. I will order the carriage
for you. Perhaps you had better take Mrs. Hall."

She came up at Richard's request; but Mabel decided to
go alone; a sudden sense of responsibility had come upon
her, and she took it up with patient, sorrowful gravity.

"It's a sore, sore trial," the housekeeper said. "No one
but God can comfort you;" and then she turned away with
tearful eyes. Words seemed so useless!

It was a harder task than Mabel had imagined. How
pitiful the fair little faces looked in their black bonnets!

So it is — we never become accustomed to death, but every time it seems new in its sombre belongings. The dressmaker took her orders with a quiet air, that was really sympathizing; but Mabel was glad to return to the silent house, and be again under the roof that covered her great grief. Richard had been very busy, and did not return until dinner.

The storm of the preceding night had ceased, yet the day had been cold and cloudy, just relieved, late in the afternoon, by a little sunshine. They clustered in the familiar sitting-room, where Richard tried to talk away the first strangeness of their grief; not by bringing up other subjects, but speaking of the dead father, who lay below, as one whose new life had already commenced in Paradise; who was looking down on them with the same loving heart and fond eyes that had been their comfort here. He had entered into the blissful rest of the redeemed, and now they were to strive to meet him at the last day. The low, gentle voice charmed away their grief; the sobs came at longer intervals as the twilight closed in around them. Tessy had crept up into Richard's lap, and the three elder ones were clasped in each other's arms.

"I hoped Robert would be at home before this. I ought to go out a little while," Richard said.

"Don't;" and Tessy, reaching up, clasped her arms around his neck. "Please don't; we have no papa but you, now."

He kissed her, and thought a moment, saying, "I will make a note answer. Light the gas, Mabel, and bring me your writing desk."

Turning the burner towards him, she lingered a moment with the desk in her hand, and then said, gently, "Get down, Tessy."

The child moved slowly, her large eyes filling with tears; but Richard changed her to one knee, and took the desk upon the other. "I think we can manage it," was his hopeful reply; "I only want to write a few words." So Tessy kept her seat, as she would have done on her father's lap.

The note was not very brief, after all; but when he had sealed and directed it to Miss Ada Townley, and asked Mabel to send it immediately by Martin, he clasped his little sister to his heart again, and rocked slowly backwards and forwards, thinking of the life that lay before him. And it was something to think of. He was within a fortnight of his wedding day. He had given his father a most solemn assurance that he would love and care for these orphaned ones. Would not something need to be relinquished? His trip abroad, perhaps; and the bridal must be delayed. But when he described that death scene to Ada, he knew she would feel as he did — that his duty lay here, for the present. She would not refuse to come and share it with him, perhaps; and in spite of his grief, a proud smile grew up in his face. Was it possible to doubt her? No, indeed. Disappointed she could not fail to be, for the trip to Europe had been one of her promised joys; but for his sake she would be content.

A quick ring at the door startled them all, and an instant later Robert was in their midst. Many tears were mingled with their kisses, and the silence spoke of tender grief more eloquently than words.

"Come here, Tessy," Robert said, as he sat down.

She clung timidly to the elder brother, with a child's naive preference, and climbing into his lap again, said slowly, "Richard's papa now."

Robert Bertrand was past eighteen, tall, well developed, and unmistakably handsome. His eyes were nearly black, proud, sparkling, and defiant; very unlike Richard's, which were a soft, liquid brown. His forehead was high and fair, less broad than his brother's, and clustered about with rings of shining hair. His chin was girlishly round, and dimpled; his lips beautifully curved, red, and somewhat full. When he set them firmly together, they shadowed out

an unpleasant meaning, that, as years passed on, might be
both selfish and cruel ; now it was ease-loving and indifferent. His face was full of restless force — the index to a
nature hard to govern, and extremely self-indulgent. There
was a great contrast between the two. Richard's face was
essentially *good*, not wanting in harmony and nobleness. It
was trusty, where Robert's was proud ; tender and affectionate, yet with none of that indecision often mistaken for
good nature. There was a fibre of almost womanly love for
all who were weak and suffering running through his heart ;
he could be patient to the last degree, and self-denying, but
every thought was marked by conscious rectitude. Once
committed to a cause he knew to be right, there was no
swerving with him.

As a family they had lived in perfect harmony, unconscious of any discordant elements. Mrs. Bertrand had loved
Richard sincerely ; and though the doctor's sense of justice
had been too correct to admit of favoritism, Richard's
seniority had made him companionable, while the others
were too young. Robert had occasionally chafed a little,
but always yielded ; now, however, he seemed to take his
place at once as an equal. He listened, with evident
emotion, to the sad story ; but his questions and comments
jarred a little on Mabel's bruised heart. She could not
recur to the sad event without tearful eyes, and frequently
Richard's voice seemed tremulous with sobs ; yet she checked
herself by the thought, "He was not here ; he did not
see it all." And when they kissed Richard "good night,"
she clung to him with something of the feeling of dependence she had hitherto held for her father alone.

The next day was quite eventful. The children's aunt
came, and there were various consultations, that broke in
upon the sacred solitude of grief. Aunt Sophia was too
deeply touched not to refrain from adding to their tears ; so
she reserved her questions for Mrs. Hall. Indeed, it seemed
as if the business of life *must* be gone through with, even if
hearts did break.

Late in the afternoon Richard went to call on his betrothed. The meeting could not be otherwise than sorrowful. The sudden shock, coming at an important period of their lives, rendered them both grave. It brought their whole existence more plainly before them; led them to see the thorns in every path, the wounds that must bleed, despite the love that so eagerly sought to bind up the bruised heart; taught them anew on what frail tenure all human hopes were held. Nearly an hour passed in comforting assurances on Ada's part, before he gained courage to say, —

"Dearest, our marriage will have to be delayed. There must be some new plans for the future, and weeks may elapse before we can make definite arrangements."

"I know," she answered, soothingly. "I will wait patiently and willingly until fall, and in the mean while, if I can be of any assistance to you or yours, command me to the utmost. It is surely not too much for me to say that your sorrow and joy are alike mine."

"Thank you." The pressure of the hand said still more — that no trouble or grief could long cloud their way with this perfect faith between them.

The funeral had been appointed for two o'clock on Saturday. Quite early Dr. Bertrand was placed in his coffin, dressed so naturally that it seemed impossible to think of him otherwise than as asleep. There was a slight discoloration on one temple, but the face was fair and placid — a face to linger over in the tenderest passion of grief. The children gathered in the large parlor, to which the body had been removed, and watched for the last time. The violence of grief had spent itself; tears were not needed in this saintly presence. Looking on him there, it seemed as if he must awake at length, and clasp them to his heart again — the children he loved so well. Richard passed quietly in and out until the friends began to assemble, when he and Robert took their places beside the others. How vividly every word and look of that last evening came before him!

How comforting the assurance he had received ! how sacred
the promise he had given a few hours later !

It was Tessy's hand that took the fragrant wreath from
the coffin, and laid it inside, on her father's breast. The
last kisses and last tears were given, and they were led
out of the apartment. The rest was like a painful dream :
the ride to the church, and from thence to the graveyard;
the solemn burial service, the lowered coffin, and the last sad
rite — " Earth to earth, ashes to ashes, dust to dust, looking
for the general resurrection at the last day." Thank God
for *that* hope, amid so much darkness.

An hour later the family assembled in the doctor's office,
and listened to the reading of the will. Lawyer Guilford,
an old and tried friend, performed this duty with grave
kindliness. After a few preliminaries, it gave to Richard all
medical books and instruments, while the house, and all other
such property as the doctor might die possessed of, was to
be equally divided among the five younger children when
Tessy reached her majority. If deemed advisable, the house
could be sold at any time, and the money placed at interest,
the income devoted to the maintenance and education of the
children. After this followed a special remembrance to
every one, a small gift to each of the three servants, and the
appointment of Richard and Mr. Guilford as executors and
guardians.

The house was large, with a hall through the centre;
on one side, a parlor; opposite, two rooms; the front one
an office, the other a sort of study, library, and general department. Opening the door of this, the lawyer beckoned
hither the elder sons, and unlocking a desk, remarked
quietly, " You will find all necessary papers here; but I
wish to say a word before I leave you. Were you aware the
house was mortgaged ?"

" No ! " exclaimed the brothers, in a breath of astonishment.

" I have some explanations to make, then. A short time
ago, when your father was setting apart your fortune," — he

bowed to Richard,—"he thought it better to make a new will, as the other had been drawn up prior to Mrs. Bertrand's death. He told me then, that, several years before, he had indorsed for a dear friend, who proved sadly unfortunate; and having at that period no ready money, he had mortgaged his house for five thousand dollars. He had paid one thousand since, and intended, as soon as possible, to clear it entirely. This plan has been frustrated; but I think, after all claims are settled, you may have enough perhaps to liquidate this debt, if you choose to do it. Any suggestion I can offer will be freely given."

"Thank you," Richard said, mechanically, while Robert asked, in a more eager tone, if he knew who the friend was.

"I do not. Allow me a few more words. It may surprise some that Dr. Bertrand died possessed of no greater wealth; but he has left an honorable name, and was a most benevolent man. A family like this, with no mother's economy, must necessarily be expensive. Doubtless you can make important retrenchments. Take plenty of time for the matter, and believe that I shall always have my friend's interest at heart. I think you will find your own business all correct, Mr. Richard; your father took great pains with it. And now good day, as I suppose you will do nothing further at present."

The brothers bowed. As the door closed, Robert threw himself on the sofa with an expression of extreme dissatisfaction. "To think how it has ended!" he began, with a scornful curl of the lip. "I supposed father was worth twenty thousand, at least. What is to be done?"

"He made no such pretension," Richard said, gravely. "We will wait a while before deciding."

"It's very well for you to talk, Dick. You have had a splendid education out of father, and now can fall back upon your own fortune; while this is my first year at Yale, and likely to be my last, for anything I can see."

"Let us leave the subject now," was Richard's response.

"You may go, if you like; but I don't stir until I have examined some of these papers. Whom do you suppose father *could* have indorsed for?"

"We will talk of it when I return;" and Richard went to attend to the remaining friends. Having disposed of them, he ran up stairs, and found the resignation of the afternoon had given way to wildest grief. Even aunt Sophy could do nothing but weep. Mabel's firmness had failed entirely. His comforting voice seemed to restore them; but the sobs had scarcely ceased when the tea bell rang. Mabel lingered to bathe her face and smooth her hair. Coming back to the shelter of his arms, she said, brokenly, —

"Richard, aunt Sophy and I have been talking of what must come presently: do you think we shall be separated, even if you should—" and her voice broke down completely.

He had to make an effort to regain his. "No;" and he was glad he could say it; "there will be no parting at present, and I shall not be married until fall."

Her answer was a convulsive kiss.

After supper he followed Robert to the library, who began in a triumphant tone, ere they were séated, "Well, I have solved the mystery!"

"Who was it? Some one father must have loved dearly;" and Richard, bethinking himself of the words spoken that fatal night, — "I couldn't refuse him; he had your mother's eyes," — anticipated Robert's reply of, "Your uncle, Richard Aubrey."

"I found it in father's journal," he continued, opening the book. "It was before mother died. Of course he didn't suppose he would lose it; but then came the fire, when uncle Dick was burned out, his removal to Central America, and his sickness and death there. Still, I do not think it was father's place to pay it."

"It was any honorable man's duty," Richard answered,

warmly. "I am sorry he indorsed; that being done, however, there was only one course."

Robert moved uneasily in his chair. "Certainly, the law could compel him to pay it. I didn't exactly mean *that*. The thing is just here, Dick: if it had been *my* mother's brother I would not say a word; but we children are five thousand dollars poorer for the speculation, while it doesn't touch you in the slightest. My share of it would take me through college."

A deep crimson suffused Richard's face, as he replied, hastily, "I understand you, and will see to all college expenses."

"I will not wrong the others," Robert said, with an assumption of justice. "If the matter looks right to you, it may go."

"None of you shall suffer through *my* uncle," Richard exclaimed, with a little pride.

"You see, Dick," Robert began, as if half ashamed of his suggestion, "if we were all grown up, it would be different; but you have had more than any of us in your education, and —"

"I promised father, just before he died, that I would do all I could toward filling his place. No one shall want for anything while I live. I think you can trust me."

The solemn, yet tender voice sobered Robert a little. "You *were* going to be married, Dick," he said.

"It will not be until fall, and I have given up my trip to Europe." No one knew how hard it was for him to say that. "When you come home for vacation I shall have decided on what it is best to do; till then, all things will go on as before."

"There's some railroad stock, and a little money in the bank. What do you suppose the house would bring, Richard?"

"I hope there will be no necessity of selling it until I can become the purchaser," was the quiet answer. "Since you

have begun, we may as well go over the papers together;'
and he drew his chair towards the desk.

Everything was in tolerable order — letters laid by them
selves; bills and business accounts rightly arranged, and
the ledger written up to the last day of the doctor's life
Then there was a journal-like volume, containing simple
entries of the day's events, that told more than many
lengthy paragraphs. He was too healthy-spirited a man to
go into any morbid analysis of thought; yet it contained
many touching glimpses of home life. It was here Robert
had found the particulars of the mortgage, and this was the
only account of his unfortunate indorsing. Richard prom
ised himself a sad, sweet pleasure in reading it at some
future time. The clock struck ten, and a light tap at the
door interrupted them.

"Let us put these away for to-night," Richard said, open
ing the door to Tessy.

"I came to kiss you. We were all going to bed," was
the half-timid exclamation.

He took the child in his arms, and as she buried her face
in his soft beard, she murmured, "O Dick, I love you
dearly! dearly! Do you think God will ever make you
die?"

For answer he held her tightly, and kissed lip, cheek, and
golden hair; then carried her up stairs, where he said good
night to the rest. They all looked up to him now as the
head of the family.

3 *

CHAPTER IV.

The lines of our life may be smooth and strong,
  And our pleasant path may lie
Where the stream of affection flows along,
  In the light of a summer sky;
But woe for the lights that early wane,
  And the shades that early fall,
And the prayer that speaks of the secret pain,
  Though its voice be still and small.

FRANCES BROWN.

THE head of the family! This was what Richard Bertrand
thought, as he sat in his room, weary, and yet wakeful.
What a change a week had wrought! Then he had been
musing over such visions as young men are wont to dream
of; a girlish wife and baby faces growing up in his household, whose helpless, clinging touches give to parents wisdom
and patience. Instead, ties not his very own sprang up to
fetter him with a double chain of love and duty. It was not
such a care-free path as those rambles over the old world,
with his chosen wife beside him. What wonder if he
glanced at that lost way with sorrowful tenderness? Already
cares and sacrifices began to stare him in the face. Could
he make his position harmonize with his affection? The little scene with Robert told him he had not a parent's authority, and that his rule must be one of love. A fine sense of
honor ran like a silver chord through his nature, and he felt
it would be right for him to pay off this mortgage with his
own fortune, no matter how overstrained the action might
appear to others. His father had behaved with scrupulous
generosity and delicacy in never mentioning the fact of his
having indorsed for Richard's uncle, and it touched him to

the heart. Yes, he would clear the house from debt, and
then — some provision must be made for the family. His
father's practice was extensive; he would doubtless succeed
to a large share of it. If he could keep them all together
for a few years! And then thoughts of Ada arose. Would
she be happy here?

I think it was well Sunday came in the midst of their grief.
It sanctified it, and added a tender solemnity to the memory
of the dead, and gave Richard his true position at once — the
place he was to fill through years of mingled joy and sorrow.
He took his father's seat in the church with a feeling of grave
awe, and those who looked upon his manly figure and truth-
ful face, prophesied it would be worthily filled.

He hesitated a little whether he should go to Ada that
night, then decided to remain at home. They could not
sing, as was their usual custom; but Richard read to them:
afterwards they fell into a sweet, sorrowful talk of him who
had gone from their midst, and was keeping the eternal rest
that remained for the people of God.

"' A day which shall be known unto the Lord, not day, nor
night; but it shall come to pass that at evening time it shall
be light,'" Mabel said, with her lingering good-night kiss.

"At evening time," Richard repeated. He did not dream
then how often he should have need to comfort himself with
the words.

Monday morning brought the stir of busy life. Robert
was called into conference with his brother, and all immediate plans laid before him. There was a sad parting with the
girls, and Richard drove him to the depot, offering a few
brotherly snggestions that were received with an attentive
air. But a feeling of intense relief came in his face when he
found himself alone; and he said, almost audibly, —

"Dick *is* a good fellow, and I must be careful. Wasn't I
lucky to make my peace with the learned and reverend faculty? Suspension just now would have been — well, it
didn't come, thanks to fortune; so there's no use of borrowing trouble."

Then followed aunt Sophia's departure. It was natural she should feel anxious for the children's welfare, as their mother had been her only sister; and she offered to take the two younger ones, in case they decided to break up the household.

"You are to be married soon, I believe?" she said to Richard.

"Not until fall, and I may remain here then. It is my wish to keep the family together. I think father desired it."

She could not object to this; but as Mrs. Hall helped her put on her wrappings, the subject was re-discussed.

"I'm afraid it will not work," she said, slowly. "Mabel is growing up, and may want to be mistress in her own house, and Miss Townley won't feel disposed to accept of the second position. Then, he is only their half-brother, and we cannot expect him to give up *all* to them. Poor things, they will never find another friend like their father!"

Mrs. Hall sighed and hoped it would end rightly, but was a little doubtful of two families living in perfect peace, when both would have such a strong claim on "Mr. Richard."

The next event in order was the mortgage. Mr. Guilford was a little surprised at Richard's proposal, but simply said, "I hope you have considered the matter well;" and then went about the business in his ordinary manner. Some days elapsed before it could be finally settled; but when Richard had freed the house from its encumbrance, and placed a thousand dollars in the lawyer's hands to Robert's credit, a great weight seemed to have fallen from him. Now the question of retrenchment must be seriously considered.

This was a difficult subject for a young man. The house was large, to be sure, yet it was all needed; and it was not possible to do with less than the three servants: Mrs. Hall, a sensible, middle-aged woman, who had filled the post of housekeeper since Mrs. Bertrand's death, and was a most excellent manager; Ann, the maid of all work, a good-natured Irish woman, whose tastes were certainly promiscuous as regarded employment. As a girl she had served apprenticeship to Mrs. Bertrand, married, and after a brief essay at housekeeping, had come back during the illness of her mistress. Her husband having been taken as coachman and gardener, Martin and Ann Burns might well be considered fixtures. Martin was especially valuable, if he did grumble a little now and then, for he was sober, honest, and industrious. None of the servants could be dispensed with while the family remained here.

And to go away! It sent a quick pang to Richard's heart. Dr. Bertrand had come here after his second marriage, and this was the scene of Richard's boyish years, as well as his thoughtful, happy manhood. He could remember every improvement, and how he had sometimes assisted in planning. The house was situated at the northern end of the city, in a quiet, shady street, whose sidewalk was bordered with patriarchal elms. The grounds, though small, were tastefully laid out, a handsome court-yard in front, with miniature lawns, whose dark green Norway pines made a pleasant gloom. The house was double, the pointing roofs over the dormer windows relieving its squareness. To the right, partially hidden by trees, stood the carriage-house and barn. The rear commanded a lovely prospect. It lay on the banks of the Passaic, the slope terraced by a series of steps, the upper ones being devoted to flowers, and the lower to fruit and vegetables; ending by a thick stone wall at the water's edge. Here was the boat-house, whose building Richard had superintended, and he could almost feel the thrill of delight with which he had welcomed the dainty "Jessie," his boat. Here were fruit trees he had trained, rose-cuttings bestowed by friends, and a host of flowers he had taken delight in cultivating. Then the rooms! there was not a nook or corner but held some pleasant memory for him; all had been hallowed by the presence of that dear father. No, he could never willingly go away.

He summoned Mrs. Hall, and they took a review of the housekeeping department. He found his father had supplied every thing with a most lavish hand, and that Mrs. Hall thought an important reform might be commenced here. She lingered after they had arranged their plans, her face so plainly showing something left unsaid, that he asked, with a pleasant smile, —

"Are there any more suggestions? I am a new hand at the business, you know, and will take the least hint kindly."

The little woman's face flushed, and she said, quite humbly, —

"I *should* like to speak of one thing, if you wouldn't be offended, sir. It's not my place; but I've seen more of life than you, — women's lives, I mean, — their likes and wants, and sometimes little jealous feelings that make a household miserable. People who love dearly do not always know just how to make each other happy. If it isn't too bold a question, — wasn't you thinking of being married, and bringing your wife here?"

"I *did* think about it; in the fall, perhaps;" and Richard's color rose a trifle.

"What I wanted to say, Dr. Richard, was this. Miss Townley, being the youngest of her family, and having such a fortune, never has had anything to try her patience, or any feelings or wishes beside her own to consult. I dare say she loves you very much, and looks forward to a happy life with you, thinking, like most young creatures, that the highest joy is having you all her own. And here are the children, very fond of you, and used to having their father all to themselves, for he was always thinking what he could do for them, and was so indulgent, so patient, with their little tempers and rare disputes. Now they all cling to you; indeed, you are filling their father's place; but when a new claimant for your love comes ———"

"You are afraid there might be some trouble," he said, in the calm tone of a man who felt certain of perfect accord.

"It's right and natural for a wife who loves her husband beyond all else, to wish to be first with him—to want all his leisure hours. No one could blame her for it. But the children would have to be put off, and might feel neglected. A restraint would come hard at first; they're so affectionate, and were used to so much freedom with their father. It's trying to a man, when he loves both parties; and it's difficult for both parties to agree, when they look at the same thing in a different light. You'd be the shield, with one side gold, and the other side silver."

"Well," said Richard, cheerfully, "how shall I keep the peace?"

"I can't answer that, sir. But if you tried the plan and found it did not prove agreeable, I was thinking how much pleasanter than sending them among strangers it would be to hire a cheap little cottage, and let me take charge of them. I could do all the work, and make them happy, I think, and you could watch over them. When I remember how much I owe your dear father, I feel as if I ought to spend my very life for his children's happiness. He came to me when my husband lay dying, and my poor baby too ill to go out of my arms, while I was almost wild with poverty and anxiety. O, I can never forget his goodness, and how he comforted me after they were gone, when I came near dying with loneliness and grief myself. I feel as if I daren't meet him in heaven, unless I do all I can for his;" and Mrs. Hall broke down in a sobbing fit.

Richard was moved to the heart. He took her hand kindly, and said, in a voice of emotion,—

"How much I thank you for this generous offer, I cannot put in words. I honor you, too, for so practical a plan; and if the time should ever come when such a division seems necessary, I shall gladly avail myself of your suggestions. Believe me, I am eager to do my whole duty by them; they were my father's last charge."

"I hope you'll pardon me if I've been over-bold, but I

couldn't bear to think of their being separated while they're so young. Miss Mabel will grow up a sort of mother to the rest, and I know we can make a pleasant home. They have so few relatives that they'll always cling together. Their aunt·Sophia would do anything in the world for them, but she has such a large family."

"If my plan will not work, we must try yours," he said, kindly.

After Mrs. Hall had left him, he dropped his forehead on his hand, and fell into a reverie. How many difficulties rose in his path! More than once some slight incident had made him feel his actions would be more severely criticised because he was a half brother to the rest. The suspicions that had been scarcely suggested, wounded his keenly sensitive soul. He understood how this home, delightful as it was, might not be so happy for Ada. He would be compelled to divide his attentions. There were lessons, little troubles, and much demonstrative love, that he could only check by positive coldness. How could he teach Tessy the first kiss did not belong to her? Would he wish to estrange them?

No, indeed; he loved them too well; and he resolved, come what would, to keep, in the truest manner possible, his promise to his dead father. If Mrs. Hall hardly dared meet him in heaven, with an unperformed kindness between them, how much more he, a well-beloved son, in whom his father reposed the highest confidence!

Yet it would take the most entire devotion to repay Ada for her disappointment in not going abroad. It was her right to have some voice in a matter that so deeply concerned herself. Suppose she should not wish to come and share her husband's time and love with so many. She *was* rather exacting. He had hitherto liked the jealous regard that could not spare a word nor caress. But how would it answer when they all came to live together?

A rush of children through the hall dispersed his troubled thoughts, and he rose to meet them. Fresh from school,

with rosy faces, and somewhat boisterous greetings — Archie
begging for a little help in his Latin, Lily petitioning for a
ride on Saturday; and Tessy, clasping his arm with both
eager hands, hopped beside him, intent on studying locomo-
tion on one foot.

Mabel's voice sounded from the hall above, —

" Come, children, the dinner bell will ring in five minutes,
and you are not ready."

Lily went up the steps two at a time, and Archie made
noisy attempts at imitating her. Richard swung Tessy with
a sudden force, landing her three steps up. She gave a gay
little laugh, and said, in a delighted tone, —

" O Dick! you're as strong as papa; he used to do
that!"

CHAPTER V.

All as God wills, who wisely heeds
  To give or to withhold,
And knoweth more of all my needs
  Than all my prayers have told.
                            WHITTIER.

Two months had elapsed since Dr. Bertrand's death. Changeful childhood rallied and grasped eagerly at the pleasures of life, in order to fill up the chasm of loss. Merry laughs once more woke echoes through the quiet house, and occasionally Lilian broke into a bird-like song. Richard had been very busy. His father's patients had poured in upon him in numbers that could not fail to be gratifying; yet it rendered the prospect of a long absence unfortunate for his position as a doctor, if not absolutely impossible. The new cares and responsibilities had somewhat broken in upon his devotedness as a lover, though his betrothed had consoled herself with a visit to New York for gayeties she could not well ask Richard to share at home. She had been kind and sympathizing, and borne her share of the grief tranquilly. Still he was anxious for a more thorough understanding of their future.

One lovely May evening they went out for a walk. He had a purpose in this, for he wanted to be beyond the chance of interruption. The night air was fragrant with the breath of young trees, and the varied odors of spring. The soft blue sky, with its tender stars, seemed to have a peculiar nearness to human hearts and human wants. The tremulous air brought vague memories of lost joys, dreams unrealized and forgotten, save in such hours.

"How beautiful!" and Richard paused. They had turned into High Street, and gaining a little eminence, the whole city lay at their very feet, softened in a flood of silver light, serene as if all in those homes were perfect peace.

"Yes," Ada answered slowly; "but think, Richard, what such a night would be in Venice with the songs of gondoliers, or roaming through the palace gardens of the old world. I am longing for fields of olive and figs, and where purple grapes glisten in the long reaches of a still fairer light than this."

"It would disappoint you very, *very* much not to go?" His voice had a touch of winning gentleness in it.

"O, I *must!* You know what I said about waiting! By fall you will surely have all family arrangements completed."

"Matters are very different from what I expected," was his grave answer.

"Your father was not so rich as people supposed?"

"It is not that alone. I promised my father in his dying moments that I would love the children as he had loved me — take care of them — befriend them."

"Of course it is your duty to love them; but surely there is enough to support them without any effort of yours. May I make a suggestion?"

"Certainly, dearest."

"Could not the house be sold, and the money properly invested? Would it not make sufficient for the children's support?"

"O, I couldn't give up the house. I should never find another spot in the world so dear! I hope some day to be able to purchase it, for the girls will doubtless marry and seek other homes. I have half a plan, Ada, if you are willing."

"Well." Her tone was not at all encouraging.

"I do not think it will be possible for me to go abroad. I find there is not enough left to support the family without some exertion on my part. I am in a fair way of succeeding to much of my father's practice. If you were willing to

marry me, and share my lot for awhile, I know I could make
you happy. At least, we might try. Will you not come?"

"Richard," Ada began slowly, "I may perhaps offend you
by what I shall say; yet I think it my duty. I do not approve of such arrangements. I do not feel capable, or even
willing, to take charge of such a household, neither should I
be satisfied with a secondary position. I will gladly share
what I have with you in travelling, and afterwards in any
manner that seems best. Surely there would be no difficulty in reëstablishing yourself on our return. Besides,
you have a tolerable fortune. I shouldn't starve on it if
mine were all gone;" and she laughed with assumed gayety.

"It is not so large as it was. I have had occasion to
spend half of it." His voice was quietly firm. The truth
was best told now. Yet he felt there would be an outbreak,
and summoned not only resolution, but tenderness.

"Five thousand! What have you been doing, Richard?"
she asked, sharply.

"My duty, only. After my father's burial I found he had
mortgaged the house to enable him to pay two notes he had
indorsed for my uncle, my own mother's brother."

"He left you nothing, and expected you to pay that!"
she said, indignantly.

"He *did* leave me a great deal," Richard answered with a
little wounded feeling. "A handsome library, and a most
complete as well as expensive set of instruments; besides, he
never spoke of my paying the debt. But in order to have
you understand why I have taken these particular views of
duty, I must tell you some of my past life. At my mother's
death, my uncle and aunt Aubrey took charge of me, keeping me until my father's second marriage, and utterly refusing the slightest remuneration. My grandfather divided his
property equally between uncle Richard and myself. My
father never touched one penny of either principal or interest; supplying all my wants himself. Uncle Richard was
prosperous for a while; but a disastrous fire, which swept

away nearly all his earnings, was succeeded by a long illness.
Afterwards he took his family to Central America, where he
seemed to have a fair prospect of redeeming his losses. In
several of his letters that I have since found, he expressed
the most earnest determination to repay my father at the
earliest opportunity. He took a fever and died, and aunt
and the children went to California. For two years we have
heard nothing from them. In my father's last moments he
pleaded tenderly for uncle Richard, although I did not understand the full import until Robert discovered an acknowledgment of the indorsement. He suggested the only course
I should have followed; for it is true I have had more than
the others."

"I do not think it right or fair. Your father did not consult you in the matter of security, and you are not bound in
the slightest."

"Only by a sense of honor, and respect for myself."

"It was unjust for Robert to speak of such a thing. They
will never be as generous for you."

"It was *my* relative, and not theirs — one who had loved
me fondly. And if I can repay my father a little for his
kindness to me, I ought to make some sacrifice. Besides, I
have so much more than they will inherit."

"If they were your own brothers and sisters, it would look
more reasonable for you to spend your life for them." Ada's
tone was bitter.

"I do not believe their mother ever said of me, ' If he
had been *my* child, I should have felt it my duty to do more
for him.' I cannot imagine any one more devoted. I would
do a great deal for the sake of the pleasant life I led with
her; indeed, we are as much brothers and sisters as if she
had been mother to all."

"Yet I will protest against your spending your life and
your fortune for them! You belong to *me*, at least if I have
not been crowded out of your heart."

Both her words and manner pained him; yet he answered
gently, "I do not expect to devote my whole time to them,

only just now when they have lost so much ! Think, Ada, how many more years I had *him* — years of tender love and unwearied counsel. God made me a son and a brother before I became a lover, and a little while at this period will surely not detract from my permanent happiness. You must know my love for you is beyond question."

"A divided heart," she returned, coldly.

"No, not divided. I love *you* no less, and the others no more, than I did three months ago ; but God has placed new duties in my way. I dare not neglect them."

"You would rather relinquish me ?"

"Ada !" The whole strength of his nature came out in his tone, as if there was a bound she might not pass.

"Forgive me, Richard. I love you dearly, and you try me beyond endurance. I acknowledge you have a sacred duty to perform towards your brothers and sisters. If you invest their property well, and send them to good boarding-schools, what more can any one ask ? "

"Boarding-school !" he repeated in surprise. "And Tessy nothing but a baby ! "

"Sister Mary doesn't consider Clara a baby. She is about Tessy's age, I believe, and quite womanly."

"I don't know how they could endure separation and a life among strangers."

"It would be the best thing you could do for them. They will certainly be spoiled if you go on this way ; and of course every one will blame you."

He thought of one who never considered them spoiled, or a trouble ; who never wearied of their caresses ; never frowned when dimpled arms almost strangled him ; when eager feet followed him from house to garden, and childish voices plied him with questions ; or when they sat upon his knee, and buried their soft fingers in his hair. Their love had been so active, never content with a quiet assurance of once for all. Could *he* be the one to chill their young hearts with lessons of coldness? Alas ! how hard duty had become ! He summoned courage to say, cheerfully, —

"You may think differently of the matter, Ada, when you have considered it well."

"It is useless to hold out false hope," she answered quickly. "I *could not* be happy in the life you have planned. I will wait, therefore, until you have time for me."

This was the woman he had relied on so confidently! the one who was to share toils as well as pleasures with him. He was chilled to the heart by her coldness, her want of sympathy, her lack of appreciation for the struggle he was going through.

They turned down the street in which Ada lived, and no further word was spoken until they reached the house, when she said, "You will come in?"

"Thank you, not to-night, dear." His voice was not quite steady, but his kiss as fond as ever.

"Good night." There was none of the eager persuasion she was so ready to use generally.

He walked away slowly and sadly, with a sense of pain at his heart. It was well he could not see the flushed face Ada carried up to her sister's room, nor the scornful smile with which she threw herself on the sofa.

"Where is Richard?" asked Mrs. Taylor.

"Gone home to the bosom of his family!" The reply was bitter enough.

"Will he never have affairs straight?"

"He has called me into council;" and her eyes sparkled with an angry light. "What do you think of his wishing me to give up Europe, marry him, and assist in the care of the children? Quite a generous offer, — was it not?"

"Shall you?"

"Wouldn't you advise me to?"

"No, Ada, I should not. You are young, and have had no experience with a family. Then they are only his half brothers and sisters; if they should turn out badly, you and Richard would always be blamed. Their father indulged them beyond everything. In a month's time they would walk over you pretty effectually, and there would doubtless be a disagreeable separation. No, it is not a wise or prudent plan."

"I *do* mean to go to Europe; that will settle the question. It would be a mercy to take him away, for they will make a perfect slave of him. Listen to this —" and Ada repeated the story of his paying the mortgage.

"What quixotism!" and Mrs. Taylor gave a little provoked laugh. Her sense of honor had long ago been buried under the dust and rubbish of fashionable life.

By the time Richard reached home he began to ask himself if it was absolutely necessary to sacrifice his own happiness, if it came to that. Mrs. Hall had spoken truly; it *would* be difficult to stand between two interests, and yield the proper share of affection to both parties. He let himself in with his latch-key, and though he would rather have avoided every one just now, he had fallen so in the habit of running up to the children's sitting-room, that he stood in the doorway before he thought.

Mabel had a book in her hand, and Tessy was sliding off the lounge, rubbing her eyes.

"Tessy!" and his voice had a touch of sharpness in it. "What are you doing up, this time of night?"

She sprang to his arms. "I didn't kiss you before you went out, and I could not go to bed. Dear, dear Dick!"

"She pleaded to sit up, and I could not refuse her," interposed Mabel, gently.

The touch of the soft face had already disarmed him. Clasping her to his heart, he satisfied her with repentant kisses, and sent her away. Then he took up Mabel's book, — a French work she had been studying, — and turning the leaves idly, said, with a careless endeavor, —

"Bel, how would you like to go to boarding-school?"

"O Richard! I couldn't endure it, and now of all times." A white terror crept up in her face.

"It is not so very dreadful. Some boarding-schools

are quite civilized institutions. And if Lily went with you?"

"Do you mean it? Must we go away? I think it would break my heart to leave home and part with Tessy. O, please, Richard, do not send me."

"My darling, don't distress yourself. The idea came into my head, and some girls like it. I did not mean to pain you." He twined his arm around her, and her fair head drooped on his breast. O, if God would only give him strength to be faithful to the old home affection! Some day Ada might look upon his high trust in the same light he did. He *must* " endure to the end." Yet an indefinable influence seemed playing a jarring discord in his soul, with a hand mercilessly cold.

CHAPTER VI.

And though one wearies by the way,
And hearts break in the sorrow,
We'll sow the golden grains to-day;
The harvest comes to-morrow.
                    GERALD MASSEY.

A SCAMPER through the yard and up the piazza, a mysterious tiptoing through the hall, and quite a "company" knock at the office door. Richard knew well who the invaders were; their smothered laughs would have betrayed them, as well as their noisy raid up the yard. Entering into the spirit of merriment, he stole behind the door before he said, "Come in." It was opened a little way, and a voice in droll Irish inquired, "Is the docthor in?"

There was no answer. The door was pushed wider, the question repeated, and Tessy's golden head began to make sunbeams. Her wandering eyes opened to their full extent as she exclaimed in a disappointed tone, "He isn't here, Archie."

"Why, yes, he is; didn't he say, 'Come in'?" and the next instant Tessy gave a cry of delight, as Richard rushed out and caught her in his arms, imitating her voice as he asked, "Was it the docthor you wished to see, darlint?"

"O Dick, we want to go sailing, after dinner."

"It's office hours, and some poor Irishwoman might come; but if Mabel will promise to raise a white flag in case of distress, and you will be sure to see it, I *may* be induced to consent."

As they walked through the hall, he placed one arm around Lily's neck. She bent to kiss the hand; and fan-eying a tear dropped on it, he gazed earnestly at her. The bright eyes were brimming over.

"I couldn't help it, Dick;" and her voice trembled. "It was so like what *he* used to do; and when you laugh, there comes just such a light in your eyes as used to sparkle in his. Dear, dear papa!" and with a little sob she put both arms around Richard's neck.

Mabel called them to prepare for dinner. The meal well over, they led him down to the boat-house, and shortly afterwards went skimming up the river, as merry as larks.

But that evening, when the children were dismissed to bed, and Lily deep in her lessons, Mabel watched her brother's figure as he paced up and down the garden walk. His head was bowed, his hands clasped behind him, his whole air one of sad thoughtfulness. She stole out to him, and taking his arm, said, beseechingly, "May I walk with you, dear Richard?"

"Certainly."

"I want to talk, too. I have ever so many questions to ask."

"Well," he said, encouragingly.

She hesitated a moment, then began slowly : —

"I think I ought to know a little about our situation, Richard. I am the eldest girl, and will some day manage for the rest. I have been keeping accounts for Mrs. Hall, the past month, and learning what it costs to support a family. How much have we besides the house?"

"Two thousand dollars, and a sufficient sum for Robert's education."

"We could not go on this way, then, unless you were in practice?"

"Don't distress yourself about that, dear. If I had purchased such a chance, I must have paid a good price for it; succeeding to it, I ought certainly to share the profits with the others. You must look upon it as a debt due the estate. It's so much pleasanter than sitting on the watch for patients,

and wondering when one will get established; and it is a
great comfort to go among those who loved *him*."

"Every one did," was her fond rejoinder.

"My highest ambition is to be such a man. I often think
of this, in connection with him — 'being dead, yet speaketh.'
We must love one another the better for his sake."

This strengthened Mabel for what she most wished to
say.

"Before *that* night, Richard," — her voice was very low,
— "you were to be married. I have thought much about
it lately. It does not seem right to take your time and
affection from what should be the great hope of your life.
Yet if you support us — "

"I am young, and can wait," he exclaimed, hopefully.

"I don't want you to wait; that is what troubles me.
And, Richard, I wonder if there could not be some compromise, such as marrying Ada, and bringing her here?
The house is large enough, and we should all love her so
dearly. I would try to keep the children from annoying
her, and do what I could for her happiness. Will you not
ask her, please?"

He mastered his emotion with an effort, for he had a trial
in store for her. "My darling," he said, "have you considered the subject thoroughly? Wives are not exactly
like sisters. I suppose a man learns to love his wife so
well that he prefers her to all the world. Would you like
me to be taken from you, even though we lived in the same
house?"

There was no moon; but the light from the window sent
a long ray over their path, and by this he scanned her face
eagerly. She did not know how much he had at stake.
Looking up with the proud nobleness of entire truth, she
answered, —

"O Richard! did you think I *could* be selfish when you
were doing so much for us? It would be *right* to have you
love her best. I could not be satisfied unless I saw it so;

but what we lost in you we should gain in her. She would
be so much to me."

Do not blame the lover too severely, if, at that moment,
he contrasted the two women he had known most intimately;
for it seemed as if Mabel had suddenly blossomed into
maturity, and was worthy of a place in the front rank. He
remembered the sweet unselfishness of her childhood, her
readiness to sacrifice herself for another's enjoyment. If Ada
were here, might she not learn to be tender and considerate,
not for *him*, — he could trust her love there, — but for his,
the children so sacredly bequeathed to him?

"Will you tell her," Mabel continued, "that we are longing to love her and call her sister, and that, if she will only
come and try us, we will be forever grateful? I think we
could not miss of being happy."

"Thank you," he said from his full heart; but it was sorely
troubled as he recalled Ada's words and manner when they
had discussed the same subject. He comforted Mabel, and
determined, after waiting patiently a while, to make one
more effort.

There are natures at once exacting and self-renouncing,
feeling keenly any drop that is withheld from the measure
they receive, yet desiring others to be satisfied with what it
pleases them to give. Ada would have yielded her fortune
willingly to Richard, been content to devote her whole time
to him; but she must do it in her own way. If he had been
left alone in the world, he would have found no more faithful and loving friend. She had never learned to study
another's happiness. Her life had been passed at boarding-
school and the homes of her two sisters, both married to
prosperous, indulgent men, and seeking their happiness in
mere worldly pleasures. With these specimens of conjugal
ease before her, Ada had planned her own. Amid the delights of a foreign tour, they would doubtless have assimi-
lated more readily; for Richard would have been devoted,
and she radiant with an excitement that often cunningly

puts on the guise of love. When the quiet of every-day life came, he might have missed and longed for some old dreams, and understood how much too late it was to expect them.

Now, Ada felt herself wronged. She said, a hundred times, she was willing to give up *all* for him — to positively forget sisters and friends, if need be; but, in return, she wanted him wholly. His family must be quite a secondary consideration. He might manage their property, send them to school, or see they had a home somewhere, and his duty would be done. Of course, when they visited her, she expected to kiss them fondly, and treat them in a familiar, sisterly fashion, only they must not be troublesome.

Both parties delayed a new discussion. Ada mistook Richard's fear of giving pain for indecision. She determined to gain her point by a little feminine strategy, and that fond appealing to his love which so often wins its way through the firmest heart. Susceptible as he was to impressions from those he loved, he was rarely mastered by impulse. He could not forget the first sacred ties of life at another's bidding, no matter how well loved that other might be. Unconsciously to both, they were drifting apart. Richard resolved, after much sorrowful consideration, to postpone the union for a while, if Ada resolutely refused to share his present home.

Summer came on radiantly. One grave blossomed in beauty; one household learned what it was to have " treasures in heaven." The duties and pleasures of life came to them as they come to all, and were taken up cheerfully. Grief does not always mean weakness.

Aunt Sophy had petitioned for a good long visit from "the children." Ada and her two sisters were going to the White Mountains, and Richard had promised to devote a brief period to them. At this juncture Robert returned.

Hitherto they had been united by similar affections and tastes, as if one soul pervaded the household. But it was evident Robert began to indulge some new traits. He was full of fun and frolic, petted the younger ones, but avoided both Richard and Mabel, and seemed coolly indifferent to their regard. He sauntered into the library, one morning, where Richard was writing letters, and threw himself at full length on the sofa, watching the gliding of the pen, until his eyebrows contracted impatiently, and fitful flashes of light escaped through the jetty lashes.

"Dick, my dear fellow," he said at length, "do you mean to write all the morning? I want a little conversation with you."

"I can attend to you, also," was the reply. "What is it?"

"There's a party of my college chums going to Lake George, to have a capital time boating, fishing, and camping out. They are to start on Monday next, and I've promised to join them."

The tone was carelessly independent.

"Is there to be any reliable person in the party?"

"Frank Conway's uncle lives there; he's old and steady enough, I suppose, and will keep an eye over us."

"How long will they stay? and have you any idea of the expense?"

"Six weeks or so. A hundred dollars will do me, I fancy."

Richard turned towards him, and said, slowly, "I do not approve of the plan. Suppose you go to aunt Sophy's instead; you enjoyed yourself there last summer."

"Cape May!" was the disdainful ejaculation. "It's good enough for the children; yet there *is* a possibility of such a delightful scene palling on the senses after a while. No, Dick; nothing short of Lake George for *me* this summer." There was a resolute line above the eyebrows, and the lips shut determinedly.

To persuade was useless. With good-natured firmness, Richard said, "I think it too extravagant just now; especially as you spent sixty dollars more than your allowance last term."

"I only want my own. You need not trouble yourself to hoard up money for me," was the rather sulky answer.

"A thousand dollars will not do everything, Robert. You have made an unfortunate beginning."

"Well, if I choose to spend my own, that's my affair. Hermit-living isn't at all to my taste; so don't make me angry by preaching on the text economy. I'm bound to go; and I'll raise the money some way." The fire that sparkled in his eyes was not pleasant to contemplate.

Richard was sorely puzzled. He could not exercise a father's authority over this young man, although he felt he was beginning a dangerous course. Sealing his letters, he said, gravely, "I'll see Mr. Guilford."

Robert lighted his cigar as he returned, "Well, I've given you fair warning. I know I can borrow the money."

Richard spent two hours in calls, before he drove to the lawyer's office. The clerk was alone.

"Where is Mr. Guilford?" he asked.

"O Dr. Bertrand! I supposed you knew he was ill. He went home yesterday noon, and has not been down since."

He drove to the house immediately. Mrs. Guilford met him with an anxious face.

"I am so glad you have come," she began. "I wanted Mr. Guilford to send for you yesterday; and this morning, when James went down, you were out. He is seriously ill, I fear, and has been slightly delirious for an hour or two."

The sick man started as they entered his room. His face was flushed, his eyes sunken and wild. At Mrs. Guilford's announcement, he rallied a little, and held out his hand, saying, "O doctor! I believe I was half asleep."

Dr. Bertrand made his examination, and asked a few necessary questions. Mr. Guilford collected his thoughts with an effort, and answered slowly,—

"I have not felt perfectly well for a week, but the weather

has been very warm, and I was so busy, I thought it came
from overwork. Yesterday I rose with a most excruciating
headache, and felt too weak to stir. I spent a couple of
hours at the office, and then came home, thinking a good
rest would set me up; but I had a high fever all night.
However, I dare say your skill can bring me around in a
day or two."

Richard studied the symptoms thoughtfully, and then
asked, in a calm tone, "Have you any objections to my calling in Dr. D——."

"Dick, my boy, what is it?" and Mr. Guilford started
up. "Your father never shirked a truth, and I always hon-
ored him for it. If you fear anything serious, I ought to
know before my mind gives out. I've had hard work to
keep straight this morning." He fixed his eyes keenly on
the young man, whose face changed a trifle under the scrutiny.

"You have every indication of typhoid, I think," was the
grave answer; "and though my skill might be sufficient, I
should feel safer to rely on Dr. D——'s greater experience."

"As you like; although I have as much confidence in
you. I am aware there are some things beyond a physician's reach. Does it promise to be severe?"

"I think it does. I wish I had seen you sooner."

Mr. Guilford sank back with an expression of exhaustion.
After a long pause, he said, "There is a little business I
must attend to."

Richard hesitated. He knew how necessary extreme
quiet was; he also knew there *was* a chance of his never
being better able to finish any earthly task, and consented.

"Stop at the office, and send Jarvis up, please."

Something besides directions struggled through the young
physician's mind — a remembrance of his father's death,
and the blessed consolation that he had been among those
who "die in the Lord." Was there not a duty owing to

the soul as well as the body? He leaned over the bed with
an earnest face, and said, in the gentlest of tones, —

"Dear friend, is it well with you in either event?"

A weak, helpless light in the sick man's eyes, with an imploring gesture of the hands, was the only answer. Richard
left the apartment quietly. His own perplexity he must
bear alone. Robert must go, and risk all improper associations. He would be powerless to restrain him.

CHAPTER VII.

Sorrow and silence are strong, and patient endurance is Godlike,
Therefore accomplish thy labor of love till the heart is made Godlike.
EVANGELINE.

NOT finding Dr. D—— at home, he remembered an engagement with Ada, and drove at once to Mrs. Taylor's. His betrothed met him with a bright face, and said gayly, as she ushered him into the drawing-room, —

"How good of you to come just when one wants you! We have made our final decisions. But how grave you look! What new trouble has been added to your list?"

The flippant tone pained him, yet he answered pleasantly, "Never mind me. What are the arrangements?"

"We are going earlier than we thought — next Tuesday. Mr. Taylor can stay only two weeks, as his partner is going to California. The party will consist of Mr. and Mrs. Taylor, Mrs. Ashley, you, and myself. In ten or twelve days Mr. Ashley will rejoin us, and you, like a good child, will remain with us until we return."

He thought of Mr. Guilford, and was silent.

"You shall not make any excuse," she began, with girlish petulance. "For once I am resolved to have my own way."

"Listen, Ada." There was some authority in his tone. "Mr. Guilford, my father's cherished friend as well as my own, is seriously ill with typhoid fever. At that period he will have reached the worst. No physician would leave a patient, at such a moment, to go on a pleasure tour. Affection as well as honor binds me."

"You can never do anything I ask of you! I think sometimes that you have not the slightest regard for the tie between us; that where I go, and what I do, are alike indifferent to you. I'm not sure you would have felt at all hurt if I had left you without a word."

"Ada, you are ungenerous. You know I have been looking forward to this journey as a great pleasure; but could you counsel me to leave Mr. Guilford at such a time?"

"Doubtless there are as skilful physicians in the city as yourself," was the cold reply.

"If I did not value my reputation, common gratitude would bid me remain. If the tour could be delayed a week —"

"It cannot. We are all ready, and shall go with or without you. I confess to some mortification in owning to my sisters that *my* lover puts his duty to others on a much higher round than his duty to me. When it is your pleasure to attend to *me*, I shall be happy to know the fact." Her tone was bitter, her face flushed and haughty.

"I will join you at the earliest day possible. If you think, Ada, that, in giving you pain, *I* do not suffer any, you are mistaken."

She would not unbend. "I have no more favors to ask of you. When your duty leads you in this direction, come."

"You are angry."

"I am hurt — wounded to the quick. Your whole manner has changed towards me. If you are tired of — of —" and her rapid breath compelled her to pause.

He rose and stood before her with much authoritative pride in his manner, and his tone was almost stern, as he said, —

"Ada, this is child's play; nay, worse. It is wicked. We two, who expect to be nearest and dearest through life, have no right to torment each other with it. You know I love you — that my heart has never wandered for an hour. I am confident you would despise a man who could be weakly tempted to forget duty and honor. If I neglected others, what safeguard would you have?"

"Please yourself. We will not quarrel about it." Her tone was provokingly complaisant.

He rose to go. Her chilling manner never relaxed, and their adieux were coldly spoken. With a heavy heart he sought Dr. D——, and the two proceeded on their errand.

Mr. Guilford was rapidly growing worse. He did not recognize either of them, when they aroused him from his stupor.

"You are doing the best that can be done," said Dr. D——. "The disease has so much the start of you that it will be difficult to manage. Poor Guilford! What a pity he did not ask advice earlier; but that is ever the way with these strong, hearty men. They think themselves invulnerable."

"And your opinion is —"

"That it's a serious case. Steady nerves and a cool brain are what you must bring to the trial, my young friend. Guilford has a strong constitution, and is a temperate man; that's in his favor. But the hot weather is against him, and his delirium will doubtless be very exhausting. But we will hope for the best. Come to me in any doubt."

"Thank you." He could not think calmly when the life of a dear friend was in jeopardy.

He hurried home for a little rest and quiet; but as he was hanging up his hat in the hall, an angry, boyish voice caught his ear.

"You're mean and hateful, Rob Bertrand, that's what you are! I wish you'd go off again, for you plague me to death, and I don't like you one bit!"

He walked to the piazza and surveyed the scene — Robert cool and tantalizing, Archie flushed and tearful. He held out his hand to the child, and said, sorrowfully, —

"Who is angry and rude?"

"O, Dick! but you don't know how he torments me!"

"What a little fool you are, Archie!" and Robert sauntered down the steps.

Richard led the child to the library, and spent his leisure in listening patiently to the story. The dispute had been trifling enough in the beginning, but Archie was passionate, and smarted under a sense of injustice he could *feel* better than explain. It was no light task to conquer him with kindly patience, to convince the child he was not to sin, even under provocation. Just as the dinner-bell rang, Archie clasped his arms around his brother's neck, and said, in a voice that was still humble with sobs, "O, Dick, you are the best man in the world! I love you almost as I used to love papa."

When they took their seats at the table, he passed quietly around to Robert's place, and said low, but frankly, as he held out his hand, "I am sorry I was so rude to you."

Robert gave the hand a little pinch, and laughed.

After dinner Richard walked in the garden with the children. He was surprised to find how soon a wrong example was beginning to bring forth fruit. Robert's brilliancy was so captivating that the insidious poison took a broad sweep before it declared itself. Would *he* be strong enough to counteract the influence it might have on Archie? More keenly than ever he felt the responsibility laid upon him by his father's death. With silent fervor he prayed for guidance, for patience, and a hopeful heart.

How full of pain that bright, beautiful summer day had been to him! Where he had looked for roses, thorns had pricked him. Where he had gone for strength, he had found weakness. But there was one never-failing Friend, and in this hour of perplexity he went to Him who had said, "My grace is sufficient for thee."

Robert had lighted his cigar immediately after dinner, and strolled out. It was late when he returned, and Richard, lying wearily on the sofa, was thankful not to be disturbed.

After breakfast the next morning, he summoned his brother to the library. As Robert noticed the grave, determined face, he fortified himself with some arguments he

had been running over in his mind; but the precautions were
needless.

"I could not discuss your proposed trip with Mr. Guilford
yesterday," Richard began in a kindly manner, "for I found
him very ill. I have therefore concluded to let you go under
protest. I do not approve of the plan. I think, with your
means, it is extravagant; yet I feel myself unable to make
any other arrangement that would satisfy you. I do not expect to have a father's authority over you, but I want to feel
assured, Robert, that there is a cordial brotherly affection between us. I want to have confidence enough in you to trust
you anywhere, and believe you are doing nothing you would
be ashamed to have our father know. I want you to think that
however much my judgment may differ from yours, I have
your interest and happiness at heart. Will you do this?"

"You're a good fellow, Dick, but I wasn't made after your
pattern. There's different blood running in my veins, and I
cannot get along in this humdrum style. You need not feel
afraid, though. I can take care of myself;" and Robert
glanced around with a proud air of self-sufficiency.

"You are young, and of a nature that meets temptation
half way; but O, Robert, for our dead father's sake be careful. Remember, we are to strive worthily to meet him at
the last."

"Don't preach to me, Dick! It always stirs up my blood,
and just now I don't want to say anything cross to you. I'm
not any worse than other young men, although being a saint
does not run in the list of my accomplishments."

Richard wrote him out a check. "Do not forget," he
said, "that this lessens the money for your education.
Think before you spend it."

"I have thought, and 'my heart's in the highlands.'
Thank you for all, Dick;" and taking the check, he bowed
himself gracefully out of the room.

Richard wrote some letters, and then proceeded to his
daily duties. Mr. Guilford was much worse; but besides this

he had no very severe cases. He was glad of a spare half hour before dinner to devote to Ada, for he had experienced a strange uneasiness since their parting.

"Miss Townley had gone to New York," the servant said, briefly; but, before he could turn away, Mrs. Taylor fluttered through the hall, and in the most solicitous of tones, inquired for Mr. Guilford.

"We are all so sorry, and feel greatly disappointed at your not being able to join our party, but of course a friend like Mr. Guilford demands your first attention. You must follow us as soon as you can."

Her cordial tone quite reassured him, and he answered, "You cannot regret the interruption more than I do. As soon as it is possible for me to leave Mr. Guilford, I shall come. When will Ada return?"

"On Saturday. Mr. Taylor brought her a note last night from Mrs. Ashley. There's some shopping to finish, I believe."

He left her with a lighter heart. Anger had not been the cause of Ada's sudden departure, and it was evident Mrs. Taylor did not blame him very severely.

He came home to find the scene of Archie's late quarrel in pleasant confusion, and the two brothers agreeing capitally. Robert was displaying some handsome fishing tackle, and a box of flies that interested Archie wonderfully. His rifle, powder-flask, a dainty hunting suit, and a wide-brimmed straw hat, had all undergone inspection. Tessy was watering the jasmine with his drinking-cup, an ingenious affair that afforded her much amusement. Robert was in a charming mood, and after dinner romped with the children, and sang them a host of droll college songs, making most grotesque faces to accompany them. Tessy seemed to be delighted with —

> "Old mother Scraggins couldn't go to meetin',
> 'Cause she hadn't two shoes for to put her feet in;
> Meetin', Meetin',
> Couldn't go to Meetin',
> 'Cause she hadn't two shoes for to put her feet in."

The week ended and a new one began. Robert started off in the highest of spirits. Caution and advice were so evidently useless, that Richard did not proffer them; but his heart yearned over the handsome, wayward boy.

On the following day he went to New York with his betrothed's party. He felt that Ada had not quite forgiven him; and as visions of the pleasant tour rose before him, the sacrifice seemed almost too great. Under a mask of careless good humor, Ada managed to give him many a stinging wound, and at the last, while the bell was ringing, in the midst of his assurance that he would rejoin her at the earliest possible day, she whispered, "I have half a mind to fall sick. When I am married, I shall be ill all the time, for the sake of keeping you attentive."

His glance was reproachful. They had never parted in so indifferent a manner. For the first time there entered into his heart a doubt, not of her constancy, not of her devotion, but whether he had chosen the woman who would care for his happiness above all things.

6

CHAPTER VIII.

A strange, sweet path formed day by day,
How, when, and wherefore, we cannot say;
No more than our own life paths we know,
Whither they lead us, why we go.
MISS MULOCH.

WITH an anxious, prayerful heart, Dr. Richard Bertrand awaited the issue of his friend Guilford's case. It was the first real responsibility since his father's death, and that event had made him pitiful and tender. He felt keenly for the loving wife and young children who would need the careful guidance of such a parent for years to come. Through the fearful crisis he never left him. Taking his station at the bedside, he noted every stage of the waning delirium until it became incoherent mutterings. The terrible fever strength began to subside; the wild, eager eyes grew dull; the hands fell like dead weights; there was a lingering transition into heavy slumber, marked by spasmodic gasps and stertorous breathing. Midnight passed; the gray dawn came up in the east. Mr. Guilford's pulse grew weaker, and his face assumed a pallid hue. The fever had gone, but whether life would not follow it, seemed a doubtful question. He despatched a servant for Dr. D—— as soon as he heard the household astir.

All that human knowledge could suggest had been done. For an hour the two watched; then they noted a faint change; the pulse revived, a calmer sleep succeeded.

"If he has strength for a day or two, he will come out safe. It has been a severe case, and, Bertrand, you deserve great credit," said Dr. D——.

"I never felt before how entirely in the hands of God the issues of life are," Richard replied, solemnly. "When our best is done, we have to wait for *His* fiat."

"True, true; but a less cautious man might have killed him in three days. Didn't I hear something about your going abroad?"

"My father's death prevented it;" and a little flush rose to Richard's pale cheeks.

"If you will take an old man's advice,—and your father had some faith in me,—you will not leave this path until you have made your mark. The next ten years here will be invaluable to you, if you expect to stay in the practice. I predict a fair future."

"Thank you;" and Richard bowed his adieu.

All that Mr. Guilford would need for several hours was extremest quiet. After seeing Mrs. Guilford take her station in the darkened room, he departed. The fresh summery air seemed strange as it blew in his face; indeed, so tensely had his nervous system been wrought upon, he could scarcely realize for the first few minutes where he was. He took a long, brisk walk, and reached home mentally refreshed, but physically tired.

"How pale and weary you look, but not despairing," was Mabel's greeting. "There is hope for Mr. Guilford."

"A little. It was a terrible night; but I am thankful I remained. And now, Bel, I'm going to sleep an hour or two; do not let me be disturbed."

He bathed his hands and face, and was just settling himself on the sofa when Mabel entered the library.

"I've made you a nice cup of tea," she said, with a smile.

"Your face tempts me to try it," was his response.

She arranged his pillows, shut out the sunshine, and sat down by him with a book in her hand.

"What's that for?" and an arch light crossed his face.

"I'm going to read you to sleep, as I used to papa,

when he was fagged out; and you like ‘ In Memoriam ’ so much.”

He closed his eyes, and listened to the clear, liquid voice, until the room floated away, and in its stead came dim pictures of meadow greens, with the tender ripple of silvery brooks, the murmur of forest trees rocking in the breeze, delicious fragments of music, and remembrances of fragrant airs, steeped in odorous summer blossoms. A vague sense of beauty and comfort stole over him. Two hours later he awoke refreshed, and found himself alone.

He ran up stairs to Mabel, and exclaimed, laughingly, —

“ What a charming nurse you are! I’m afraid you have not a very high opinion of my endurance, when you see how one night’s work used me up ; but I shall take matters easier another time. Now I must hurry off, and finish up my calls before dinner. There’s your pay ; ” and he kissed the rosy mouth.

By Saturday there was a fair hope of Mr. Guilford’s recovery. Richard was discussing this, and their own plans, as they sat on the balcony, in the star-lit evening.

“ And so, Bel,” he said, “ if you can be ready by Tuesday, I’ll take you all down to aunt Sophy’s, and stay one night ; then on Thursday I shall start for the White Mountains.”

“ O, please, Dick,” cried Lily, “ put it off until Wednesday. Lucy Ogden’s birthday party is on Tuesday, and we are all invited. They’re to have a splendid time, with a supper on the lawn, and the fireworks Lucy couldn’t have Fourth of July because she was sick. I wouldn’t miss it for anything ! ”

“ Wednesday, then,” said Richard. And on Monday one letter was despatched to Cape May, and another to the White Mountains.

Everything went on prosperously. Tuesday morning Mabel spent in looking over the children’s clothes, and making preparations for the journey. Lily and Archie inter-

spersed their dinner with glowing anticipations of the party.
Tessy's plate was sent away nearly untouched, and she only
played with her dessert of pine-apple. Richard noticed this,
and also her flushed face and sparkling eyes.

"You have been playing too hard this morning," he said.

"O, I didn't play at all ; I went to sleep on the sofa."

He drew her to his knee, and took the little hands in his.
They were feverish ; so he said, gently, —

"Suppose you take a ride with me, and then come home
to Mabel. It will be better for you than going to the
party."

"O Dick !" She drew a long, quivering sigh, and her
eyes filled with tears. "Please do let me go ; I'm not sick."

He had been studying fever symptoms so long, that he
fancied he must have grown nervous over them. He looked
at her earnestly ; but the beseeching face was too much for
him.

"Never mind, pet ; don't cry. You may go if you will
promise not to run too much, or eat up all the candies ; and
do not get frightened at the fireworks."

She kissed Richard with convulsive fondness, but in a few
moments was laughing gayly at some of Archie's nonsense.

A sudden summons for Dr. Bertrand interrupted the after-
dinner conversation, and he hurried away. Mabel dressed
the children, and Martin took them in the carriage. Tessy
looked so bright and pretty that she dismissed the fears
Richard's words had called up. It was only a child's intense way of anticipating pleasure.

Richard was busy until quite late in the evening. He felt
rather disappointed, as he had intended to have a nice long
talk with Mabel, before their separation. Letting himself
in with his latch-key, he encountered her at the foot of the
stairs ; and even in that subdued light her white face startled him.

"Tessy !" he exclaimed, at a thought.

"I am so glad you have come ;" and Mabel clung to him

with a frightened grasp. "Mrs. Ogden's nurse brought her back just at dusk. She had complained of a headache, and at last cried to come home. I bathed her and put her in her crib, and she fell asleep for a little while, but awoke so wild that I had to call in Mrs. Hall."

By this time they had reached the apartment. In her little bed lay the child, talking, laughing, and crying, in a breath; her face crimsoned with fever, her eyes staring vacantly around. Richard took the hot hands in his, smoothed away the golden curls, and tried to calm her.

"It's brother Dick," he said, soothingly. "Tessy remembers brother Dick?"

She made an effort, as if to recall her wandering senses; but it was useless.

"She has not recognized me since she woke," Mabel said, choking down the fear at her heart.

Mrs. Hall was very anxious, and obeyed Richard's orders with speed and quiet. The carriage drove into the yard, and the gay voices floated up through the open window.

"Bel," Richard said, quickly, "go down and keep them as still as you can. They must not come in here; I want Lily to sleep elsewhere, for I shall stay with Tessy."

She ran down and managed to allay their apprehensions, mingled as they were with bits of pleasure — accounts of the fireworks, the lawn full of colored lanterns, and sorrow that Tessy could not have seen it all. It was some time before she could quiet them sufficiently for sleep, and then she returned to Richard. Tessy lay dozing now; but her eyes were half open. She looked into her brother's face with a feeling of awe, and said, just under her breath, —

"Is it typhoid?"

"No, not that. We will see what it proves in the morning. And now, dear, I want you to go to sleep, for to-morrow you may have to play nurse, and overstrained nerves won't do."

He kissed away her half-tearful pleading, and led her to

the door. Through those long hours of the night he thought not only of the danger, but the new disappointment that had befallen him.

At early dawn Mabel was down again. Richard had fallen into a light doze. Tessy moaned uneasily, but was not restless. Even in that pale light she could see the scarlet face and arms in strong relief against the white pillow and nightdress. Like a flash the truth thrilled through her, leaving her cold, but calm and strong. When Richard stirred she went to the sofa.

"O Mabel! I did not mean you should come in the room until ——"

"It is scarlet fever," she said, in a steady voice. "I am not afraid."

He drew her down beside him, asking, —

"Do you want to take care of her?"

"As if I *could* give her up to any one else! Our precious baby papa loved so well."

"I would rather have you; and there is no danger if you are careful. If you are to take office under me, you must learn first not to be wasteful of your strength. I want you to have your breakfast every morning before you do much around her; and you must walk in the garden for fresh air. I will see if Mrs. Parkhurst cannot take Archie and Lilian for a week; it will make less care for you, and we shall be able to keep the house quieter."

"Do you think ——" and Mabel's tears finished the sentence.

"I have a good deal of hope, dearest. My experience of the last fortnight has taught me much. Yet we can judge nothing for the present. She is very ill, with a most dangerous disease. Get your prayer-book, Mabel, and let us read together."

It was the twenty-seventh of the month. Among the psalms for that day was the one hundred and twenty-first. How comfortingly these sentences fell : —

" Behold he that keepeth Israel shall neither slumber nor sleep. The Lord himself is thy keeper; the Lord is thy defence upon thy right hand.

" So that the sun shall not burn thee by day, neither the moon by night."

Ah, yes, here was the stay and support. When human love grew weak and fearful, the everlasting arms of divine strength were folded about it. They were to be kept from all evil, watched over by One who could never know weariness. Mabel gathered courage, and looked steadily on the way before her.

Opening the window blinds, the fragrant air rushed in, heavy with night dew that had lain for hours steeping in honeysuckle and roses, and the odorous dampness of the river. Tiny threads of vapor curled upward, clinging tendril-like to the shore. Afar, the horizon seemed studded with bars of sapphire and emerald, while faint, arrowy streaks of gold shot up, and were lost in the filmy blue overhead. Then the glory of day burst slowly through the crimson and purple veils; tree and shrub were burnished with the glowing tints, save where in shadow lurked a weird, fleecy mist. As drifts of rosy cloud floated across the sky, the very air grew tremulous with radiated heat; the freshness turned into languor, and the promise of a long, hot summer day dawned upon them. But Mabel knew who had said, — " So that the sun shall not burn thee by day."

A solemn awe fell upon the household. Instead of Ann's lively repartee and gay laugh, she went about with a great weight on her heart. Mrs. Hall sat up stairs and sewed, so as to be within call. Mabel was grave, and her eyes had a startled look in them, as if she could not quite reconcile herself to the sense of danger. It took her back to those sorrowful days whose shadow had only lightened, not departed. The little sufferer lay moaning and tossing, restlessly, with no light of recognition in her eyes. As Mabel watched, this seemed the hardest of all.

The day was an almost stifling one. Even as the sun went westward, the flickering currents of air seemed to shake out rays of molten gold. · There was no breeze stirring, and all nature drooped exhausted. Tessy's fever raged terribly. As Richard stood gazing at the burning face, he said, slowly, —

" Mabel, do you think you could cut her hair? It is so warm, clinging about her face."

She brought the scissors, and with a trembling hand slowly severed the shining rings that were fast becoming matted by heat and restlessness, one by one. and laid them in a box of keepsakes. How would they be taken out? As little golden remembrances of one gone to heaven, or to be smiled over at some happy reunion, when the child's voice was again the gayest of all? Only God could tell. Her tears fell silently upon them. O, how powerless poor human love was at its best estate! It was well that faith could believe, through all the blinding agony, that God was a Father who remembered mercy.

Late in the evening Mabel was dismissed, with injunctions to go to sleep as soon as possible, and Richard watched through the quiet night alone. It was not strange, perhaps, that something besides Tessy should linger in his thoughts. In two days he had hoped to see Ada. How would she bear this new disappointment? Was there some strange fatality between them? He brought his writing desk, and began a letter to her; yet, disguise the fact with never so much love, he felt he could not lead Ada to look upon his duties in the same light that he did. He could not open his whole heart to her. Alas for love, when there must be reservations and fears! Its divine essence is gone, its electric chord is weakened. More sacred than ever seemed his promise now, and looking down the future, he felt the years, only, could release him. No wonder such a conscience should shrink and tremble with tender, yearning pain.

Another and another day of heat, blinding sunshine, and the agony of dread. The little sufferer lost some of her wildness, and sank into pitiful moans, as she tossed her arms about, or lay with her eyes half open, regardless of the faces pleading in wordless pathos for one gleam of recognition. Then there came a time when they counted hours, moments, and prayed as they only pray, who stand shivering at the entrance of the dark valley, for one beloved; when they scarcely breathed, and learned how little they had hoped, when they came back from utter despair, and glanced in each other's faces, with a low cry of relief.

After this Mabel had much more to do. With returning consciousness Tessy's wants increased; and the childish restlessness, the petulant, humorsome fancies, might have tried any other than a loving heart. There were no traces of weariness in her face, no impatience in her tones; indeed, her thorough gratitude gave her strength for all demands. Richard used to watch this assiduous tenderness with a curiously strange feeling. Was it inherent in all women, or could Mabel be a higher type of her sex?

Lilian and Archie came home. Familiar voices floated on the summer air, and rang through the house so lately silent with the chill of apprehension. Tessy, pillowed on a corner of the lounge, or nestling in Mabel's arms, listening to the sweet old songs she loved so dearly, her face reduced to baby proportions, her scanty locks just waving around her head, her thin little hands too weak to grasp anything, was the central attraction. How happy they all were! And one Sunday, when Richard carried her down to the parlor, so Mabel might play their evening hymn while they all sang, their satisfaction was complete. Could he be the one to break up this pleasant home circle?

Aunt Sophy had written for them as soon as Tessy could bear the journey. Mabel was very willing to go, and sincerely sorry that Richard's trip had been delayed.

"When will it be safe to start?" she asked.

"Next week, I think. The sea air and a little bathing will soon bring the roses to Tessy's cheeks."

"O," laughed Lily, "half a wave would carry her to Europe, and a breaker land her in the China Sea." Tessy's recent efforts at walking had amused the two younger ones greatly.

The child made rapid progress. Richard took her out for short rides, Archie petted her when she was restless, and Lily arranged dolls, dishes, and toys to her liking, twenty times an hour. Then, when the weary eyes were turned to Mabel, she was soothed into refreshing slumbers, and nature wrought for her with silent power.

Again the packing commenced. This time there was no interruption. Mr. Guilford came to say good by, and was delighted with their bright faces. Since his illness he had loved Richard like a son.

CHAPTER IX.

The man is the spirit he worked in; not what he did, but what he became.

With self-renunciation begins life.

CARLYLE.

THE day was bright and clear, and there was a fresh breeze as they steamed down the bay. The purple hills of Staten Island gleamed with the peculiar golden bronze of the later summer, and the low-lying Jersey shore was bathed in a mist of dun amber. The waves crept slowly shoreward, drifting into fantastic shapes, whose foamy crest pranced along, and then, breaking, scattered the pearly spray far up on the land. As they left the city behind them, the distant ships looked like flocks of sea-birds, outlined against the blue sky.

Tessy sat in Richard's lap, her pale little face and his devotion attracting more than a casual attention from the passengers. She watched Archie and Lilian in their eager enjoyment, glanced at the places Richard pointed out to them, and was presently lulled to sleep by the motion and the monotonous music. More than one mother's face kindled into a sweet smile over the picture they made.

At the end of their sail, aunt Sophy came to meet them in a large family carriage, and bestowed upon them the warmest of welcomes.

"Poor baby," she said, taking Tessy's wasted hand. "If it had been any other season of the year, I should have come as soon as I received your letter. Nearly every one is alarmed about scarlet fever. I don't see how you managed so well, my dear;" and she gave Mabel a fond smile.

"Mabel proved a most excellent nurse," Richard rejoined.

"And you know I had a physician always at hand," was Mabel's arch answer.

While aunt Sophy listened to the story, Archie amused himself with attempts at driving. Presently they reached a large country-house, whose numerous additions were more suggestive of comfort than architectural beauty. Two boisterous cousins nearly smothered Archie and Lily with kisses. Aunt Sophy led the way up stairs to a spacious apartment, whose white curtains, checked matting, and maple chairs looked cool and inviting.

"This is the best I can do for you," she exclaimed, glancing at Mabel. "Lily must share Dora's room, and Tom can take Archie in charge. I've been crowded with boarders this summer, but I've kept this room in spite of all. Now I'll go and send your trunk up. Wouldn't you like to have supper here this first night?"

"A very delightful proposal. But think of the trouble."

She answered Richard's look with a laugh. "Trouble! No, indeed. I'm only too glad to have you all down here;" and she bustled off in her cheery fashion.

Mabel refreshed herself and the children with a plentiful ablution, and by the time she had them all in order, aunt Sophy reappeared with the tea-tray. Lily gayly proceeded to arrange the table. Such nice creamy biscuits, such dishes of fruit, and for Tessy a little broiled bird. Aunt Sophy took the head of the table, and soon made them all feel at home. Her warm heart and cordial manner were wonderfully enjoyable.

The next morning Richard left them, though not without many charges concerning Tessy and the two others, who seemed disposed to run wild.

"Never you mind," said aunt Sophy. "I've managed them many a time before. As for Tessy, she'll be so plump and rosy on your return that you will hardly know her. And now, little ones, kiss brother Dick good by, and come down to the kitchen with me."

After his duty was fairly performed, and no pleading eyes met his at every turn, Richard was all impatience. Delay and disappointment had strengthened his desire for Ada. Now that he had a right to shut out every other thought, he was almost surprised to find her so dear, so well beloved.

The party had gone to Newport. It was late in the afternoon when he arrived, and just allowing himself time for the briefest toilet, he hurried down to the spacious hotel parlor. Summoning a servant, he despatched him with a message for Miss Townley.

The reply was that Miss Townley had gone out, but Mrs. Taylor would be down presently.

Ada had not received his letter, then, or she would surely have been the first to greet him. He paced impatiently up and down the room, glanced at the gay groups among the shrubbery, and found it hard work to restrain himself. After what seemed to him an interminable while, Mrs. Taylor entered, and greeted him cordially, yet with perceptible constraint.

"I am so sorry Ada is out; but Mrs. Ashley was anxious for some sea-coast views, and the day was so fine for visiting them, they thought it best not to wait."

"Do you know if she heard from me this morning?"

"I was out until nearly noon. I do not think she expected you to-day," was Mrs. Taylor's non-committal reply.

It was some comfort for Richard to believe the mails at fault. He walked up and down the balcony with Mrs. Taylor, and as the best means of quieting his mind, related the events of the last few weeks, and questioned her concerning their White Mountain trip. Then Mr. Ashley came sauntering towards them, and Richard's first eager question was, "Where did you leave the ladies?"

"Me? O, I have not seen them since about four. They have quite deserted me, I assure you; won by a fast horse;" and Mr. Ashley laughed with the easy grace of a man of the world.

"Mr. Livingston, an old friend, has taken them out," explained Mrs. Taylor.

Richard's disappointment deepened almost to disapproval.

"Don't look so sober, doctor," began Mr. Ashley. "When you see those magnificent grays, you will not wonder. Everybody is frantic about Livingston's turn-out, especially the women."

At this juncture the supper bell rang. "Since we have to play the roll of the deserted, we may as well do it with a good grace," said Mr. Ashley, gayly. "Accept my arm, Mary. Come, doctor."

"Perhaps we had better wait," suggested Mrs. Taylor, as she noticed the expression of Richard's face.

"Nonsense. You remember Mr. Livingston's description of the beach by moonlight, and Ada's saying the only time to ride there was after sundown. They will not be back these three hours. Don't look so disconsolate, doctor; this Newport bewitches the women."

Richard followed them reluctantly, wondering if there could ever come a time when *he* would be so indifferent to *his* wife's absence. Mr. and Mrs. Ashley were certainly a most fashionably independent couple. Each placed implicit confidence in the other, and neither was jealously inclined. Perhaps, too, love had some powerful rivals in both hearts, and kept uncomplainingly in the background. Mrs. Ashley was careful of her own and her husband's honor; Mr. Ashley was proud of having his wife admired, and not peculiarly sensitive in any respect.

The moments after supper seemed intolerably long. Declining Mr. Ashley's invitation to a game of billiards, he watched the throngs promenading the walks, half listened to the music, and at length, weary of the gay scene, wandered down the avenue, taking one of the paths leading to the beach. Disappointed and restless, he was anxious for the time to pass; and never did seconds seem more leaden. He walked on in a vague hope of meeting the carriage, and when he turned to retrace his steps, found he had gone much farther than he intended.

He came up to the long balcony, flushed and anxious; but the first sight that met his eyes restored immediate composure. There stood Ada Townley in the beauty and brilliancy of an exquisite evening dress, her round, white arms gleaming with costly bracelets, her face one dazzle of animation. No sign of expectation or longing, no glance down the walks for the coming of some one dearer than all these. *Was* he dearer? If so, **how** could she stand there in careless grace, and talk to that tall, handsome man, who did not attempt to conceal his admiration? A fiery-pointed pain shot through Richard's heart; jealousy first, then dreary despair.

He was almost beside her before she raised her eyes. There was a light in them he did not like. She held out her hand, and said, cordially enough, —

"O Dr. Bertrand! Mrs. Taylor was quite distressed about your sudden disappearance. I think I have been home nearly an hour — is it not?" and turning, she introduced her companion.

Richard responded courteously; then, in a low but authoritative tone, said, "May I ask the favor of your company a few moments?"

She seemed irresolute at first, but the pressure of his hand upon her arm was not to be mistaken. "Excuse me," she said in an undertone, meant only for Mr. Livingston; "old friends have a claim on one's indulgence;" but softly breathed as it was, Richard's quick ear caught it. His intuitions were in an electric state, and biting his lips to keep back the rush of anger, he led her down the walk. For some time neither spoke.

"Did you receive a letter from me yesterday or this morning?" he demanded at length.

"Yes, last night." · Her manner was cool and careless.

"You must have expected me then. O Ada!"

"No, I confess I did not. You have disappointed me too often, of late, for me to believe until I saw you. I was not sure but some one would conveniently fall ill at the last moment."

Her heartlessness roused him, and he said, rather sternly, —

"Do you imply that I sought an excuse for not joining you earlier?"

"I don't imply anything. I know that no request of mine has found favor in your sight for a long while. Every one seems to have a stronger claim on you than I?"

A new fire sprang up in the soft hazel eyes, and outraged love asserted itself. In a tone steady with deep power, he said, —

"Since you think me capable of subterfuge or wilful deceit, and can no longer depend on my affection, you cannot wish to marry a man so lost to honor and truth. I release you from a promise that must have grown irksome."

It was foolish, doubtless, but he expected even then to see her disclaim these cruel assertions, look up with imploring eyes, and give some sign of love. Vain hope! Carelessly beautiful, indifferent to any past memory, she answered, with a haughty inclination of the head, "As you please."

He led her to the balcony, wished her good night, and turned away, feeling she was already half won by Howard Livingston. In that first moment he thought calmly of her being another's. He pitied himself as if it had been a third person, so little did he realize the great shadow fallen upon him.

Ada turned to Mr. Livingston with an easy grace, and as if some explanation was needed, said, nonchalantly, —

"For two years I have been engaged to Dr. Bertrand — a girlish fancy that I have outlived in the last six months. We have just dissolved the bond."

He bowed with a pleased look. There was nothing for

her to regret in the exchange. Of late, she had felt the position Dr. Bertrand's wife must fill was very little to her liking. Here was a man to whom she would be *first* always, superior to her old lover in those points she cared most for. She could retain her position in society; no troublesome domestic details would ever be forced upon her, and life would prove a perfect round of pleasure. Although she inwardly congratulated herself on her improved prospects, she gave a pitying thought to Richard, and said to herself, " I could have made him very happy if he had not been so set upon those foolish whims." She was relieved to learn that he left early the next morning.

Mrs. Ashley congratulated her openly. She had never cordially approved of Dr. Bertrand, her theory being that it was much more sensible to love a rich man than a poor one. Since affairs had proved so obstinate, she had been secretly favoring Mr. Livingston, quite determined to have him for a brother-in-law.

Mrs. Taylor kissed her, and said, —

" I am heartily glad, my dear. You never could have given satisfaction in such a family. It would have been worse than marrying a widower."

Two weeks later Ada Townley went home the affianced of Howard Livingston.

In the mean while the party at Cape May were well cared for. It took but one day for Lilian and Archie to recommence the old life laid down the preceding autumn. To them there seemed no change, except the few strange boarders, and the inches Tom and Dora had grown in a year. Aunt Sophy took entire charge of them, and Mabel was left to the undisturbed care of Tessy. She felt keenly the alteration her father's death had made, and would continue to make all the coming years. She had grown older in those brief months. Care came to her not as a burden, but a portion of life that it was her duty to accept willingly. She missed Richard sadly, and tried to resign him with the pure unselfishness of her nature, knowing the time must soon come when another would be first and best to him.

Tessy's days had been rounded into perfection by a ride down to the steamboat landing. But on Saturday both horses had gone out with the large carriage, and Mr. Sheldon's pony, which Tom often drove, was busy also. The child's eyes filled with tears of disappointment.

"Why, we don't expect any one," Mabel said, cheerily.

"I know it, but it seems like a little piece of Dick to see the steamboat and all the people. O Bel! can't we walk."

"No, darling, not that distance. Richard would scold us for such a crazy step."

"What is the matter, Snowdrop?" said stout, good-natured Mrs. Chesterton, coming up the steps, and patting Tessy's head. Mabel briefly explained the difficulty.

"Mr. Chesterton has had Mr. Grey's old Hero and the little wagon. I do not believe he has taken them back, and you may as well use them as not," the lady said.

Mabel thanked her, but declined. Tessy's eyes overflowed. Mrs. Chesterton found her husband, and brought him to the balcony.

"Why, yes, Miss Bertrand; take them by all means. I told Mr. Grey I'd be home about dusk; so he won't expect his horse until that time. He's so lazy you need not feel a bit afraid. He couldn't run if he tried."

Aunt Sophy insisted as well. Bell and Tessy were lifted in, and drove off in triumph, the little one's face full of intense satisfaction. The eager eyes and flushed cheeks gave Mabel a strange presentiment of something like evil. She begged to go faster, that they might be in time to see the passengers land.

"What *is* the matter, Tessy? Don't get so excited; no friend of ours is coming," Mabel said, gently.

"But some day Richard *will* come." Then, after a long pause, in which her eyes wandered over the crowd, she gave a rapturous cry, and grasping her sister's hand, exclaimed,

"He *has* come! Look! there he is, our own very Dick! He is waving his handkerchief," and Tessy nodded in reply.

"Why, I don't see him," returned Mabel, slowly. "Tessy, you must be dreaming."

"He is leaning over the edge of the rail. There, now he's gone."

"I have not had a glimpse of him."

Tessy's eyes wandered over the throng in curious expectancy, and grew perceptibly grave. Then the whole face was overspread with sunshine, and following her glance, Mabel saw Richard.

He pushed through the mass, and came forward, his eyes bright with earnest affection. Tessy reached out her arms to him, and was kissed again and again.

"Why did you think of coming for me?" he asked, in surprise.

"O, we do every day," was Tessy's joyous answer.

"Because you expect me?" and he laughed.

"Not *quite*. And Bel didn't want to come to-day, but —"

"You made her, I suppose, little tyrant. You look improved already. Are you not going to offer me a seat? or do you purpose to have me walk?"

She sprang up, and as soon as he was settled, nestled in his lap. Mabel bestowed wondering glances on him, and asked for the third or fourth time if he was well.

"Entirely so." He put the reins in Tessy's hands, holding his own over them, and bending down, whispered, "I was not wanted at Newport. I have come back to be all yours."

The words gave her a pang as she took in their full meaning. Yet she hardly knew what an aching heart the tender manner to Tessy covered.

They were all overjoyed to have him back so unexpectedly. Lily and Archie had quantities of adventures to relate. Indeed, Mabel scarcely had a look at him until they were all sent off to bed, after he had, as a special favor, sung Tessy to sleep. Then he bade Mabel find a shawl, and come to walk on the beach with him.

The tide was going out, leaving the shining sand smooth as a floor. The dim and lonely reaches of the broad ocean flowed onward with a sad, mighty pulsation, the slow, regular swells breaking into a rhythmic melody — a grand chant of ceaseless sorrow. Along the western sky sailed fleecy islands in a sea of wondrous azure. Above them were hosts of golden stars, the crown of the summer night. It was just the hour for a fond confidence, and Richard opened his heart to the fair girl blossoming into pure and lovely womanhood. Her tender sympathy soothed him immeasurably. He said calmly, but not in despair, that his dream of love was over. Henceforth he was to fill the position of elder brother in its truest, widest sense. There was nothing to come between him and his duty now; no temptation to lure him from that precious household.

It was well, perhaps, that Mabel did not see all. Alone in his room, with the sorrowful midnight stars for watchers, he laid aside the mask from his heart, and glanced at it, as he only might do for many a weary day to come. He did not so much regret Ada; he seemed to understand now the wants and trivialities of her nature, the petty trials to which she would have continually subjected him. He was content to have her choose another. But the keen sense of desolation after he had shrouded the corse of a sweet first love, and silently borne it to a place of sepulture, was what remained with him, and left a nameless pain. As in death no faults are remembered, so he recalled the earlier days of their acquaintance, when love was haloed with the rose-hue of newness. Could any after passion be so sweet? He said then for him there could be no second spring. The grave in his heart could never outgrow its greenness. He felt how truly, how tenderly, he had loved.

And so came one of life's sorest lessons to Richard Bertrand. Was it to teach him patience, forbearance? He took it in that wise, quite humbly, as a little child. He remembered who had said, " All things shall work together for good." Others had walked in shaded pathways, and found rest at last. And for him, hereafter, love and duty would be as one word.

CHAPTER X.

So many feet that day by day
Still wander from the fold astray.
GOLDEN LEGEND.

As it was impossible for Richard to remain at Cape May, he compromised with the children by promising to come once a week during their stay. Tessy improved as if by magic. When September arrived, aunt Sophy begged for another month, but Mabel longed to be again at home. Mrs. Hall and Ann were delighted with their return. Robert came back in a high state of satisfaction, and had plenty of adventures to relate to the younger ones. Yet there was something in his light-heartedness that rather pained than pleased. Excitement and enjoyment appeared to be his continual study. He possessed the brilliant and dangerous qualities that make men favorites of society and slaves to temptation. Easy and generous they are called, yet many a weary burden do they lay upon others.

Richard could only pray for him when they separated. And in his frequent letters he strove to keep up an interest in home affairs for the absent one. Mabel, who had given up school, devoted herself assiduously to the household, and endeavored to make all around her happy. Love reigned perfect among them.

It was a quiet, uneventful winter. Christmas brought aunt Sophy and the cousins. Yet the day was not gone through without tears. There was a missing voice, a place unfilled — memories infinitely tender and infinitely sad.

Ada Townley's marriage occurred at this period. It assisted Richard to recover his mental tone somewhat. He no longer asked himself, in weak moments, if he had not been hasty or unjust. No good, faithful, affectionate man can easily tear up the tendrils that have twined around his very life. He will not in a moment forget the hope that was to have made glad all his future years. He may say, "I will dream no more," but in lonely hours

> "The spirit that no exorcism can bind"

will rise from the deepest grave. But Richard's sorrow strengthened and ennobled him. He did not look on the passion dreams of his young summer with hard, scornful regret. Duty and sacrifice were no self-scourging bonds whose chain clanked with every movement. He had been "wounded in the house of a friend," but he did not forget there were others to heal. Glancing down the days yet to come, he saw himself the ready helper, the comforter in trouble, and the sharer of others' joys. He would bless their marriage vows when the birdlings left the old home nest. And if, at the last, he was left alone by the fireside, he would be content with whatever God should send him.

They went on evenly again until one March night. In the very room where their father had gayly frolicked with them that last dear evening, and kissed them with tenderest affection, they sat recounting incidents of his love, words they treasured up like fine gold, caresses

> "Dear as remembered kisses after death."

There was no storm now. For several days it had been lovely and spring-like, an earnest of the country beyond, where *he* had gone to be "forever with the Lord." And time, which sanctifies all griefs, would soften this. By and by they would come back to this night as a precious remembrance.

The golden sun of May streamed into the breakfast-room, where they were all congregated one pleasant morning.

The meal was about over. Richard sat studying his memorandum-book, and as Ann brought in the paper, Mabel took it until he should be ready.

"O, Richard!" she exclaimed, with a sudden cry of pain, while her bright face faded into ashy paleness.

"What is it, Bel?" and Richard started up in alarm.

"It's so terrible! But it can't be true. There *must* be some mistake;" and her trembling finger pointed out the paragraph.

Richard's brow contracted with more than sorrow, with shame, and a flush of indignation, as he read an account of a disgraceful riot in New Haven, in which several students had been concerned. Foremost among them, indeed, the most daring and lawless, was Robert Bertrand. He had even discharged a pistol, and slightly wounded the policeman who arrested him. No wonder Richard shivered. The hand of Providence alone had kept his brother from being a murderer. And Robert in a prison cell, a criminal!

"It surely cannot be so bad," he said, at length, loth to believe such an account, and longing to comfort Mabel. "I must go to New Haven immediately."

"Is Robert ill?" asked Lily, looking up from the remnant of her toast, in wide-eyed wonder.

"No, but in serious trouble. Perhaps it will be best not to discuss it until we know all the circumstances. So you must be good children, and not fret Mabel with idle questions while I am gone."

Mabel rose and tried to regain her composure. Mrs. Hall's entrance checked Archie's exclamations. Lily took up her neglected French, and went out on the balcony to study.

"When will you go?" Mabel inquired, following Richard to the office.

"Just as soon as I can. There is a train at noon, I think."

"I wonder what will be done."

"Robert will be expelled, if nothing worse. I must bring him home." There was a little tremble in Richard's voice.

" And we thought he was doing so nicely. O, how could he ! "

" I ought to have looked after him more closely. There are so many temptations for such a nature as his."

Mabel went to prepare the children for school. In answer to their questions, she bade them be patient, and kissed the shadowed faces with strange tenderness. Then she sought refuge in her daily duties. Richard made a few necessary calls, and ran in to say good by. At sight of his troubled face, her firmness gave way.

" Don't cry, dearest," he said, gently.

She wanted to ask him to be tender with Robert; but it seemed so like a reflection on the kind heart that was always merciful, that she could not utter it. When he was gone, she almost persuaded herself it was a troubled dream.

It was sharp enough reality to Richard — the more bitter because he had hoped much for his brother of late. Robert had spent the Christmas holidays with some friends, but his letters had been regular, his demands for money moderate, and his progress, as he had recorded it, very commendable. But Richard knew the fatal tendency of Robert's mind to evade any disagreeable truth; and a chill foreboding filled his heart. Alas! his worst fears were more than realized.

Robert was still in confinement, sullen and uncommunicative. Shame added to his reticence. His face was haggard, and retained traces of his late debauch. It was plainly evident that intoxication had been one cause. As nothing could be elicited in his present state, Richard determined to go to the college authorities.

The president received him with unaffected sympathy and respect. His own career in that institution had been highly satisfactory, and gained him many warm friends. Condemning his brother was a blow they all felt most sorry to inflict. It was a sad story. The party had been drinking and gambling until a late hour, when, sallying forth with boisterous merriment, they committed several acts of wanton mischief, ending by assaulting one of the officers who attempted to arrest them.

"I confess," said the kind-hearted president, "Robert's course has never been praiseworthy. His abilities are of the highest order. If he chose he could distance any one in his class. But from the first he has allied himself with the indolent and insubordinate. I'm not sure but suspending him last spring would have been a good lesson. But he was so very penitent, that, under the circumstances, we concluded to forgive him."

"Last spring?" gasped Richard. "Then this is not his first offence?"

"Nor the second," was the rejoinder. "He had been reprimanded before last March, when he committed an act of such flagrant disobedience, it was judged best to suspend him for a while. I was writing to your father when the announcement of his death reached us. After a long conversation with Robert, we concluded to try him again. I thought him a good deal improved after his return, and hoped his grief would prove a permanent benefit. Your father possessed my entire esteem and confidence, and for the sake of his family I trusted Robert had decided on a better course. Up to Christmas of the present year his conduct appeared very satisfactory, but I am afraid it was a superficial reformation. Many depredations have been committed to which it seemed impossible to find a clew; but it appears now that Robert headed this party. I spare you details; it is sufficient to know in what it has culminated. Believe, my dear young friend, that you have my warmest sympathy."

Richard felt sick at heart. The long-continued deceit that had unblushingly braved a dead father, and while running at riot had preserved a semblance of honor, filled him with dismay. How could one so young in years, and with Robert's home associations, become so perfect an adept in duplicity?

"It will be better for him to leave the city," suggested the president, kindly. "His associates are bad, his habits expensive and irregular. He needs an entire change of life and pursuits. If you could lead him to turn his attention to some active mercantile business, he might do better."

Richard went away sorrowfully, stunned by the sad story. Could *he* have been more watchful? The attempts to gain his brother's confidence had been met with specious falsehoods; even the dear father's trust wickedly betrayed. How dark the future looked! He hardly dared hope, but he prayed fervently for strength to perform his whole duty.

The next morning he visited Robert again. Kindly, but firmly, he demanded the whole truth, and a list of Robert's debts, stating his intention of paying them immediately, so that his departure might be honorable in this respect. No reproaches passed his lips, less for fear of exasperating Robert than from pity for his own sore heart.

Robert paced the small room in silent attention, his mind divided between a desire to openly defy Richard, and shake off all authority, and the benefit of a partial concession. Penitent he certainly was not, and was more angry at having his misdeeds brought to light, than ashamed of committing them. Of the trouble and disgrace he had brought upon the family he scarcely thought.

"To remain here is simply impossible," Richard said, when he found his brother in no haste to reply. "Give me your assistance therefore, and let us finish as speedily as we can."

"It's my own money," was the ungracious answer. "If I choose to spend it, it's no one's business."

"It's some one's business to see it paid," was the grave rejoinder.

"Don't grudge a fellow what belongs to him. You succeeded to a ready-made practice, so *you* can't complain."

"Not wholly for myself, either. You know there was not sufficient income to support the family without sacrificing the house."

"What should you consider its value?" and Robert paused in his walk.

"It is worth from twelve to fifteen thousand, I suppose; but in regard, I rate it more highly than that. Every year it will go on increasing in value."

"I've a proposition to make. Will you buy me out?"

Richard thought a moment. It would assuredly lessen his trouble and anxiety; he could foresee there would hardly be a peaceful moment until Robert had wasted his inheritance. On the other hand it would be snapping the link that gave him the only remaining power over his brother. Could it be right to purchase his ease by a prospect of greater temptation for Robert? O, how he longed for strength and wisdom!

"No," he answered, slowly, "not until you are nearly or quite of age."

An angry light shot up in Robert's eyes, but he found himself mastered. Sinking into his former sullen apathy, he tossed some notes across the table. Bills for oyster suppers, champagne, and cigars, carriage hire, and a schedule of various sums of borrowed money. Richard looked at the aggregate in dismay, and then asked if there could possibly be any more.

"A trifle perhaps — fifty dollars or so."

"O Robert! How could you be so foolishly, wickedly extravagant?" It was the first indignant outburst Richard had uttered.

"I'm not asking you to pay it," was the harsh rejoinder. "Young men might have lived on nothing in your day, and enjoyed it; but it's not my style. Don't make a fuss: it is not necessary for me to go through college; so what I spend in one way I shall save in another;" and he gave a heartless laugh.

Further conversation was useless. Richard went about the business in hand with a depressed soul, yet was relieved to have it finished. He settled the fine with which Robert's misdemeanor had been punished, and then turned his steps homeward, taking with him the sympathy of many true hearts.

More than once he asked himself what was to be done with his brother.   As he glanced at the face still handsome, despite its moody expression, and thought of talents that might make him an honor to his family, he felt that he could not give him up without an effort.   He must be more watchful, more prayerful, and strive to fulfil the duty laid upon him. Alas! thorns beset the path in too many directions.

CHAPTER XI.

And if along with these should come
The man I held as half divine,
Should strike a sudden hand in mine,
And ask a thousand things of home.
TENNYSON.

THEY were nearing New York, when Robert started from his indifferent mood, saying, suddenly,—

"I'm not going home, Dick."

"Not going home?" was the astonished rejoinder.

"No; my nerves are not equal to facing Guilford just now, to say nothing of an eager and excited crowd of friends, all anxious to learn the cause of my sudden arrival in their midst;" and in spite of his nonchalance, a deep flush crossed his face.

"I would rather have you."

"No, Dick; you'll be more comfortable without me. Let me go to aunt Sophy's; otherwise I shall stay in New York and try my luck."

The relief it promised made Richard doubt its propriety; but he found Robert was determined not to meet Mr. Guilford at present. Cape May, at this season, had fewer temptations than a city; so he acquiesced, and the brothers parted with some semblance of affection.

Richard went to Mr. Guilford immediately, and related the whole story. The lawyer was not much surprised, and, after discussing the matter, proposed to visit Robert at his aunt's, and learn what course of life he intended to pursue.

"If you only would," the young man said, gratefully.

"I will not believe any son of your father can go so utterly astray. We may save him yet."

"Thank you;" and Richard wrung his hand warmly.

A gloom fell over the household at the knowledge of Robert's misconduct.

"It seems almost as if some one was dead," Lily said, in a hushed voice; and the two younger ones clung to Mabel, as if she could shield them from any like danger. To Richard she was more considerate than ever, striving in daily kindnesses to bear a part of his burden.

If Richard cherished a hope of Mr. Guilford's influence, it was completely crushed on that gentleman's return. He found Robert haughty and unmanageable, alike insensible to threats or remonstrances. What step to take next perplexed them both; but Robert fortunately solved the difficulty by falling in with the captain of a trading vessel, who needed a clerk, and shipping immediately. The voyage would last four months.

By degrees they settled to their former pleasant life. The garden was a source of unfailing interest to Bel and Lily, and Richard took up botany with them. Mabel's tastes were mostly domestic; but Lily flew hither and thither with the airy grace of a humming-bird. Richard laughingly declared it was a marvel she ever knew anything perfectly. And so, while the elder trained the flowers, the younger stood over them with her book.

. "Office hours," as the children termed the time from dinner until evening, were a great delight to them all. When Richard was not occupied with patients, they claimed him relentlessly. He enjoyed it also. In the midst of the merry group he seemed to quaff the sweet reward of his labors, and forget the cares.

They were on the lowest terrace, one July afternoon, watching Archie's attempt at managing a pretty sail-boat. He was to acquit himself creditably before Richard's eyes, on a short voyage, ere he could be allowed to "dare the treacherous ocean," as Lily drolly termed it. They laughed at his mishaps in tacking, and cheered him when successful; but bringing the boat safely into port was a rather difficult achievement for the young navigator. He had barely succeeded, when a frank, hearty voice, just above them, exclaimed, —

"'Come and see for yourself how I manage at the head of a family, and partake of an old chum's hospitality.' Wasn't that the invitation?"

They all turned, and saw a fine-looking man, about Richard's age, with a genial face, now crossed by a mirthful smile at the astonishment his unlooked-for appearance created. To the elder ones he was not quite a stranger.

"Why, Philip Gregory! If it wasn't a faultlessly clear day, I should suppose you rained down;" and Richard shook his friend's hand warmly.

"No, there's nothing supernatural or unnatural about me. I came like a Christian, and a citizen of the nineteenth century, rang at your hall door, and was ushered in by a servant; deposited my travelling-bag on the floor; and when she said you were all down here, watching Master Archie try his new boat, I thought I would treat you to a surprise. If you don't believe me, go and look at my little black bag, marked P. G., in white letters."

Lilian laughed outright, and then blushed.

"My dear Philip, a thousand welcomes! Where have you come from? and are you not tired?"

"So tired I long to throw myself under that tree yonder," was the answer, in an affectation of breathless fatigue. "But first, please do the honors of a householder, and introduce me to your family. This surely isn't little Bel?" and he held out his hand, as if quite convinced of her identity, notwithstanding his implied doubt.

"Even so. And this is Lilian; and this, the baby of your day, though they have all been babies in your day, I think;" and Richard folded his hands around Tessy's soft face.

"Six years since I have seen one of you! And Dick, old friend, don't you feel quite venerable, with two such tall, blooming daughters by your side?"

Mabel blushed this time. Indeed, Mr. Gregory's glance expressed as much admiration as it was possible for a look to reveal.

"Don't I do credit to the whole race as *paterfamilias?*" asked Richard, straightening up. "Shall we go to the house?"

"Not if you'll let me have that seat I mentioned away back at the beginning of our conversation;" and with an easy grace he threw himself on the grass, leaning his shoulder against the old elm tree.

A call from the youthful sailor attracted Richard a moment. . Returning, he seated himself by his friend, and drew Tessy down on his knee.

"I'm afraid I'm in some one's place," said Mr. Gregory, picking up a book. "Here's Kane's Expedition, miles and miles away from the Polar Sea. Who is so frosty-minded this weather?"

"I was reading it," rejoined Lily. "It is a good cool book for a hot day."

"Then I suppose at midwinter you regale yourself with Central Africa, the Tropics, or Mount Vesuvius."

They all laughed.

"I can hardly realize it, Richard," his friend began, in a softened tone. "After rambling from land to land, it is delightful to sit down in the shade of the tree where one talked life over with his first friend. I never had any home in those days, or in any days, save when I came here;" and he sighed a little.

Archie advanced on the scene of action, or rather repose, dressed in a pretty sailor's suit of blue and white, fashioned by Mabel's dainty fingers, and underwent the honors of an introduction with commendable self-possession.

"How well I remember my first vacation here!" Mr. Gregory said, with animation. "Richard used to take me out on the river, and taught me to row and manage a sail, though I was much older than this young man. I considered them marvellous exploits."

"Where has your memory gone?" laughed Richard. "You were fifteen, I think, and Archie is past twelve."

"I have the remembrance of being an awkward, over-grown boy, frightened half to death by the appearance of two little girls in white dresses. I had an idea this was a sort of Aladdin's palace, and would vanish if I spoke a loud word."

"And how mother petted you into courage," Richard added.

"Yes, and the happy summers, until six years ago, the last dear time I made one of your number. And do you recollect, Mabel, — Miss Bertrand, I mean, — how I took you out sailing one evening, and staid so long that — everybody thought we were wrecked?"

Mabel knew what the sudden pause and the "everybody" meant — the picture of her father, standing on the lowest step, and gazing up the river; the fervent ejaculation and fond kiss. That name was a sweet note in their home music; so she filled up the pause with tenderness, saying, —

"And how glad papa was to find us safe!"

He knew by the tone that he would be allowed his old place in the household, and to share their sorrowful memories, as he had in past days partaken of their joys. His voice was low with emotion, as he answered, —

"He was so good and kind. Not only then, but all times."

"Yes," Richard rejoined. "Each day we learn what we lost with him."

"You hardly let us miss him," Lily said, in a soft whisper, as her fingers crept through Richard's hair.

It seemed so natural then to go over those sad days with one who had loved their cherished dead! As Mabel listened to the sympathy that partook of divine trust, as well as earthly affection, her heart warmed strangely towards Philip Gregory.

Afterwards, when she and the children had gone to the house, the friends took up the years that had fallen between since they last saw each other's faces. At school and college they had been chosen friends; but Philip's long absence in Europe, attending an invalid and querulous grandfather, had broken in upon their intimacy. Letters had missed, rendering correspondence uncertain; and though Philip had mentioned his return a year previous, this was their first meeting. Richard related the circumstances of his father's death in simple, earnest language, that showed his deep feeling.

"This was why you gave up the journey to Europe?" Philip's eyes asked another question, for his friend had once announced his intended marriage, with all a lover's ardor.

"Yes." And Richard briefly went over the episode of the past summer. He felt the fond clasp of the hand, more truly comforting than words could have been just then.

"And now your story?" he said, when he had finished.

The childhood that had been happy to Richard was spent by his friend in a lonely house, with a morose, unsocial old man. The first visit to Dr. Bertrand's opened Philip's heart to a new and wonderful world. Not only friendship, but religion, had come to him like a revelation. In this house he had learned to know God: under this very tree he had chosen to enter his Master's vineyard as a worker. When his grandfather heard of this resolve, his anger was fierce and deep. The boy should not throw himself away. He would have no canting parson among his descendants. Immediately after Philip had graduated, he declared his intention of taking him to Europe. In this extremity the young man applied to Dr. Bertrand for advice. It was simple and straightforward. His grandfather had reared and educated him; he was the only near relative the poor old man had. To leave him now would be ingratitude. His duty was in "that state of life to which it pleased God to call him." So Philip Gregory took up his cross; left behind him dear friends and sweet hopes; bore patiently with fretful complainings, real and imaginary illnesses; looking steadily forward to the answer of a good conscience as his reward, until God should set him free, and open the way for a higher service.

Philip recounted his wanderings in lands rendered sacred by song and story. He made no hardship of those exiled years.

"But I thought you were to inherit his fortune?" Richard said, with a little astonishment.

A warm color suffused Philip's face, as he answered, in a low tone, "I could not submit to the conditions."

"What were they?" The tone was not curious, but pleasantly authoritative.

"We never agreed on religious subjects, you know. It was the one bitter point between us; and at last he said, if I was resolved to become a clergyman after his death, I should never have one penny of his to waste on such narrow, bigoted notions. One day he angrily made a will, disinheriting me; and then held it before me, promising to destroy it if I would give up my folly. Many a time afterwards he placed the temptation before me. Don't think me miserably weak, Richard, if I confess there were moments when I almost yielded. I used to fancy how much good I could do with such a fortune; but the denunciation rang in my ears, 'Woe is me if I preach not the gospel.' I could not sell my birthright for a mess of pottage, even if I was fainting on the highway. After a while the subject dropped. Sometimes he would threaten to send me away, but in his weak state he was too much at the mercy of servants. Yet the last days were very pleasant. He always regarded me with a sort of tyrannical idolatry, much as he had treated my poor mother. During the winter at Florence he behaved

with more consideration, and sometimes would follow me
about with strange, wistful eyes, that seemed to have a tender regret in their depths. One afternoon he asked me to
read whatever pleased me. Occasionally I had taken up the
Bible; he used at times to like its grand imagery. I turned
to Isaiah now, and read quite a while. Presently he put out
his hand, saying he was sleepy. I don't know how long I
held it. I was watching one of those glorious sunsets, and
thinking of the country beyond this glowing sea of purple
and amethyst. When I turned he looked very peaceful, and
laying his hand gently down, I went to give some directions
to the servants. After the physician came I ordered lights.
He had not stirred from the position in which I left him; but
the soul had fled. What passed at the final moment is known
only to God. No one dreamed of its being so sudden ; but
I was more than thankful he had died at peace with me."

There was a silence of some moments. The shadows under the tree were lengthening, and crimson, instead of gold,
was sifted through the leaves.

"He was buried at Florence," Philip resumed. "Baltimore, his native city, profited by his wealth. I have only
the small portion my father left me ; but it will be more than
sufficient for my present purposes. I am thankful no duty
towards him was left undone."

Richard's clasp of his friend's hand tightened. How full,
how compassionate it was, both understood. "You have
done nobly," he said.

"Don't praise me. I have often doubted my own faith,
my love to Christ. How many times I longed for a good
talk with your father to set me right! I meant to come
to you immediately; but I met Mr. Chaloner, the old Hilton
clergyman, in Baltimore, and he persuaded me to begin at
once. I had not a day to lose ; so I went to studying with
an earnest purpose, knowing well your faith could trust me
for all it was impossible to convey in letters. O Dick, my
friend, how pleasant it is to be here again, and find you un-
changed amid so many changes ! "

" And you have begun your true life now," Richard said, with a grave smile. " May God prosper you in it."

" Amen." The young man's tone was deep and reverential.

" Where is Mr. Chaloner ? " Richard asked, presently.

" At Rothelan, up the Hudson. The dear old man considers it an earthly paradise, and has spoken for my vacation ; but first love had an earlier claim."

The dying sun was leaving behind him seas of amber and crimson, and a fine white fog came creeping down the river, stretching out threads of filmy beauty to catch the rays of opaline splendor, and weave them in a thousand fantastic shapes. The friends rose, and walked slowly up the garden path. Tessy was coming to meet them.

" Mabel said I should call you to supper," she began, shyly, looking at Philip from under her long lashes. " And — it's on the balcony."

He put out his hand, but she clung to her brother. Glancing up, his eyes took in a charming picture. The balcony almost hidden, and fragrant with honeysuckle blooms ; the table with its snowy drapery, pure white china, and cut glass ; two vases of flowers, brilliant and artistically arranged ; dishes of luscious fruit ; a plate of choice biscuits, just tinged with richest brown, and some dainty cream-cakes.

This little feast was in special honor of their guest, as the late dinner rendered such a meal unnecessary. Richard was compelled to leave them shortly afterwards, and Mabel accepted her position as hostess with a quiet ease and dignity. She had some difficulty in restraining Lily's high spirits, as Mr. Gregory's lively sallies brought her out almost too rapidly.

They were engrossed with music when Richard returned, held captive by Mr. Gregory's fine performance. His masterly hand evoked a strange pathos from the full, deep chords, or broke into soft, faint murmurs, that floated out on the night air, to die amid summer sweetness.

Presently he found a well-worn copy of Handel's " How beautiful are their feet," and persuaded them into singing it with him. Mabel's voice was soft and clear, like the ripple of a forest brook ; Lilian's contralto, rich and deep. As the grand melody swelled out in notes of exquisite beauty, Tessy crept up on Richard's knee, and twining her arms around his neck, said, with a quivering sob in her voice, —

" It seems just like Heaven — doesn't it ? O Dick, if the clouds could only open, so we might see papa for a moment ! "

CHAPTER XII.

But who could have expected this,
  When we two drew together first,
Just for the obvious human bliss,
  To satisfy life's daily thirst
With a thing men seldom miss?
                    ROBERT BROWNING.

It would have been impossible for a guest like Philip Gregory not to fraternize thoroughly with the Bertrands, even if there had been no old remembrances to fall back upon. But now there was a charm in those boyish recollections that roused Richard from his too literal present. There were many elements in both natures that would have harmonized under any circumstances; but with the griefs and experiences of the past, and a sense of brotherly love that had outlived years of separation, came a still stronger regard — the superstructure of a lasting friendship, built on an imperishable foundation. To Richard, an intimate friend of his own age, viewing things youngly, and enjoying with the ardor and keenness of a rich, overflowing nature, was indeed a luxury. Both had made some painful sacrifices, had been strengthened with the same faith, and taken up a future widely different from their fair, first dreams. Richard was grave and rather calm of temperament — one of those souls that accumulate gradually, and wait for a strong central fire to rouse their highest emotions. Unselfish in a great degree, it was invariably his custom to hope first for others, and in some cases take no note of himself — one of those spirits oftenest misunderstood. Philip would have been as ready for sacrifice or noble deed; but in him there was a certain warmth and desire, a faculty of seizing the golden

9 *

time of enjoyment, of taking present happiness with almost boyish ardor. Richard needed a salient influence like this to start anew the hopes of his heart.

In another way he was very attractive to Mabel. He had been a visitor in the house when her mother was the presiding genius; he remembered the old songs she had sung, the flowers she had worn in her hair, and books she used to read — little trifles that came back with a forceful tenderness to the girl's heart. Besides Richard, no one ever talked of her mother. To the younger children, their father had so thoroughly supplied her place, they rarely looked back with the longing regret common to motherless children; so the peculiar nearness of the relation had been felt more exclusively by Mabel. Philip seemed intuitively to understand this, and was never at fault with the shy girl.

Indeed, he seemed almost to have the gift of ubiquity. He romped with Tessy, sailed in Archie's boat, talked, sang, went out with Richard, and indulged Lily's never-failing inquiries about the countries and curiosities he had met with. For one so apparently thoughtless, she evinced a strange fondness for descriptions of travel or natural scenery. Everything on this point was devoured with avidity. She soon became absorbed in Philip's brilliant word-pictures. He was terse and vigorous, possessing the rare faculty of transporting his hearers to the scenes that moved his eloquence, until they fairly beheld with his vision. And when he lingered in the glowing orient, or sailed slowly over tropical seas, his very voice sank into summer ease and indolence, until Lily laughingly declared if she was not so deeply interested she should certainly go to sleep.

Richard insisted that she resembled the skipper's wife in Eothen, "who had an inquiring mind and an irresistible tendency to impart her own opinions, and looked upon her guests as a piece of waste intellect, to be carefully tilled," which seemed to amuse Philip exceedingly.

A week passed rapidly. They had done absolutely

nothing, and unanimously declared that Philip must remain longer to be entertained. They would sail up the river, and spend a day in the woods; they would go to Passaic Falls, and take rides to Eagle Rock, and all places of interest in the surrounding country; and he consented without requiring much persuasion. Their dinner in the woods was a decided success, and their rides wonderfully enjoyable. They had not been so happy since their father's death. Richard expanded into new life.

Philip entered the parlor one evening where Mabel sat amusing herself with some old-time ballads. She glanced up in surprise.

"I thought you had gone with Richard," she said.

"There was a medical association on hand, I believe; so I concluded to return. Where are the children?"

"Tessy, tired out, is asleep; the others are in Mrs. Charlton's, playing tableaux. Shall we follow them?"

"It is too fine a night to remain in doors. What do you say to a moonlight row? It will be my last chance, for I must go to-morrow."

"Well," she said; and running up stairs for her shawl, paused a moment to inform the housekeeper. Mr. Gregory was waiting for her on the balcony, and they walked slowly down the path, drinking in the intense loveliness of the night. The moon was at its full. Great golden stars seemed melting into blue ether, and white, weird drifts, like phantom fleets, floated across the sky. Every tree and shrub seemed frosted with liquid silver, and each wave of the river tipped with a diamond crest, while the reflexes trembled in pearl and azure. The air was fragrant with late roses, honeysuckle, and the aromatic odor of the trees.

Assisting Mabel into the boat, he pushed out so as to clear the shallow shore. He liked to linger in these green glooms at the river's edge, and watch the slender spires of shrubbery, that, waving to the slightest breeze, sent troops of dancing images over the tremulous reaches of water.

Slow, faint swells of the outgoing tide, rhythmical plashes of oars, the voice of a flute, and the far-off echoes of some singers, filled all the air with melody. It was as if the drifting motion carried them to the very verge of fairy-land.

Did they know whither they were hastening? that in their very midst, bounded neither by shining river or shadowy shore, lay a land of bliss more potent than those magic realms of eld, and he who treads them is a captive as secure as if fay Vivien's chain had wound him three times about? No; the full pulsation of both hearts was too new to be interpreted. Philip Gregory's thoughts had not deepened into desire. In coming back to the Bertrands, he fancied he took up the old life, and was content.

During that brief fortnight, a change had come over Mabel. The roses, the summer, and herself, all blossomed together. She drank in large draughts of quiet, measureless joy; her intuitions became refined, her whole being permeated with a glow of emotion at once tender and profound. Fearlessly she left behind the golden glory of girlhood's untroubled sea, and became a woman. No lingering regret, no troublous misgiving concerning the future! O the blessedness of faith that comes to many with their first love! Let us take courage, and thank God that it is so.

They went far off for a subject of conversation. Something about the Nile, clustering palms, fragrant waxen lotus blooms, wild Egyptian or Arab melodies that left Shelley's sweet song ringing through her brain: —

> " The wandering airs, they faint
> On the dark, the silent stream;
> The champak's odors fall
> Like sweet thoughts in a dream;
> The nightingale's complaint,
> It dies upon her heart —."

After Philip Gregory turned the boat, an exquisite silence fell over them. His heart took in the picture Mabel made, to the minutest detail. The willowy form, the stately head, with its luxuriant bands of soft-brown hair rising out of the snowy, fleecy wrappings that fell loosely around her shoulders, the fair face, with tender, drooping eyes, the slender hands folded in her lap, — how lovely it all was!

Floating on in this idle manner, neither noticed a sail-boat that, from dilatory management and lack of favorable wind, was making eccentric tacks across the river. Impelled by a vigorous hand, it flew shoreward, and met Philip's bark with a violent concussion. Mabel sprang up, and with the cry of affright there was a flutter of a shadowy dress across his vision, a scream from the opposite party; and obeying the first impulse, Philip found himself reaching through the water with strong arms for something dearer than life.

"See what you've done now, Jem!" said a coarse, but not unkindly voice. "Didn't I tell you to leave that sail alone?"

"Who thought of a boat being here? I never saw them until we struck," was the rejoinder.

The first speaker brought Philip's boat around, and sprang into it, with instructions to his companion to "hold on for life." As Philip reached the surface, he cried, cheerily, "Here!" and stretched out his arms for the burden. There was no alternative; so Philip resigned it, and scrambled in himself.

"I'm awful sorry," said the man; "but it's darkish right along here, and we never saw you. I wouldn't 'a done it for a mint of money. Think the young lady's hurt?"

"No, she has only fainted."

"Perhaps we better help you," said one of the girls, leaning over the side of the boat.

"No, thank you; we shall soon be home;" and seizing the oars, he sent the boat along with vigorous strokes, hardly daring to breathe until he came in sight of the house. Then he raised the fair head, and rested it against his knee. There was a languid flutter of the eyelids, a faint movement of the lips, and he clasped her to the heart that still quivered

with intense emotion. Murmuring in a low, convulsive tone,
"O, my darling! my darling!" he covered the face with
passionate kisses.

She lay quite still, encircled with one arm, while with the
other he brought the boat around, and fastened the chain.
Lifting her tenderly out on the coping, he found her able to
stand. When he would have taken her in his arms again,
her girlish bashfulness protested. "I can walk," she exclaimed. "I am not hurt."

"Thank God!" was all he said. Then she felt herself
borne up the terrace steps, and through the garden, as if she
had been thistle-down. Releasing her in the hall, where the
gaslight sent shadowy rays through its globe of ground glass,
he glanced earnestly in her face a moment. It required an
effort to deny himself the words he most wished to say, but
her paleness gave him strength. "Shall I call Ann?" he
asked, instead.

She was trembling violently, partly from fright, and partly
from flashes of feeling that ran over her like seas of fire one
instant, and the next chilled her with keen frostiness. She
was glad to lean on his shoulder, and said, with childish entreaty, "Take me up stairs first."

The confidence evinced by her request thrilled him with
joy. He bore her to the sitting-room, and had just laid her
on the lounge, when Ann emerged from an opposite apartment.

"O Miss Mabel!" and she held up both hands.

"Hush, Ann; it was only a slight accident. Not a word
to any one to-night. Mr. Gregory is wet through also."

"Yes, I must leave you," he said, in a lingering tone, as
if it pained him to go. Then he pressed her hand to his
lips. She flushed redly.

"And the doctor not in!" ejaculated Ann, recovering a
little from her surprise.

"Well, I don't need him;" and Mabel laughed at the ludicrous aspect of affairs. "He wouldn't know where to find

me any dry clothes — all I want just now. Will you get them?"

As thanks for her assistance, Mabel briefly went over her adventure, trying to keep her voice steady, and her face from that troublesome crimson. Lily came flying up stairs, and the sisters began to prepare for bed, for Mabel felt anxious to hide herself from everybody. It seemed as if they were all going to demand her secret immediately.

Half an hour later Philip tapped lightly at the door. "How is Miss Mabel?" he asked, in a low tone.

"O, she's comfortable, and in bed. Didn't she come near getting drowned, Mr. Gregory? Are you quite sure?"

"Yes;" and he laughed a little. "I should not have let her drown. We were in no great danger, though. Good night;" and he was off, for he heard Richard at the hall door. He had no wish to take any person into his confidence that night, but he spent a long while in prayer, thanking God for more than one blessing.

It was not very early when he came down the next day. Pausing in the hall, he caught a glimpse of a white morning dress, with violet trimmings. Obeying his first impulse, he entered the parlor. Mabel paused in her work, laid down her gay feather duster, and glanced up with a beseeching look, her face all one rosy flush.

"Are you quite well?" he asked, hurriedly, "and recovered from last night? I don't know what I am to say for being so careless: we were so in the shade that I was more to blame than the other party. I should have kept better watch."

"And I should not have started up. It was partly my fault."

There was a long silence. They stood by the open window, their hearts beating audibly. Then he drew her gently towards him, and without questioning the face, pressed his lips to hers. A faint, tremulous motion answered him — her first kiss; and in that mute caress the soul of her girlhood passed into Philip's keeping.

"I have hardly any right to say this," he commenced slowly, "beginning my life over again, as I am; but when I perilled your safety last night, I learned how dear you were to me. Can you wait, Mabel, for what I hope to offer you by and by?"

She hid her face on his shoulder with the abandonment of perfect trust.

"The sweetest of all answers," he said, raising it and kissing the quivering lips. "You love me even as I love you."

Richard looked in at the door. "O!" he exclaimed, turning away.

"Come here, Richard; we want you;" and Philip held out his hand, adding, with a little heightened color, "the usual reward of hospitality."

Richard grasped the extended hand warmly. In his face was fullest approbation.

"Don't answer until you have heard my story," Philip said, with frank ingenuousness. "You may not feel like trusting me with any of your treasures;" and in a voice that had to be governed a little to keep it calm, he related the events of the preceding evening, not so much to excuse what might seem a hasty proposal, as to satisfy his own frank nature. Mabel listened with downcast eyes, and crimson face, as Philip went over the still incomprehensible moment when love had so suddenly surprised both hearts. Richard read the expression perfectly.

"My dear Philip," he began, in a full tone, "you can hardly understand my satisfaction. Had the power been in my own hands, I could not have chosen more wisely for her. I know I am right in saying the position you will have to offer her will be more in consonance with her own tastes than mere worldly aims. As for the years of waiting, if your love is true, — the real fine gold of life, — it will be unchangeable. If not, it is best to learn the fact before the irrevocable word is spoken."

"As if it *could* change or fail!" and Philip Gregory passed his arm proudly over Mabel's shoulder, while she half unconsciously placed her hand in his.

Was it strange a pang of desolation should pierce Richard's heart at sight of this perfect faith? A waft of memory swept a furrow through the waving grass, and disclosed the ruined temple in his soul.

"No, no," he returned, hurriedly, "I have no fear for you, and Mabel's heart is truth itself." Bending down he kissed the fair face.

She clasped her arms around his neck, and exclaimed, in a self-reproachful tone, "O Richard! I ought not to love any one better than you;" yet the lingering cadence confessed that she did.

"If it was any one but Philip, I might not consent so readily," he replied, gayly, as the breakfast bell rang.

She ran away to cool her cheeks; but Archie upset all composure a moment afterwards, by crying out, "She didn't look a bit like a drowned girl!"

They were barely seated, when Lilian began a lamentation about this being Philip's last day, declaring it was positively cruel in him to leave them with so many promises yet unfulfilled.

"I'm not quite as hard and unpersuadable as the Rock of Gibraltar," he said, gravely; "so, Lily, if you will make out a very tempting programme for another week, I may take in Newark on my way back."

Thus encouraged, Lily began to count up the books there were still to read, the places that absolutely ought to be visited, and made such a formidable list, that Philip declared himself quite vanquished.

"There!" she exclaimed, triumphantly, and with charming *naïveté*, "you were wishing yesterday, Bel, that he would stay, and I dare say you never thought of coaxing him."

Lily's keen eyes might have discovered that there was a

secret, if Richard had not rushed to the rescue. On leaving the breakfast-room she carried Philip off in triumph, but was vexed to learn, a while later, just as she finished a little favor for Richard, that he had gone to walk with Mabel; and it was nearly dinner time when they returned. The parting was brief and full of hope for all.

That evening Mabel came to Richard of her own accord, as if she needed the seal of his words to assure herself all was right. There was no mother to soothe the blushing cheeks and palpitant nerves, no girlish friend, in whose fond bosom she could confide her trembling joy; but he made amends for all, with his tender thoughtfulness and wise counsel.

And thus Richard Bertrand made another essay in his position as head of the family. Unconsciously he had come to lean on Mabel since the stay of his own heart had been wrenched away. The nobleness and purity of her character attracted him strongly. But instead of keeping her for a friend all the future years, he was suddenly called upon to yield his claim for one that must inevitably grow dearer and more absorbing. There was a little pain, but no jealousy; he loved Philip too sincerely for that.

One by one they would go to other homes — those happy, loving children! He could not quite banish the lost dream of his own past — the hope that should have made fadeless sunshine for all time. As he grew older and graver, amid cares and duties, fair young girls, with fresh, eager hearts, would pass him by. Yet he did not regret Ada, nor think impatiently of the charge so solemnly given him. He remembered a wise hand had written, "It is good for a man that he bear the yoke in his youth." Far better than a weightsome cross in after life.

CHAPTER XIII.

"God sets some lives in shade, alone;
    They have no daylight of their own;
    Only in lives of happier ones
    They see the shine of distant suns."

THE annual visit to Cape May, that had been thrown into
the background by Mr. Gregory's unexpected arrival, was
now discussed. To Lily's surprise, she found Mabel quite
disinclined for the journey; and as Richard did not press
the matter, the number of travellers dwindled one half.
But Archie had no fancy for giving up his anticipated pleasure, and Lily gravely announced the fact "that she could
have all the fun she wanted at aunt Sophy's, and be back by
the time Mr. Gregory came."

As for Mabel, she hardly dared take a comprehensive
view of her own happiness until the house was quiet, and no
curious eyes remained to come upon her suddenly at some
defenceless moment. In the long days that followed she
had plenty of time for thought. Her first feeling was one
of surprise. Her own estimate of herself was lowly; she
wondered how a man, brilliant and talented as Philip
Gregory, could have dreamed of choosing her. And then
the life he had marked out for himself, — could she ever
become a fitting companion for such a man and such a
destiny?

Her communings might have been more troubled than
pleasant but for Richard. He smoothed out the tangled
path of difficulty, restored the drooping courage, and was,
as Mabel afterwards told Philip, a perfect Mr. Great Heart.

He understood readily the charm such a pure nature held for a man of quick resolution, refined and enthusiastic, yet continually occupied and excited by human interest. Philip could mould it, with his force of character, into whatsoever shape he liked. She was gentle, but not weak; yielding, yet not indolently passive. Her high, true faith, her generosity, tempered by a fine sense of justice, would be excellent qualities in her new life. She also possessed that graceful dignity which was winning in itself, and demanded from others a certain respect. Even the very obtuse would not be likely to trample on her.

During that brief separation she received two letters from Philip. With a delicacy only the highest mind could have evinced, he startled her with no rapturous declarations of love, and asked for no answers until he came himself. The weeks flew by rapidly. Indeed, she was hardly ready when the frank, electric voice greeted her, and the earnest eyes demanded their full meed of affection.

They had one delightful day to themselves — a day in which they sat under the old elm, and, as Philip said, "became acquainted with each other." It was an odd state for Mabel, who had never yet dreamed of a lover.

"How little I thought, a few weeks ago, that, before I went back to college, two new and blessed hopes would be added to my life, that for years had looked so solitary," Philip said, musingly. "In Mr. Chaloner, I have found a more than friend — a father. O Mabel, I wish you could see that little nest among the hills! The village proper is back a short distance from the river's edge, the old gray stone church and vine-embowered rectory forming a sort of connecting link. To the right, all along the river, the scene is beautiful, and varied by numberless charming summer residences — some standing on hills with sloping lawns, some hidden among rocks and trees. There is scarcely anything in all Italy more lovely. Mr. Chaloner has been at Rothelan nine years, and the people love him devotedly. His long, white beard, and the flowing hair that clusters about his temples in loose waves, give him a benign, patriarchal appearance. He is nearing seventy, yet he is earnest and vigorous in all good works, patient with poverty and ignorance, and O, so kind to the little ones! Three years ago he lost his only son, who was shortly to take holy orders, and become his father's assistant."

"How sad!" Mabel returned, in a tone of truest pity.

"Yes.; I wonder it did not entirely break him down. His faith and resignation are beautiful in the extreme. And now, my darling, I come to something that concerns you, or must at least have your assent."

"Concerns me?" was the wondering rejoinder.

"Yes; are you not linked in with every thought of my future life?" and he drew the fair form nearer to him. "Before I left Mr. Chaloner, he made me an offer that was at once generous and affectionate. He will need an assistant; indeed, he ought to have one now, but the place seems sacred to him, because it was destined for his son. Judge of my surprise when he asked me if I would be willing to come by and by."

"And you will," she said, in a tone scarcely less sweet than the south wind that went whispering above them.

"Would you like a country life? Mr. Chaloner wishes to be rector at Rothelan while he is able to toil in the vineyard. He has a small income of his own, but, at best, the salary of the assistant would not be very large. Then the two families would have to make one — at least, that is his idea. The rectory is roomy enough, and in addition to this, he gave me a word of advice, especially relating to you."

Mabel colored, but looked incredulous.

"He suggested I should marry, and bring my wife there;" and Philip raised the sweet face to note the effect of his communication. "I might do better, you know," he said, with a smile, "and you *may* prefer something grander."

"O Philip!" The tone was tenderly reproachful.

"My darling!"

"It must be as you wish," she said, with quiet determination. "If I trust you with my heart, can I not trust you with all things else? And Mr. Chaloner has been your friend so long."

He could not forbear kissing her.

"Yes," he went on; "to Mr. Chaloner and your father I owe all that is and will be truly good in my life. He was the clergyman at Hilton, where I first met Richard at boarding-school. And now from Richard's hands I take one gift, and from his I am offered another. Everything seems to come to me, when a few years ago I used to think I had given up everything."

"All things shall work together for the good of those who love HIM," Mabel said, with sweet seriousness.

"It seems a long while to look forward, yet two years will pass quickly. I have much to do in that time."

"And I, also. O Philip! you must help me to grow strong, that I may be fit for my station. It is such a great and holy work, that I tremble lest I shall fail you when you most need help and comfort."

"We will remember who 'giveth liberally, and upbraideth not.' *He* must be our perpetual guide." And in the quiet of that summer afternoon, both hearts cried unto Him.

The next day Lily returned, bright, vivacious, and coquettish. Richard, however, proved himself equal to the situation. He planned nicely for the lovers, and so engrossed Lily that more than once she excused herself to Philip with an important air. The week flew on rosy wings.

"I shall not be so generous at college," Philip whispered, an hour before his departure. "You must send me good long answers to my letters, and if it is possible, I may make you a flying visit at Christmas."

Mabel remembered, just then, she had never written to any one except her father and Lily. She trembled at the prospect before her.

A little later Robert came home, taller and handsomer

than ever; the brown hue of his complexion imparting a foreign look. He had gained a jaunty swagger that certainly sat well upon him, the only thing that could be said in its favor. His trip had not greatly improved him, neither had it increased his taste for business. He slept late in the morning, was imperious and sulky over his solitary breakfast, lounged and smoked through the day, and was frequently out until midnight. His influence on the children was anything but desirable. In his ill-tempered moods he fretted them beyond endurance, and at other times indulged them and interfered with everything like order. He did not seek to conceal his habits, but talked of drinking, gaming, and fast horses with the easy *insouciance* of a man of the world. Richard tried patience and love, ably seconded by Mabel; and though no words were spoken, their troubled glances mutually confessed each attempt a failure.

Another trait in Robert's character was likely to prove a serious source of trouble. He was indolent as well as selfish. When he had spent the wages of his trip at sea, he evinced not the slightest desire to seek a position that would give him independence, but applied unhesitatingly to Richard for money. There was not a thought of jealousy or self-interest in Richard's heart; yet he knew it was necessary to take a firm stand, or he would be answerable in some degree for his brother's ruin.

To this followed angry taunts. "He was not born a miserly old skinflint; he wanted to take the comforts of life, and he meant to have them. He wasn't spending any one's money but his own." And to out-general Richard, he had recourse to the old trick of borrowing. On making this discovery, Richard called in Mr. Guilford.

"The best plan for you," said the guardian, "will be to obtain some regular employment. I will interest myself in anything you prefer, for I desire to see you settled. You are well aware, that at your present rate of expenditure, you would waste your portion before you came of age."

"That's my own affair," was the haughty reply. "All I ask of Richard is to buy out my share of the house. He may as well do it now as a year hence."

Mr. Guilford candidly stated his objections to such a plan, and tried to rouse the young man to a sense of duty, but only succeeded in making him extremely angry.

"Very well," he said, with flashing eyes, "since you are both determined to send me adrift, so be it;" and he marched out of the office in high indignation.

"Let him go!" exclaimed Mr. Guilford, in answer to Richard's perplexed and sorrowful look. "It is time he was thrown on his own resources. With his abilities it is a shame for him to be idling and keeping the company he does."

"If one could only be sure of the right course with him;" and Richard sighed.

"My dear friend, you have tried gentle means until the very verge of weak indulgence has been reached. Few brothers would have done as much. Had your father lived, he would have found governing Robert no easy task. I wonder the shock of his death did not sober him. It only proves how deeply rooted the evil is."

The interview left Richard greatly disheartened. To fail with the first-born of the family he had promised to watch over was a painful thought. His heart cried out, from its inmost core, "How shall I give thee up, Ephraim?"

For a fortnight nothing was heard of Robert. Then he made his appearance, in his usual easy, off-hand manner, and announced that he had secured a situation in a broker's office in Wall Street, and also a boarding-place. Richard demurred a little at the latter arrangement.

"You ought to be glad to rid the house of me on any terms," he returned, rather bitterly. "And as for me, I've had enough of governing. You may keep your superfluous care for the girls."

"At least," Richard answered, "I want you to feel that

this is still your father's house — the place where his children will ever be welcome. I want you to come and go as you choose; we, at least, shall never forget how tender a claim you have on our love."

The bold eyes sank under the clear, fearless gaze they encountered. Conscience woke for a moment, and warned Robert the path he was in would lead to shame and destruction. But self-indulgence was strong upon him; desire, so often gratified, hurried him from thoughts of repentance.

Mr. Guilford made some inquiries, and found Robert had told the truth respecting his new situation. He was not favorably impressed with either member of the firm; and when he found how small the salary was, he felt assured a young man with Robert's fondness for society, and expensive habits, could not live on it in such a place as New York. He deemed it his duty, however, to warn the employers not to let him draw on them for a larger amount, as he did not care to have the property entangled in such a manner.

Robert soon learned this, and his passion knew no bounds. He wrote angrily to Richard that he would have no more of this spying and interference. "I offered to sell out to you once, and you refused; now I want you to understand, once for all, that I shall raise money in any manner I please. I can do it, if I am under age."

This threat decided Richard. He answered to Robert that he would find a sum placed in Mr. Guilford's care, on which he would be at full liberty to draw at any time.

It was nearly Christmas when this troublesome affair was settled. Yet, through all the perplexity, Richard did not forget Mabel's young hopes. His delicate tenderness, his thorough knowledge of Philip, and perhaps, too, his own costly experience, enabled him to guide, where her timidity might have betrayed her into some false step. Her letters came always under cover to him; thus she was spared questioning and embarrassment. There were hours when he took comfort from the pure, perfect affection ripening before him.

Mabel tried to understand that in accepting Philip's love she had also accepted his life, and endeavored to fit herself for her new sphere. She went at housekeeping with remarkable ardor, studied her music indefatigably, and amused Richard by various attempts at solid reading. Yet she did not neglect the duties nearest her. The sisters, so well loved, demanded and received their full share of attention. Archie clung to her with fond, boyish pride, compounded of love and admiration. Only one had remained proof against her sweetness and affection, and yet even he had paid her a curious sort of respect.

Philip's visit was brief, and made general by the festivities of the season — hardly satisfactory to so ardent a lover as he had become; but he bore the disappointment with becoming equanimity, and looked forward to summer.

Another spring shone and blossomed over them. They were all very happy. Even Robert forgot his anger, and paid them flying visits. He had changed his situation for a better one, and, all things considered, had not been immoderate in his demands on Mr. Guilford. Richard ventured to indulge in a little hope.

At the commencement of vacation Richard sent the three younger children to aunt Sophy's, declaring he could not spare Mabel for a full fortnight yet. She blushed a little consciously over this; but before the kisses of separation had grown cold upon her lips, new and blessed ones mingled with them; and in the quiet of those pleasant days Philip had no rival.

It was their first real love-making. Hitherto she had been shy, and passively acquiescent. Philip had paid homage to youth and innocence; but now the man's strong, ardent, and not easily satisfied nature demanded a return. Once fully opening her heart, even she was surprised at its depth and capacity. She grew brave enough to connect every day and hour of the coming time with him for whom she should spend it. And he pictured visions of their years together — of the work they would do, of the hopes that would blossom and unfold before them; sweet days, when he should take her into his own keeping; when their two lives would blend into one perfect soul union. Her tender gravity would restrain his impetuous spirit, his exuberance counteract the tendency to pensiveness that the events of her early life had given. As Richard watched them, he inwardly gave thanks that the two, so evidently formed for each other, should thus meet on the bridge of life.

So they walked through shadowy twilights, talked, read, sang, or gave themselves up to blissful dreams, that have survived Eden, and blossom in as dewy freshness for all as for the first mother. To Mabel's care had been committed a loving, loyal heart, that must evermore thrill at her lightest smile, and sorrow over her smallest grief. When wearied by painful discords and rude cares, it would come to her for rest, comfort. No longer her own! She knew now what Richard had hoped; she dimly guessed what he had suffered.

Then she went to rejoin the children. When Richard came for them, he was accompanied by "Mr. Gregory." Of course it was impossible to keep the secret. Lily was surprised, piqued, and pleased. Aunt Sophy was delighted, kissed Mabel, and cried over her, and predicted a bright future. As for Philip, he enjoyed his position of acknowledged lover immensely.

The last night of their stay they went to walk on the beach, where, two years before, she had paced the sands with her brother. But the murmurous sea kept time to happy heart-beats now, and the stars glorified their pleasant way. Philip was more than ever in love with Rothelan, and built his castle in spare corners of the rectory, which seemed equally as absorbing as Spain.

"He was so kind and fatherly," was the remark, after a long dissertation on Mr. Chaloner, "that I couldn't help telling him how sweet a hope my life held. And, dear, he was so pleased! He has made me promise to come to him just as soon as I am ordained, and thinks, as I do, there is no need of delaying the marriage. Can it, shall it be, my darling?"

She started, and all the pulses of her heart sent their crimson blood to her face. She was thankful for the night, for the purple darkness. His wife! It had seemed like a distant dream to her; she could not bring it to this peaceful present. It was too strange, too exciting.

He misunderstood her emotion. "Will you not like to go?" he asked.

"Thy people shall be my people." The fair face grew sweeter and tenderer beneath the soft stars of the summer night.

"This will be the most blessed year of my whole life, because at its close, if it please God, I shall realize my two best hopes. O darling, how good God has been to me, to *us*!"

CHAPTER XIV.

In a valiant suffering for others, not in a slothful making others suffer for us, did nobleness ever lie. Every noble crown is, and on earth will ever be, a crown of thorns.

CARLYLE.

THE September sun, with its ripening tints of umber, lay warm and golden on walk, terrace, and river. All that lovely day the Bertrand mansion had presented a picture of still life in exquisite detail. The children at school, Mabel alternately musing and sewing some dainty trifle, and even Richard being pleasantly idle, with leisure to look over accounts, and read some choice books. A spirit of peace brooded in the very atmosphere. He remembered long afterwards the sweet, restful calm of this day. It was as if he had turned out of the hot, wearisome highway of life, and lingered a while in some cool valley.

Just as they were summoned to dinner, Robert made his appearance. They welcomed him warmly, although a little surprised at his coming. His manner was cordial, and full of that easy grace always distinguishing him; but Richard fancied the lines about his mouth were tense, and his brow more than once was knit by some sudden and unpleasant thought. Therefore he was not surprised when Robert took his arm and led him down the garden walk.

"Dick," he said, at length, "I want you to grant me a favor."

"You are in trouble again," was the sad rejoinder.

"Yes, and no. I want to turn over a new leaf in good faith, Dick. I confess I've fallen into company and habits

11

that are rather troublesome and expensive, and I can't seem
to make a new beginning here. I have a chance in California, with a large shipping firm, of a good salary; so I
want you to buy out my share of the house, and let me go."

"To California! And you are sure there is nothing else
— no difficulty? I must have the whole truth before I take
one step;" and, as Richard's steady eyes confronted the
handsome face, it flushed and grew uneasy, as with an air
of bravado he answered, —

"My dear fellow, how dramatic you are! I haven't mur-
dered, nor forged, nor stolen. I am considerably in debt,
for somehow I hate to ask Guilford for money. It makes
me feel as if he was paying my debts gratuitously. But
when I take a new start it shall all be different."

"When do you want to go?"

"Saturday, by the Northern Light. The person whose
situation I am to take, expects to come home in about a
month. He's tired of the place, I believe, and I'm tired of
this; so we're even."

"It's very sudden," Richard said, slowly, not at all convinced that this was the real reason.

"So, if you'll let me have all my money, it will make
affairs easier for me. I want to straighten up everything
before I go."

Richard knew by past experience that asking direct questions was useless; so they discussed the journey and the
separation. Robert seemed really grateful and appreciative;
so he felt that it might be the best step that could be taken.
California was not the place of all others he would have
chosen, but to oppose would gain him nothing at all.
Presently they returned to the sitting-room, and announced
the coming departure. There was a great outcry of astonishment at first; then Robert quieted and interested the
younger ones with descriptions of the golden land, until
the pleasant talk quite took the edge off their sorrow.

Mabel was thoughtful, and sought opportunity to whisper, —

"What sends him away so suddenly?"

"I don't know anything more than he has told," Richard replied.

The following morning the brothers went to Lawyer Guilford's. Richard saw him alone, and explained the matter in hand.

"It's rather irregular, you know, Robert being under age. He may cause you trouble hereafter."

"I think he means to act in good faith. We want the house valued, and I am to lend him the amount, taking his part as security. He has promised to sign off as soon as his birthday comes. But I want everything securely arranged, so that he will not be able to dispute any point, in event of my death."

Since Dr. Bertrand's death the place had increased in value somewhat, and Richard was too honorable to defraud his brother of a penny. Robert appeared to be in a most amicable mood, and acceded willingly to every suggestion. His extravagances since leaving college were deducted from his part, and the remainder was left subject to his order.

"Give me a check for a thousand," he said. "I want to engage my passage and make a few purchases."

Richard filled it out and handed it to him. He just paused to say, "I shall be home this evening," and bowing to both gentlemen, walked off in his jaunty, independent fashion.

"I am glad for your sake that this troublesome business will soon be over," Mr. Guilford remarked.

Richard sighed. He was thinking just then of another prodigal, who took his portion and went into a strange country. He could not feel quite at ease.

It was midnight ere Robert returned. The next morning found him in charming spirits. He scarcely left Mabel's side, and evinced the warmest interest in her future. Indeed, he won her over completely; and after school he rowed the children a long way up the river, amusing them with songs and stories. And on Friday, his last day home, there was a menagerie in the city, and a very fine concert to be given in the evening; so he persuaded Richard to allow him to take the children to both. They were wild with delight. The grave elder brother looked after them as they set off. What bright, happy faces! Even Robert's was glad and smiling, and he felt self-condemned at having unjustly suspected him of wrong doing.

"O, is that you, Doctor Richard?" Ann asked, as he let himself in with his latch-key. "Will you have dinner now, or wait until the children come?"

"Wait, by all means; I'm in no hurry. Any calls?"

"There are two people in the office, who have been waiting this hour to see you and Master Robert."

He drew off his gloves deliberately, entered the library, and walked through to the office. The "two people" were a stout, business-looking man, and a tall, hard-featured woman, whose face indicated shrewdness and determination. Neither was very prepossessing. He merely gave them a glance, and said, courteously, "You wished to see me?— Doctor Bertrand."

"Yes," responded the woman. "Your brother's goin' to Californy — isn't he?"

"He expects to."

The woman gave her companion a significant nod, and then said, "He sails to-morrow — doesn't he?"

The answer was in the affirmative.

"I want to see you both together, when he comes in," the woman said, settling herself back in her chair.

More puzzled than he cared to show, he rang the bell, and ordered Robert to be sent to him as soon as he returned; then took up a paper, and from behind it cast furtive glances at his visitors. The woman was undeniably coarse and masculine, her dress a strange mixture of ill-taste and glaring color. She had a rough, weather-beaten look, yet did not seem old, although her black hair was slightly grizzled. What *could* she want of them both?

Presently a host of gay voices sounded in the hall. Rober*
opened the door with, " What did you want of me, Dick?"
and before his brother could reply, the woman confronted
him. He sank into the nearest chair, the brilliant face fad-
ing into pale ashen gray, while a quick gleam of fear and
hate shot out of the astonished eyes.

" So, my fine bird, you haven't slipped out of my hands
as easy as you thought for!"

The taunt seemed to reanimate him. A blazing ray of
passion brought the color back to his face, and he ground
his white teeth together with a half-suppressed oath, as he
demanded, " What in the fiend's name brought you here?"

She laughed triumphantly, took a cool survey of the face,
absolutely distorted with rage at having been thus foiled in
his schemes, and said, in a tantalizing tone, —

" Keep your temper, my young gentleman! There's lots
of business to be settled afore I stir out of this house. You
was goin' to dodge me all so fast, but you've found I could
be right spry when I started. You ain't in Californy yet!"

Robert was too angry and excited to speak. Richard
turned to him, saying, calmly, " What does this woman want
with you? If she has claims upon you, settle them immediately."

She turned her eyes steadily upon him, and exclaimed in
a high, shrill tone, —

" Yes, I've got claims upon him, and I ain't goin' to be
bullied out of 'em either. You rich folks think you're lords
of the world, and kin do what you like; but you won't do it
here. I'm bound to have satisfaction! I've got law on my
side, and some money that I ain't afeard of spendin'. Mebbe
your young man 'd rather tell his own story, though."

" Tell it yourself. Your tongue is glib enough," was the
sullen rejoinder; and Robert buried his face in his hands.
If he could have spared Richard the coming pang, he would
have undergone any torture at that moment. Shame, anger,
and a bitter sense of defeat rankled in his heart.

11*

"He married my gal last Feb'uary, or at least pretended so; and now he's goin' off without leavin' a dollar for her or the baby that's to come. My friend here's an officer, and you'll pay han'somely for this piece of work, or you'll go to jail. That's the long and the short of it."

The dinner bell rang at this juncture. Richard opened the door, and bade Mabel not wait for them, then shut it carefully, and closed the window. "Now," said he, with quiet authority, "I am ready for your story. Tell it briefly as possible."

"You needn't be so uppish!" and the woman bridled angrily at his calmness. "I shall tell the truth, which is more 'n *he's* in the habit of doin', I guess;" and she nodded her head towards Robert. "He'd been comin' to my place a spell, with a lot of young bloods, when one night he saw my gal. He took to followin' her home from school, and bein' mighty pleasant with her. I didn't put her in his way, nor ask him to fall in love with her; but he kept hangin' round, sendin' her books and sich, until I see she begun to like him. The gal was too young, and innocent, and pretty, to be fooled with. So I told him, plump and plain, if he wanted to marry her he might keep on, but if not, to make tracks, 'cause I wasn't goin' to have any trouble. He kept away a week or so; then he told me he wanted to marry the gal, but he wasn't of age, and his folks would oppose it, 'cause they was rich, but if I'd let 'em be married privately, he'd take care on her until he got his fortin. And he wanted a friend of his to marry 'em, so when he come to confess, the minister could smooth things out a little for him. Well, I got my neighbor here, Mr. Garrick, to find out how things stood, and he said he guessed the story was about straight; so I consented, for my gal thought as much of him as if he'd been made out of gold."

"You were ready enough to have me marry your decoy duck," sneered Robert.

"She wasn't no decoy duck!" snapped the woman, angrily. "You know she never 'tended shop; and you was crazy about her — you needn't deny it! Well, they was married, and he used to stay to my house a good deal. Marg'ret and he was happy as birds. After a while, 'long in the summer, he begun to slack up comin'; but the gal believed his excuses, and as he took care of her, and wasn't ugly, I thought I wouldn't find fault. But when he staid away a week or two at a time, I see she grieved about it, and asked him what he meant. He was pretty lordly, and wouldn't give me much satisfaction, but finally said, if I'd wait until he was of age, I'd see what he meant to do. He didn't come near Marg'ret after that; so Monday I marched down to his office, and asked him if he wanted to break his wife's heart by neglect. He jest give a little laugh, and asked me to prove he had a wife, and he'd promise to be devoted to her. I was awful mad, I tell you; but I kept quiet. When I got home, I found he'd taken away Marg'ret's certificate. So I come over to Jersey, to find the Mr. Fields who married 'em. He wasn't the man at all, and he said he could swear he'd never married any such persons. Then I knew we'd been tricked; and when I found he'd left his office, I put Mr. Garrick on the scent, and he soon learned my gentleman was makin' off for Californy. He's got a warrant in his pocket, and can take the rascal off to the Tombs; but I'll give you both a chance to act fair. I can make him marry the gal, or send him to State Prison!" and she gave an exultant chuckle.

"Will you walk in the adjoining room a moment?" Richard said to the woman and her companion.

"Look here now," she said, turning on him; "there's to be no conniving between you two. I won't be hard on the young scamp, nuther; I'll give him off, if he'll provide for the gal and her child. She'll do better without him, if he don't care for her."

Richard motioned them peremptorily away, and closed the door. A deathly silence ensued. It was broken at length by his saying, hoarsely, —

"Is that woman's story true, Robert?"

"God knows, Dick, if I could have taken myself out of the way before this came out, I would gladly have given every dollar I possess. I meant to have spared you this trouble; but it's my luck. Nothing ever does go right with me!" and Robert absolutely sobbed.

"'The way of the transgressor is hard.' O, how could you have fallen into such a sin?"

"I didn't think how it would end. And you know, Dick, hundreds of young men do the same thing."

Richard could have spurned his brother for this weak justification.

"What is to be done?" he asked, coldly.

"Buy them off, I suppose, for I'm sick of the girl, and can't marry her. I don't think I would have gone so far if it hadn't been for George Townley. He planned it all, and personated the clergyman. O, I could kill myself for being such a fool!"

There was no real sorrow in all this. The whole affair was utterly revolting to Richard, and a sense of shame overwhelmed him.

"Who are they?" he asked presently.

"This old Mother Davis keeps a drinking and gambling saloon, up on Third Avenue. Last winter I went there with some fellows; and one night we had been sleigh-riding, and stopped there for supper. The boys used to talk about a pretty Dutch girl there; but this evening we saw Margaret. George Townley was crazy about her; but she wouldn't even look at him. Then I met her in the street: she was shy enough at first; but I soon found out the little fool liked me. I believe I *was* infatuated, Dick; and then the old woman was so pressing! Townley said it would be a good joke, and the girl wouldn't care a bit when she grew tired of me."

Richard half suppressed a groan of anguish.

"They were as much to blame as I," Robert said, quickly, "for the old woman fairly inveigled me into it. And I dare say the girl will play the same game over twenty times."

"Is she like her mother?"

"Not a bit. I believe she isn't really *her* child. She's a pretty little milk-and-water thing ; her face bewitched me at first ; but I'm sick and tired of her now."

In spite of his hardihood, Robert's face was crimson with shame. He understood Richard too well to attempt any special justification ; but he was determined the mother and daughter should take their full share of blame.

Richard considered the matter in silence. While he could not excuse his brother's sin, he felt something might be due to the schemes of a designing woman. What kind of a mother could she be to fancy money would make amends for such an irremediable blight! How base and grovelling her soul! Richard was not at all prepared to receive such an addition to the family, even if he could have persuaded his brother into marrying the girl. Indeed, reason said, a marriage so evidently unwise when sanctioned by love, would be doubly so when the brief passion had settled into distaste. If money could heal the wrong, perhaps it would be best to accept the woman's offer.

"Why did you not tell the girl?" he asked, anxious to note the effect of his remark.

Robert started as if he had been stung.

"No, I couldn't, Dick; I couldn't; I would have gone to jail first;" and the crimson mounted to his brow. At a later day Richard understood these words; but now he took it as an evidence that his brother was not utterly lost to self-respect.

"Well," he resumed, with a dreary sigh, "let us settle it the easiest way, since she will be satisfied with money."

"I have fourteen hundred dollars still coming. I *must* have at least two hundred. The rest she may take. It's hard, but I'm thankful to be well out of the scrape."

They summoned Mrs. Davis and her attendant. The coarse, hard face disgusted Richard more than ever. After an embarrassing silence of some moments he began,—

"It would be useless to desire two people to marry who have ceased to care for each other —"

"It's a lie if *he* said so!" flung out the woman, angrily. "Marg'ret worships him, and he knows it. There isn't a thought in her heart but of him. I ain't pertikerlar about his marryin' her, though. Likely he'd be ugly, and some time leave her again. When she gets over her sorrow now, she'll be free — a blessed good thing, in my opinion!"

"There only remains one point, then: what compensation is required?"

The woman glanced eagerly from one to the other, as if studying her ground, then said, with slow, decided emphasis, —

"Five thousand dollars!"

"Five thousand!" they both echoed, in consternation.

"Yes; people who dance must expect to pay the piper. That's lettin' you off easy, when I have it all in my own hands."

Her voice and manner were so resolute that it seemed as if she delighted in the extortion. Most contradictory emotions flashed through Richard's mind. While his high and keen sense of right shrank from shielding so terrible a sin, his brotherly affection, and a belief that justice would in any case be perverted, if dealt out by this woman, rendered him cautious.

Robert broke the silence with a cool sullenness.

"I can't go that, and I won't marry the girl; so send me to prison as fast as you like. You'll have a little revenge, and no money, and the satisfaction of breaking Margaret's heart." Then he settled himself in his chair, and scowled defiantly at her.

Richard's face was impassible. She read nothing in it to encourage her; but she was not a woman to yield at the first blow.

"Well," she said, "seeing you don't mind the disgrace —"

"I'll tell you what I will do," interrupted Robert; "I

have twelve hundred dollars still left of my share of the estate. She may take that, or I'll marry her to-morrow morning, and go to California to-morrow afternoon. There is no law to keep me *here*, if I provide for my wife before I go ; " and a smile of triumph lit the haughty face.

" Twelve hundred dollars won't take care of her and a child a great many years," suggested the woman, in a lower tone.

" Then she can stand behind the bar with her pretty face. She'll soon get a new husband," was the sneering rejoinder.

The woman took a step forward, as if she would have struck him to the ground. The bitter contempt of her nature seemed thoroughly roused. Richard fairly shivered, as he listened to her withering denunciations. Not until her breath was gone did she pause. Then Richard stepped forward with a dignity not to be misunderstood.

" We have had enough recrimination," he said, in a clear, cold tone. " Take what my brother has to offer you, and for ten years I will add one hundred dollars annually to it. That is *all* I will do."

Mrs. Davis did not seem disposed to assent at first ; but when she became convinced that Robert was very much poorer than she had anticipated, and his brother fully determined to go no farther than his first proposal, she reluctantly yielded. Richard wrote out the necessary notes, and Mr. Garrick affixed his name as witness. He would have been better satisfied at seeing the law take its course, but had promised to do Mrs. Davis's bidding in either event. Robert preserved a sulky silence, and only stared at the woman's parting anathema. Then the troublesome visitors withdrew, and the brothers were left alone.

Robert was first to break the silence.

" Dick," he began, in a low tone, " if I should be prospered, I will pay every cent of that money. You shall not be the loser through your great kindness. You see now it is best for me to go away."

"Yes;" and Richard sighed wearily, adding, "Go now; if you still desire to take the children out, I have no objection to make. It may be the last time. And your secret is safe with me."

Robert moved noiselessly away, awed by the sad, patient face, so full of woe. He hated himself for having caused it, and made all manner of good resolves for the future.

CHAPTER XV.

O waly, waly, gin love be bonny,
  A little time while it is new;
But when it's auld, it waxeth cauld,
  And fades away like morning dew.
I leaned my back unto an aik;
  I thought it was a trusty tree;
But first it bowed, and syn it brake,
  And sae did my fause love to me.
OLD BALLAD.

ROBERT ate his dinner in silence, and in answer to Tessy's questions, said he had been vexed about some money matters, but they were all going out, as this was his last night. The concert was really fine; and listening to the delightful music, he half forgot the peril he had been in. Alas, that remorse in such natures should invariably be short-lived! It was not absolute insincerity, but the result of a temperament too pleasure-loving to concentrate itself strongly on any painful idea, and too selfish to follow out the picture of another's suffering. He blamed himself deeply now — not for innocence betrayed, or a sense of forfeited honor, but because he had calculated wrongly, and at the eleventh hour the disgraceful secret had made itself known. It was not the sin, but the disclosure. "I was a fool to talk to the woman as I did," was his angry self-condemnation. "I ought to have gone off quietly, and kept good friends with her until the last moment. But it's all over now, and can't be helped!"

It is true that those who sin do not always suffer the most. Richard, with his high, fine, honorable nature, his conscious rectitude and blameless life, sat crushed and trembling under the blow.   He could not meet the familiar faces; it seemed as if they would all read the terrible story in his.   As soon, therefore, as he could command himself a little, he took his hat and walked out.   There were no urgent calls on his list, but he wanted to see some suffering that he could try to lighten; for only God could lift the cloud overshadowing him.   When he returned the house was solitary.

They all kept up their spirits wonderfully the next morning.   Little keepsakes were exchanged; and Archie delighted himself with the idea that when he grew up he would go and make Robert a long visit, and have a splendid time.   Then there was the bustle of their getting ready to accompany him to the city, to " see him off."

Nothing beyond commonplace kindnesses had passed between the elder ones.   Richard felt utterly unable to say anything wiser or better than he had said many times before.   That had all proved useless.   It might be his forbearance touched Robert.   Certainly the tone was humble and earnest, with which he said, —

" Dear Dick, when I am gone, don't quite hate me.   I know I've tried your patience beyond forgiveness, but I *will* endeavor to be more worthy of your love in the future."

" God give you strength to keep the resolve," Richard responded, fervently.   " And when you think of the old home, remember there is not one heart but would ache at your misconduct, or rejoice over the slightest improvement.   Think of the pure sisters growing up to womanhood; of our dear, dead father; and, above all, of the God whom we shall meet at the last day."

There were tears and kisses; and as the steamer glided out of her dock, they all remembered the handsome face nodding a last adieu — bright in spite of the sorrow, sparkling for all its tears.   They were content to be grave and silent, and for once Richard had no words of comfort.   He was thinking of another Saturday, when one had been taken from among them, and said to himself, " Weep not for the

dead, but weep rather for him who goeth into a far country."
There were no lamentations to be made for him who was at
rest in heaven, wisely taken from the evil to come.

And so the first birdling went out of the home nest. If
Richard had failed in any duty, he humbly prayed God to
forgive him.

With childish elasticity the younger ones soon recovered
their spirits. California wasn't *quite* out of the world, and
Robert had promised to write by the first steamer. Lily
collected a huge pile of books, and went to studying the
topography of the golden land, declaring she had half a
mind to go to California for a husband when she wanted one,
as women were esteemed a luxury there.

Several days passed before Richard could summon sufficient courage to go over the late distasteful events. Recon-
sidering the subject, he was sorry he had not paid Mrs.
Davis the whole sum at once, instead of thus giving her a
claim upon him. In case of his death, discovery would be
inevitable. It was best, therefore, to remedy the mistake
as soon as possible. He shrank from a personal interview,
but there was no other course; so to New York he went.

The place was easily found — a two and a half story brick
house, unpainted and dingy looking; the lower front windows decorated with sundry tokens of what one might expect
within; a door whose sash of glass was rendered impene-
trable to curious eyes by a faded red curtain, and a rather
more respectable side entrance. He opened the shop door,
however, ascertaining by a glance that there were no cus-
tomers on hand.

It was an ordinary drinking saloon, with a beer counter
and bar on one side, and several small tables ranged on the
other, one of which contained the daily papers and a pack
of soiled cards. There was an unpleasant odor of beer and
tobacco; but the floor was freshly sanded, everything in
tolerable order, and the mistress attired in much better taste
than at the preceding interview. Her clean calico dress and

apron, and her smoothly arranged hair, improved her wonderfully.

"O, Dr. Bertraud! Good mornin', sir;" and then she paused from surprise, adding, presently, "walk in here, sir; I hope you're well, and there's nothing wrong."

"A slight matter of business merely. If you do not object, I think I would rather pay you the thousand dollars I became responsible for, and have the matter entirely settled."

She assented readily. Indeed, her eagerness for money disgusted him. While she was looking for the papers, he took a survey of the apartment. It was large and scrupulously clean; but its old-fashioned furniture was eked out by some chalky plaster vases, with red and yellow fruit, and sundry pictures of fast horses, presidents, and female faces in various stages of beauty.

"*She's* gone out to walk," Mrs. Davis said, as if she considered some conversation necessary. "He told her she oughter, and his word always was law to her; but you'll wait and see her."

Richard knew very well for whom the pronouns stood, and was thankful to be spared the interview.

"Of course she understands all connection with my brother is ended. You told her — "

"No, I hain't told her; I couldn't," the woman interrupted. "She knows he's gone to Californy, but she's too good and too innocent to guess the rest. I wish to Heaven she'd never seen your brother! Money won't do everything;" and Mrs. Davis rocked to and fro in a despairing passion.

Richard glanced up in surprise at this outburst, and said, calmly, "I wish her to be made aware of the fact. She has no further claims upon us now;" and handing Mrs. Davis a check, he took up his own note.

"I wish you'd stop and tell her yourself, if you think it so easy. *He* hadn't the courage to! O, if she hadn't loved him, and been so happy with him! There she comes now."

Richard sat out of range of the door. Something like pride lighted the woman's hard face, as a small, slight figure, clothed in a dress and mantle of soft brown, that fell around her in graceful folds, entered the apartment.

"Mar'gret, this is Dr. Bertrand," was the brief introduction.

She turned her head. The bonnet that framed in the face was mostly white, with a few drooping pale pink buds, and strings of the same color tied underneath the exquisitely rounded chin. He had been used to fair, refined girls all his life. In his fancy he had entertained a coarse, florid idea, with bold, handsome black eyes, red cheeks, and a saucy, piquant air, as belonging to this one. For a moment he held his breath.

It was not a lofty, classic face, like Mabel's; nor arch, dazzling, and regular, like Lily's. The features were child-ishly delicate, yet clearly cut; the forehead broad, with eyebrows that might have been pencilled by an artist; large, soft, luminous eyes, with rays like a coming sunrise prisoned in their brown depths; a transparent complexion, just re-lieved by the faintest peach bloom in the cheeks, and the ripe, red, beautifully curved mouth. There was a high-bred air about it that would not have shamed a princess of royal blood; and yet so gentle, so beseeching and resistless, that it went to Richard's heart at once.

She glanced at him first in shy surprise; then her lip quivered, her eyes drooped until the lashes made a long, rich fringe upon her cheeks, that were struggling with alter-nate paleness and flushing. He rose and took her hand with that courtesy natural to him, and then he remarked how small and faultlessly gloved it was, and that every article of her attire seemed to be a part of herself.

The entrance of a customer caused Mrs. Davis's hasty re-treat. She closed the door carefully behind her.

Richard stood quite still, as if in a trance. Then he noticed how the slight figure trembled as she said, depre-catingly, —

12 *

" Are you very, *very* angry ? "

The supplicating voice had a peculiar girlish ring and richness. It made one think of wafts of meadow wind, freighted with the drowsy, musical hum of bird and bee, as they float homeward in purple twilight.

" Angry ? " he repeated, as if making a confused and ineffectual effort to remember how she had sinned against him.

" I did not know *then* how wrong it was for him to marry me. I could only think how dearly we loved one another; but it has all failed — he does not care for me now; " and the sigh with which the words ended beaded the golden-brown lashes with tears.

He forgot his just indignation, his distaste of her surroundings. Truth and honor were written on that broad, white forehead — the nobleness of an unstained soul.

" My poor, poor child! it is you who are the injured one ; " and he drew her tenderly to a seat beside him on the wooden settle.

" Mother said you were so — displeased ; and — I suppose I was not good enough for Robert." The sweet voice sank to a desolate pathos.

" Not good enough! O child! if he had been as pure and true! It is you who have been sinned against, not he."

She suffered her mantle to fall loosely around her shoulders, and laid her bonnet entirely aside, displaying an abundance of satin smooth brown hair, gathered at the back in a coil of braids.

He wanted to hear her voice again ; therefore said, kindly, " Will you tell me your own story ? "

She glanced up in his face with a little shiver, mistaking its gravity for sternness. Robert had inspired her with a fear of this all-potent elder brother, and Mrs. Davis's account of him was not of a nature to allay her apprehensions. But the thought that he had a right to know gave her courage; so she began, tremulously : —

"Last winter, one evening, a sleigh-riding party came here for supper. Barbara Chrisler, the girl who used to assist mother evenings, was ill, and had to go home; so I came down stairs to wait upon them. There were only four, and they had their supper in here. I liked Robert best, because he didn't stare at me, and was less boisterous. When they came to cards and wine I went away. A few days after this, as I was coming from school, Robert met me. He was so pleasant I could not help talking; and when we came in, mother seemed real pleased. She is not my own mother, but has always been so good to me — only when she wanted me to stay in the shop, I couldn't;" and a deep flush overspread the fair face. "At Christmas he sent me some beautiful books; and as I sat in this room, generally, evenings, studying my lessons, he used to come in. It was very delightful. He wanted to take me out, but mother would not let him. I did not care, though; I was so happy I did not want anything more. I don't know how it came, but after a while we loved one another. It was so sweet! No one had ever loved me before. I had been so solitary, for mother was always busy with the shop, and Barbara used to tease me, and the school-girls laughed about my living in a beer-shop. I couldn't seem to help giving my whole heart to Robert."

A tender, satisfied light came into her eyes, as, drawing a long breath, she paused. There was a beauteous, vivid life in every lineament, a womanly depth and consciousness, that thrilled him as not even Mabel's half-whispered confidences had done.

"He wanted to be married," she continued, as a warm crimson flushed her face. "He and mother talked it all over. He said his family were rich and proud, and would try to keep him from marrying any one who was poor. He wasn't but little over twenty, and said he couldn't wait a year for the right to call me all his, and have me constantly with him; so mother consented to a private marriage. She

let me have one of the rooms up stairs, and we had such a
nice time settling furniture and arranging everything! We
were married the last of February. I couldn't think of anything, only that Robert loved me. I was to be *his* always —
to be petted and caressed, and feel safe beside him. I liked
belonging to him. Was it very wrong ? "

She glanced up fearfully. He took the small hand in his,
and said, with deep feeling, " No ; it was not wrong for you
to give your whole heart to your husband."

" All the spring we were so happy ! He used to take me
out walking and driving, and when summer came, we went
to the country for brief journeys that were very delightful.
He couldn't live here all the time, you know ; and I used to
count the hours when he was away with such a strange feeling ! It was all like a poem or a story, until he began to
bring his friends up stairs to play cards. Sometimes they
would stay until midnight. At first I used to leave them,
for I didn't like to hear their conversation ; but when I
found it vexed Robert, I remained in the room and read,
with my face turned from them.

" Then he took to staying away for days together. I
used to cry at first, I felt so lonesome ; and he would pet me,
and try to laugh me out of my foolishness, as he called it.
Afterwards he grew stern, and frightened me by his strange
ways. One night he told me I was a troublesome baby, and
no comfort to him ; so I tried very hard then not to cry,
and always to be pleasant. Mother said men seldom loved
their wives so well when it grew to be an old story. It
seems hard, for we love them better and better every
day. I did not tell mother when he was cross to me. I
felt as if I could not have any one know it ; but at last she
guessed, and they had a quarrel. He was very angry when
he came up stairs, swore at me, and said ' he was a fool to
take me ; that he might have known I would hang to him
forever, and there would be no getting rid of me.' The
words rang in my ears after he went away. I could **not**

sleep; I could only pray that, if he was really tired of me, I might die.

"He was very good when he came next time. I couldn't help loving him, but somehow it did not seem the glad old love. I trembled when he spoke hastily to me, and felt afraid all the time. I could see he was wearying of me, and my heart grew sick with intense pain. He brought me no more fruit or pretty gifts, and seemed impatient to get away, but was never so cross again. Sunday, a week ago, was the last time I saw him. He was kind and gentle, and said he had business that would take him off for several weeks. I must not get lonesome in his absence, but read, and walk, and keep cheerful. I had been so depressed and miserable that even this failed to touch me. I felt no more solitary at the thought of his going quite away than I had with his brief, hurried visits of late. My heart was so cold I could not hope for anything. Mother came up afterwards, and asked me what he had said; so I told her. She was angry at him, but I begged her not to do any rash thing. Since she could not make him love me again, all the rest was useless.

"Saturday of that week she told me he had deserted me, and gone to California; that it wasn't at all likely I should ever see him again, but he had made some provision for me. She spoke of her visit to you. I felt then all was over; that love, and happiness, and bright dreams could never be mine again. O, if I could have known this before I married him!"

How utterly dreary and despairing was the pathos of her voice! The radiant light that had made her face so enchanting, a short time before, had faded into gray ashiness. The very features sharpened over thoughts of heart-sick agony that she could not repeat even to this kind listener.

He wanted to gather the trembling little figure to his heart, to shelter her, comfort her, take her to some place of rest where peaceful days might shut out the memory of this miserable past. Not any older than Lily, perhaps ; and he shivered at the thought of his sister's passing through such a fearful ordeal. She was not less refined and sensitive, for all her surroundings had been hard and coarse to vulgarity. She had passed through the fire unharmed. Looking in her pure face, where there was not a thought to conceal, or the ability so to do, he mentally resolved to shield her from all future ill.

"My poor little girl," he said, with the grand tenderness the children at home knew so well, "your summer has been brief indeed. I want you to forget all that passed between your mother and myself. I did not know the whole story then, and judged hastily. I cannot make you entirely happy, but I can share some of your burdens — be a brother to you. Will you trust me ?"

She could not instantly divest herself of fear. His practised eye detected the feverish expectation of rebuke, sweeping through her veins with its poisonous thrill of distrust. Her cheeks glittered with an unwholesome scarlet, and the little hands he took in his were hot with painfully throbbing pulses.

"You must trust me," he resumed, in a low, assuring tone. "I will strive to do what I can for you. Life will be sad enough at the best, and you need a true friend sorely. Would you like to go away from here ?" he asked, with a sudden thought.

"O, so much ! But where could I go ?" she responded, wearily.

"I may find some pleasant place. You are tired, and must not talk any more. I shall come again soon, and we will plan a little for the future. Will you try to be cheerful ?"

"Thank you ; you are so kind !" and her eyes filled with tears.

He had some comfort to give with his farewell — some words of peace to soothe her troubled soul. Then he walked slowly out into the shop.

CHAPTER XVI.

Yet, O yet thyself deceive not ;
Love may sink by slow decay;
But by sudden wrench believe not
Hearts can thus be torn away.
BYRON.

MRS. DAVIS was leaning on her elbows, gazing into vacancy. She raised her eyes when Richard approached, and said, with a significant sneer, " Well, did *you* tell her ? "

In spite of his effort for mastery, his face flushed, as he answered with a negative motion, instead of speaking.

" I thought you couldn't. She ain't like other folks. I used to think her the queerest child when she wouldn't play with anybody, and kept to her high notions in spite of all I could do. She's good to the back-bone, too good for a place like this. I wasn't goin' to stand by and see your brother fool her, though I'll bet he couldn't. But it's a sorry, sorry thing that she ever listened to him at all; and careful as I was, the scamp outwitted me. I've about made up my mind to say nothin' now; mebbe her child won't live; and when she's older, 'n don't care so much for *him*, it won't come so hard."

There was some vulgar wisdom in this. But Dr. Bertrand caught at another fact. " She's not your own child," he said, with a blessed sense of relief.

" No, but I'd fight for her jest as soon as if she was. I don't believe any child of mine could have been so good or so han'some. A long spell ago I loved her father. If you ain't in a hurry I'll tell you how I come to have her."

He seated himself, and motioned her to proceed, feeling a deeper interest in the story than he would have cared to own.

"You see, when I was a gal, we lived at Yarmouth, on Barnstable shore. I hadn't any father 'n mother, and spun for a livin'. I was young and high steppin', good lookin' too, folks said, for my skin was white, and my cheeks red, and my hair black and shiny as satin. I used to go to all the frolics and dances ; could keep up all night, and do my stint next day without a bit o' blinkin'.

"There was a young man used to go off fishin' every year, that I set great store by. His name was Seth Tremaine, and his mother used to keep house alone when he was gone. Mis' Tremaine and I never quite hitched horses ; she was kinder religious, and thought me hity-tity, and all that ; but I didn't mind, long as Seth liked me. One fall there was a wreck on the coast, and Seth saved a gal about like *her*," nodding to the adjoining apartment. "All her friends was lost, and no one wanted her ; so Mis' Tremaine took her. She hadn't any child but Seth, and 'twas wonderful how she loved that gal. She was a pale little thing, with yellow hair, and jest sich skin as Mar'gret's. Her hands 'n feet wasn't bigger than a baby's, and her talkin' was jest like other folks singin'. Mar'gret's got a good deal of her voice.

"Next spring Seth and me began to talk o' gettin' married. I wasn't willin' to go live with Mis' Tremaine ; so Seth, he went off agin, to get enough money, with what he had, to build a house. I worked like a bee that summer, and was chipper as a cricket ; ruther gay too, for I was fond o' company, and didn't see any sense in mopin', because I couldn't have Seth always at my elbow.

"Next winter, somehow, Seth and me didn't get along so well. He was jealous and bossy, and I was too high strung to let any man trample on me. But the worst of it come one night at a frolic. I'd been spinnin' for Mis' Brown, and her son Hiram was cuttin' round after me. It made Seth mad to see him dancin' and enjoyin' himself with me; so he said, kinder short, 'he was tired of the foolin', and wanted to take me home.' I told him I could have company any time, and wasn't goin' till the fun was over. He spunked right up, and we had a reg'lar quarrel, and he told me I might take Hi, and keep him, for there was an end of all between us.

"I knew Seth loved me, and thought he'd come round all right afore long, so I wasn't down-hearted. He started off to Nantucket to his uncle's, and I went to the north side to spin; so I never see him for three weeks, an' then it was Sunday, when he come in church with his mother an' Elfy.

"I declare! I thought I should 'a turned into stone that mornin'. The parson read the banns between Elfy Howard and Seth Tremaine. I'd never dreamed o' sich a thing! But I held out, and was as high-headed as you please till I got home, when I had a good cry. I felt as if I couldn't have it so; I was willin' then to say anything if 'twould 'a brought him back. But I wasn't going to be laughed at; so I acted afore folks jest as though I didn't care.

"Between daylight and dark one night, I run into a sick neighbor's to tidy up the house a little. Seth Tremaine come with some things his marm had sent. I couldn't say much, and waited a spell for him to go; but when I found he didn't, I started myself. Jest as if he'd been waitin' for that, he got up and offered to see me home. I told him 'twasn't wuth while; but he put my arm in his, as if I hadn't spoken a word, and we walked together silent as the grave. I couldn't help thinkin' that next Sunday he was to be married to that pale little thing of an Elfy. So, as we was partin' at the gate, I said, I hoped he would be happy; but the words a'most choked me, and I couldn't keep the tears from my eyes. He turned my face round suddenly; it was moonlight, and he couldn't help seein' all!

"'Marg'ret,' says he, — and his voice had a strange, cold sound, — 'why didn't you have some tears ready a month ago?

Why didn't you say then you loved me? 'Twould 'a saved us both a world of trouble.'

"After a little, he went on to tell me how he come to ask Elfy. His mother never 'd like me very much, and was so bound up in Elfy, she coaxed him to marry her. He found out too that the gal loved him, and somehow it all come round, and his mother set a weddin' day right off. He didn't say he loved me best, but I knew it without any tellin'. He wasn't a man to go back from his word, though; so on Sunday they was married, and the next night his mother give 'em a great weddin'.

"I couldn't stay at Yarmouth; so I come to New York to visit an uncle I had here. He was sick and kinder cross-grained, and aunt was glad enough to have me stay and help take care of him. She was always on the go with a son she'd had by her first marriage, and I felt sorry for the poor old man. After a spell he grew so fond b' me, he didn't want any one else to come near him; and when he died, he left me five hundred dollars. I'd been with him four years. Aunt wanted me to marry her son; but he was a poor coot, and fond o' drink in the bargain. I didn't like him, and wouldn't have him; so we had a spat, and I felt I must look out for a new home. That very evenin' a gentleman called to see me. I went down to the parlor, wonderin' who it could be, and was clear beat to find Seth Tremaine.

"He was dreadful thin and pale. I knowed right off something 'd happened. He told me he'd seen lots of trouble. A year before, his house had took fire and burned down in the dead of winter, and they'd all jest escaped with their lives. His marm died a fortnight afterwards; his little boy took cold, but lingered along until spring, when he died too. Elfy had a baby a few weeks old at the time of the fire, and she'd never been right smart; but after the death of the little boy, she pined away, and for two months Seth had been alone with his little gal, who was called Mar'gret, after me. I couldn't help feelin' kind towards Elfy when I heard that.

'Tain't every woman that would 'a named a child after her husband's old love !

"Seth was goin' to China now, for three years, as first mate. The ship was layin' at New York, and wouldn't be ready under a fortnight; so he thought he'd hunt me up, as he knew my uncle's name. We had a good long talk, and then he come agin the next day, and told me he wished I'd take his little gal and keep her till he got back. He said it wasn't no time to talk of marryin' now, with Elfy hardly cold in her grave; but that we was the ones that should 'a been together from the first, and if God spared him to come back, I should be his wife. I was glad, I tell you! It seemed like the old times comin', for you see I'd never loved any one but Seth.

" While he was gone after his baby, I thought I'd hunt up a quiet boardin' place. Aunt was mad as a March hare when she heard what I was goin' to do, and called me all the fools in the world. Round the corner from our house there was a little shop kept by an old woman everybody called Aunty Dean. She was a good, clever soul, and I went to see if she knew of any place that might suit me. She said she had a spare room, and would be glad to take me in for company; so I picked up my traps and went there; and when Seth come back with his baby, he was real glad to find me so comfortable. He would make me take some money, and promised to send more when he wrote. I felt mightily pleased to see him lookin' so cheerful before he went away.

" Marg'ret was jest like a little doll. She never cried, and soon got fond of me and Aunty Dean. I was happy as a bird all them two years, gettin' letters now and then, and helpin' 'tend shop and sewin'. Then I began to count on Seth's comin' home. I didn't get any letter for a long while, but I knew he was true as steel, and kept from frettin'. The baby was a great comfort to me. I believe I was fond of it as if it had been my own. One day as I was wonderin', Aunty Dean said,—

"' I'd go to the shippin' house, if I was you, and see if they'd heard anything.'

" I started off. It was a bright, shiny day, and I couldn't believe there was bad news in store for me; so I asked up, chipper as you please. The men looked at each other, and one of 'em said, —

"' Why, didn't you know Seth Tremaine was lost when the Argos was wrecked ? '

" The whole world went round for a minute. I seemed stone blind. Then he went on to say that, three months before, the Argos had been wrecked, an' most all on board were lost. Some one saw the cap'n an' the mate go down together. It didn't seem a bit true at first, and I went on watchin' for him; but when three years and four years was gone, I gave up, and got low-spirited. I couldn't care for anything. Then Aunty Dean took sick, and I nursed her for a long while, keepin' house and shop; but Marg'ret was such a handy little thing, she helped more'n she hindered. When Aunty Dean died, she left me five hundred dollars; and then I begun to think over agin what I must do, for you see I had Marg'ret to take care of an' eddicate. Her father had put all his money in the ship, and that was lost as well as him. So I come up here, and found this house for sale cheap, and bought it. There wasn't anything I could do besides keep shop, and the woman who lived up stairs advised me to sell liquor, as it was a good deal better business than thread and needles.

" Marg'ret was eight years old then. I don't know what come over the child. She was smart enough, and minded all I told her; but if any one in the shop chucked her under the chin, or called her han'som, she'd cry as if her heart was broken. She seemed too good for common folks; and when I scolded her, she'd look up with jest sich eyes as her father's, and I couldn't say a word. But it was an awful bother to me, for I couldn't stir a step without gettin' some one to come in an' stay; and I found she wasn't goin' to be the slightest help to me as she grew up, she was so 'fraid of bein' looked at. All she cared for was her books. So when she and your brother fell so desputly in love, I thought mebbe the best thing I could do would be to let 'em marry. She was good enough for any man, if she wasn't rich."

Dr. Bertrand understood what she would have been ashamed to put in words — that she had begun to consider Margaret a burden. Yet she had dealt nobly with her rival's child, simply because she was a link between her old lover and herself; for there could be no true assimilation between such widely different characters. As the romance of her early womanhood became blunted by coarse contact with the world, her nature had hardened, lost its innate consciousness of better things, while the child had increased in refinement and purity. Yet it was like finding a dove in the nest of a hawk.

"Would you be willing to part with her if you knew she was well taken care of?" he asked.

"I've been thinkin' about boardin' her away somewhere. This ain't jest the place for her, and she don't like it; besides, I can't take care of a family. I'm goin' to get a gal to 'tend shop, and *her* mother wants that room up stairs; so I think you'd be doin' a kindness to take her away. But I'm bound to see her well treated, for she's got money enough to last a while, anyhow."

"I will call again in a few days," was his abrupt announcement. "In the mean while, say nothing about her unfortunate marriage. Good morning;" and he turned into the street.

A sensation of relief stole over him, a mingled emotion of pleasure and pain; and then, as his thoughts recurred to Robert, a total revulsion of feeling swept over him. He had considered him foolishly wicked before; now it was the blackest treachery. The woman's unwise haste to rid herself of Margaret had made the path easier; but what must he be who could betray this innocent child so cruelly, when

she had laid her heart at his feet in all the honor and truth
of pure womanhood?

He was thankful she did not love Robert with the absorbing passion of her first dreams. She would suffer less in the
dreary desolation that lay before her. She was still a child.
What might have proved a strong and lasting regard had
been checked by coldness and neglect; and when the thorough woman in her woke to active being, her heart would
have some blighted leaves in its unfolding, but nothing that
would need hold her back from any new joy God might send.
He could not tell why this should comfort him; he only knew
it did, and accepted the fact unquestioningly. Yet, as he
walked slowly down Broadway, revolving these thoughts in
his mind, he did not feel quite conscience-clear. He had
been weak, hasty, and partial — glad to think money could
absolve Robert from all claims. Unwittingly he had helped
the betrayer against the betrayed. His heart smote him
bitterly. Was it indeed too late? O, if he could persuade
Robert to return for one brief act of justice!

Under any circumstances Mother Davis's was no proper
place for Margaret. He must provide a new home with some
one whose kindness and discretion were undoubted — out of
the reach of idle gossip, yet not too far from him. He could
not yield her entirely to stranger hands. Who would take
a motherly interest in this poor, friendless child?

For several days he revolved the perplexing subject. Mabel
wondered to see him so entirely pre-occupied. But he had
never been tenderer to the children.

Some conversation he was holding with a patient one day
concerning a nurse, recalled to his mind a lady his father had
placed great confidence in — a childless widow, who had for-
merly supported herself by attending the sick. About the
time of Dr. Bertrand's death she had removed to a pretty
country place, in order to take care of her father-in-law, who
had been left entirely alone by the death of his last daughter.
She possessed one of those full, cheerful natures that invari-

ably carry sunshine with them at every step. He had called occasionally at the little cottage, when business took him in that direction, for Mr. Wilcox was both old and infirm. He knew, too, that the daughter-in-law eked out her small income by taking a boarder or two in the summer. The season would be over now, and he might persuade her to take charge of Margaret. She would be trusty and kind; the place was secluded, yet with Mrs. Wilcox one could hardly be lonesome. It was worth trying, at all events.

CHAPTER XVII.

O sweet, pale Margaret!
    O rare, pale Margaret!
What lit your eyes with tearful power,
Like moonlight on a falling shower?
Who lent you, love, your mortal dower?
                                    TENNYSON.

THE sun was going westward as Dr. Bertrand rode through the main street of the pretty town of Orange, turned to the right, and passed Llewellyn Park, whose short, crisp grass and groups of beautiful trees were tinted with the tawny hues of an autumn sunset. The bright yellows and flaming reds of the ripening leaves gave a warm coloring to the lovely landscape. He only glanced at it; in his heart rang an echo of cool, sweet tones, more musical than this plashing wayside brook; and the vision of a sad, tender face came between him and this dreamy beauty.

He turned down a by-road, and soon paused before a little tasteful cottage, almost hidden by two giant sycamores, through which you caught glimpses of a pointed roof and a vine-covered porch. There was a small front yard, gay with late flowers of brilliant beauty; and a wide piazza at the side, with two entrances — one nearly in the centre, the other at the farther end.

He fastened his horse, and walked up the path, bordered with scarlet geraniums. Old Mr. Wilcox sat in the hall, his withered hands clasped over the head of his cane. His face was placid, and his kind blue eyes still shone with human interest, though the silver of nearly fourscore years rested on his straggling locks.

"Good evening, Dr. Bertrand. I'm glad to see you

once again;" and he shook hands, warmly, calling, a moment after, "Mary!"

Mrs. Wilcox answered the summons. Fair, rosy, and well kept, with a genial face and hearty, pleasing voice.

"Why, Dr. Bertrand, what a surprise! You are a great stranger;" and she placed a chair for him.

There was some general conversation, which happened to turn at length on the fine season it had been for fruit; and Mr. Wilcox proposed Mary should take the doctor through the garden, and see if she could not find a peach or a pear for him. He rose with alacrity.

"Father is childish about the garden," she exclaimed, with a smile. "But we have done remarkably well with it this summer."

"I am obliged to him for sending us out," Richard returned. "I wanted to see you particularly, and ask a great favor."

"A favor?" she repeated, in surprise.

"Yes; are your boarders gone?"

"They leave next week. Old Mrs. McLean is very feeble. I doubt if she ever comes again."

"Would you object to having any one through the winter?"

"O dear, no. Winter is a lonely time with me. I can't leave father, except to run into the nearest neighbor's, and sometimes I feel quite lost. My old life used to be so busy!"

"I must tell my story first, and then trust your kindness. There is scarcely any one else I could apply to, except a perfect stranger." Then, after a long pause, he simply said, "Robert was privately married last February," and gave the main incidents of neglect and desertion. He spoke touchingly of Margaret — her youth, her friendlessness, her unfavorable surroundings, and the urgent necessity of her being in good hands; ending with, "It would be utterly impossible for me to take her home at this juncture, even if I wanted to."

"Even if he wanted to!" That, to Mrs. Wilcox, implied his unwillingness. She fancied she understood Dr. Bertrand's feelings. Robert's wife was not *just* the woman he cared to have on an equality with his sisters, but his generous disposition would not allow him to act in the heartless manner Robert had. Her pity was deeply stirred, and after a few perplexing revolutions of her mind, she said, —

"Yes; I think I could take her."

The expression of relief in Richard's face repaid her.

"Thank you a thousand times!" he exclaimed, warmly. "I wish you could see her first; but, believe me, it will be quite impossible not to take her to your heart at once."

"Your recommendation is amply sufficient. I only hope she will be satisfied."

"I can answer for her. When may she come?"

"The 1st of October, if she pleases. And your frequent visits will be a decided comfort. Indeed," she continued, warming with her subject, since she had resolved upon it, "you may set your heart entirely at rest about the secret. Her coming from New York will cover all questions; and I have no very curious acquaintances here."

"You have done me an invaluable kindness," Richard said, in a heartfelt tone. "You are sharing a great burden with me."

So the next morning he went to New York with a lighter heart. His impatience to see Margaret was so great that he could hardly endure settling the preliminaries with Mrs. Davis, though she readily relinquished Margaret to his care.

He hurried up stairs to the child's room. How neat and faultless its appointments were! The daintily flowered carpet, the light, graceful chairs, a red and white willow workstand, books and pictures; nothing very costly, but all things evincing true and elegant taste. And there was Margaret, robed in a French print, with pale tinted ground and minutest flowers in lovely coloring. At the throat and wrists it was relieved with soft ruffles, and instead of a brooch, she wore a deep, velvety rose and bud. Her hair was smooth and glossy; her feet, in tiny rosetted slippers, seemed the extreme of neatness. There was such a regard for finish in detail about her, that Richard wondered how she had managed to retain her love of order and beauty in this place.

She was shy and distant this morning. Indeed, she could not divest herself of a feeling that Dr. Bertrand was displeased, and justly so, at her imprudent marriage with his brother. Mrs. Davis's present haste to consign her to other hands wounded her deeply. From the grave face before her she judged every duty would be steadfastly performed, and having brought this sorrow and care upon him, all she could do was to acquiesce in his arrangements. She listened with quiet deference, and passively assented, without imagining regard as well as duty actuated him. It was not possible, she thought, for him to do more than forgive her; so, wrapping herself in the garment of humiliation, she took up her cross in silence, the pathetic wail of another burdened soul floating through hers with the pitiful cry, —

"O, do whate'er thou wilt! I will be silent."

Dr. Bertrand misunderstood her resignation, and felt a little disappointed. She, too, failed to read in his grave face the almost boundless kindness of his heart. So the interview was not as pleasant as the former one. But he was more than ever anxious to have her under Mrs. Wilcox's care.

The brief interval before her departure always seemed like a dream to Margaret. She scarcely crossed the threshold of the room where she had learned those strange, terrible lessons — love, trust betrayed, hopes blighted and broken; the solitary anguish of the soul that cries through black, bitter midnight, receiving no response; the cruel, lingering death of the heart's first sweet bliss. For she felt love was indeed dead. Stranger hands would take him out to his burial when she left this room; yet, until then, she could cast regretful glances in the narrow coffin. She neither longed for, nor expected, Robert's return. As she took down the pictures, she remembered the white, firm hands that had hung them, soft fingers that had threaded her hair, or held captive her little face until she kissed her way out to freedom. And here he had written in her books, " Margaret," " Maggie," " Madge." How beautifully clear and bold the letters were! It was like looking over relics of the dead; and when they were all packed, she experienced the desolate sensation of one after a funeral.

Mrs. Davis was to accompany them to Orange. Much as Dr. Bertrand disliked it, he considered it a duty, and resolved to perform his part pleasantly. But his brow contracted when she attired herself in a light gay-colored shawl, whose glaring flowers startled him.

As if Margaret read the thought, she remarked, quietly, —

" I think I would wear the brown one, mother; it is a chilly day, and that will not be warm enough."

" La, child, how you do like that dull old thing! This is a sight han'somer; " but nevertheless she made the exchange.

Margaret was unexceptionable. Her paleness showed through her veil, and her voice sounded unnatural; but her step did not waver. Mrs. Davis was chief conversationalist, and Richard felt thankful the journey was not long, and that he met no acquaintances.

Mrs. Wilcox's flower-garden was still in bloom, but the path rustled with fallen leaves. Some tempting purple clusters remained on the grape-vine, and a hardy scarlet-runner clung to the porch in all its glory of bright berries. The mistress met them on the piazza, and was too well-bred to make any distinction in her greeting. She had Margaret's trunks sent immediately to her room, and ushering the others into the parlor, said, in a low tone, to her, " Would you like to take a glimpse of your new abode while you are laying off your bonnet and cloak ? "

Margaret followed her guide. The room was large, with two windows fronting the street, and two overlooking the porch, and from thence the garden below. The walls were covered with tasteful paper, the snowy curtains drawn back by crimson cords : a pretty lounge in damask, a low rocking chair, and the French bedstead, with its pure white belongings, first attracted her glance. The door of the little stove was partially open, and the ruddy glow of coals shone out warmly, giving a sense of home-like comfort.

"Let me assist you," Mrs. Wilcox exclaimed, anxious for a nearer view of the face hidden behind the veil. "I hope you will like your new home. I shall do everything in my power to make it happy for you."

"Thank you. You are very kind," Margaret managed to say, as she raised her pleading, timid eyes, swimming in tears, in spite of her efforts at self-control.

"My poor child!" Mrs. Wilcox's sympathy rushed out with the fond, motherly clasp, that pillowed Margaret's throbbing temples on her bosom. "You are tired and frightened. Presently we'll have a cup of tea, and a nice, cheerful talk. Then, if you like, I'll help you unpack. I want to be your friend as much for your own sake as for Dr. Bertrand's, though I have known him many a long year."

Margaret pressed a yearning, convulsive kiss on the hands that enfolded her. Mrs. Wilcox substituted her warm face instead, and returned the caress fondly.

"Now, I will show you about a little," she said, cheerily, as she remarked the almost hysteric sob that half strangled Margaret. "Here is your wardrobe; and here," — opening the door to another closet, — "you will find all washing conveniences. I suppose we may as well leave everything until your friends are gone, however."

Dr. Bertrand would have been surprised had he seen the effort of Margaret's mental nature to rule the physical. A stratum of subtle strength ran through this fine soul, like flame color in an opal, visible only in certain lights. It was susceptibility, and not weakness, that made her choose silence; a knowledge that the external breakdown would be more painful to her tense nerves, than this inward anguish that was torturing her soul with inquisitorial pangs. Her deepest feelings shrank from witnesses.

"Will you please send Mrs. Davis up," she asked, when she could steady her voice. "I think it would gratify her to see my room; and they have only a few moments, as they wish to catch the return train."

Mrs. Wilcox obeyed her behest immediately.

"Well, I declare!" and the voice sounded coarser than ever, amid these quiet surroundings, as Mrs. Davis took a survey; "you've got everything nice and slick — hain't you? and your landlady seems a proper clever creetur. It's enough sight nicer than the shop; that never did seem the place for you! I hope you'll be contented. But, Marg'ret, if things don't go straight, or Dr. Bertrand gets offish, you can come back any time; it's your home when you want it. I've tried to be a mother to you, but we wasn't made alike."

"You have been very kind, I am sure."

"If your father 'd lived, 'twould all 'a been different. I shouldn't worked so hard, and might 'a had time to smart up, and be a lady. But land! it's all spilt milk. And here's suthin' for you — the money Dr. Bertrand give me. You hold on to it, child; it's two thousand dollars and over."

Margaret drew back, and said, with loftiness, "Give it back to *him*."

"He hain't no business whatever with it. It's best to keep a close watch over your own. Nobody knows jest what's before 'em;" and she crowded the money into Margaret's hand.

"I s'pose it's about time for us to start. Now, keep chipper, and don't get humsick; and if you want anything o' me, jest write a line."

"Thank you. And you must come to see me."

"It's kinder hard for me to get away, you know; but I'll come in a minute if you send for me."

They went down stairs together. Richard looked quite cheerful. Mrs. Wilcox's account had been better than he hoped for, and very satisfactory. The farewells were necessarily brief.

As they were riding back to the depot, Mrs. Davis relieved her mind of its last charges. Glad as she was to shift her burden into other hands, her conscience demanded fullest satisfaction from Margaret's new protector, and it was cheerfully given.

Margaret lingered at the window long after the sound of wheels had died away. Her pale face drooped and grew inexpressibly mournful, as the new sense of desolation stole over her. Every tie of past life had been rudely broken. She was among strangers, and the existence lying before her must of necessity be different from anything her narrow experience had yet met with. She appeared floating out on a dim, uncertain sea, with no guide.

Mrs. Wilcox came in with some fragrant tea. It was her great panacea. Then she proposed they should go at the unpacking, and bustled about with good-natured solicitude, just sufficient to keep Margaret from relapsing into entire silence. The trunks were emptied and consigned to a closet, the dresses hung up, the bureau filled, the books and pictures laid on the lounge. Then she went for a pretty set of swinging shelves, which she hung up in a recess.

"How nice!" Margaret exclaimed; and an air of interest began to blossom faintly in her face, as she arranged her books. Then she placed her cologne bottles of Bohemian glass on the bureau, and stood her bouquet-holders on the mantel-piece. Already the room began to wear a familiar look. These inanimate friends had no tendrils to be severed by removal; they smiled as familiarly here as in the place where they had been added one by one to form a group of household treasures.

"Now I must go down and prepare supper," Mrs. Wilcox said, cheerfully, "and afterwards we will attend to the pictures. When the bell rings, you will know I am ready for you;" and, as she passed out, she dropped a tender kiss on Margaret's forehead.

The child sat down before the stove, and mused in the falling twilight. Yet it was not so much thought, as that quiet abstraction from all thought — a contented idleness. The tinkle of the bell gave her a sudden pang, as if it had come too soon.

She found Mrs. Wilcox in the hall, and was ushered into a pleasant apartment, glowing with lamp-light. The table was neatly arranged, and Mr. Wilcox already seated in his arm-chair. He bowed his white head, and held out his feeble hand to the new comer, with a gracious welcome.

Margaret was too tired to eat, but she thawed out of her shyness a little at the sound of the motherly voice, so solicitous for her comfort. She remained down stairs until the tea things were put away. Then Mr. Wilcox read in a trembling voice the evening psalms, and offered a brief prayer. It was at once new and soothing to Margaret, and seemed to relieve the weary, desolate oppression. After bestowing him safely in bed, Mrs. Wilcox fastened doors and windows, and they went up stairs again.

"I'm going to show you the place," Mrs. Wilcox said, as she went on, lamp in hand, opening the door into a wide passage, at one end of which stood a bedstead and a few chairs, and at the other a door. "This is our back stairway, and leads down to the kitchen; and here's my room. You see we can leave the doors open between, if you like, and then I can hear you if you speak. There's only one sleeping-room down stairs, and it is more convenient for father. I had this hole cut in the floor, so that I could listen whenever I woke, to see if he was safe. He always keeps a little bell on his table, in case he wants anything during the night. You see I can keep good watch over you both; and, my dear, I hope you'll soon feel at home; I want you to go around wherever you like. You'll never disturb me by coming down, when I'm busy in the kitchen. Indeed, you seem so like a child, I can hardly realize that you are married."

After that tour of inspection, the pictures were hung, and they sat down to a chatty conversation, which, being about Dr. Bertrand's family, was deeply interesting to Margaret. Mrs. Wilcox had known them a long while, but never very intimately. The circumstances attending the death of the father, and the noble conduct of the son, were eloquent themes to her. Richard would have been amused if he had heard himself described as such a hero.

"The old doctor was not so rich as people supposed," Mrs. Wilcox went on. "Richard decided to assist in taking care of the children; and the lady he was engaged to marry — an heiress, by the by — was so offended, that she broke with him, and married a richer person. I don't know what kind of a heart she could have had. I would have waited years for any one so noble and generous. Indeed, if she had loved him truly, it would have been quite impossible for her ever to love another."

Margaret was glad to hear these details. She understood now why his face was grave, his voice unconsciously sad. He knew the bitter pain of desertion, renunciation. His heart had been wounded by neglect and coldness. She felt herself irresistibly drawn towards him, more deeply than if he had been perfectly happy; and she almost envied his sisters the blessed privilege of comforting him.

Afterwards, when she was nestled among the snowy pillows, watching the moon as it stole slantwise through the low windows, she thought of his kindness to her, and how,

14 *

unwittingly, she had helped to increase his burdens. She tried to believe the stormy scene described by Mrs. Davis much exaggerated. She could fancy him grieved, sorrowful, almost heart-broken, but not angry. O, would she ever be able to express the gratitude welling up in her heart like a royal flood, drowning out distrust, coldness, and want of faith? And then she thought, with Mrs. Wilcox, that the woman who once truly loved him could never love another.

And what were Richard's reveries? Now that the excitement was in some degree over, and he began to feel satisfied with Margaret's surroundings, he looked the future straight in the face, and asked himself, for the first time, if he had done wisely. A curious sort of fate had urged him on; indeed, the merely common impulses of a humanity generous as his could not but have given rise to the tenderest pity for one situated as Margaret was. With him all nobler feelings lived a full, active life. He could never pass by on the other side, whether the case were trivial, or of urgent need; and now he had committed himself irrevocably to a labyrinthine path, where circumstances only could be his guide. He pondered the subject earnestly. There was one more step he really owed Margaret for his hasty verdict against her. Opening his desk, he drew forth some paper, and began a letter to Robert — a strong, earnest plea in behalf of the wronged girl. After detailing the steps he had taken, and expressing his deepest regret that in a hasty moment he had been persuaded to espouse so flagrant a wrong, he implored Robert to hasten home, and offer the only reparation in his power. It was eloquent with truest, tenderest pleading. As he wrote, desire became faith with him; he *must* have it so. Living, burning words thronged to his pen, such as one uses only in the great exigencies of life.

Weeks must elapse before it could be sent; yet it was a relief to have it done. Then he could resign himself to dreams of the sweet face —

> " like twilight fair,
> Like twilight too her dusky hair."

Nothing that bewildered with Murillo coloring, or stood out with the force of carven stone. It was a face one longed to see at a pleasant fireside, smiling with rare, quiet happiness. It seemed the more lovely because memory was unable to portray it with salient points, and shrouded it in shadowy indistinctness.

CHAPTER XVIII.

Blest softness ! little hand and little cheek !
This is a touch so sweet, a blessed touch ;
There is love in it — love that will not change.
                              JOANNA BAILLIE.

O, let my weakness have an end ;
Give unto me, made lowly wise,
The spirit of self-sacrifice.
                              WORDSWORTH.

IT was a bleak, dreary afternoon in early December. Little, hard pellets of snow drove in fitful gusts through a biting air, that did not in the least encourage their descent. The fierce wind rattled the leafless branches together, or whirled the dry leaves in little eddies before scattering them, and the rocky ground gave back the clatter of wagon wheels.

Margaret's room was warm and cheerful, even in its solemn stillness. Most of the shutters were closed, and the fire gleam made a grateful, rosy twilight. The air had an aromatic smell, as of powerful restoratives, and on the pillow lay a thin, white face, framed in with clustering brown hair. The blue-veined lids were closed, and the golden-fringed lashes rayed over cheeks of marble. The small, stirless mouth had lost its ripe hue. The repose looked painfully like death.

Dr. Bertrand bent over her noiselessly; but by an acute intuition her languid eyes unclosed.

"I must leave you now," he said, in a voice sorrowfully sweet. "You must be very good and quiet, and not worry about anything. I shall be up again on Thursday."

He passed his cool hand over her forehead, and then took her passive fingers in a clasp gentle, but tenderly strong. He had been fighting with death for her, and she knew what that clasp expressed. A peaceful light stole over her face, a trust that told each had fathomed the depths of the other's heart.

He went out quietly. She listened to the last footfall, then weakly and weariedly turned a little. She could not see the soft, pinky flesh her hand lingered over with a thrill of deliciousness; she only knew it was hers — a part of her own life. She cried gently, in a transport of love, pity, and grief.

"O baby," she said, in murmurous, broken tones, "how kind, how good he is! And yet, I almost wish we had died. We should have had each other in heaven, and God would have loved us, poor and weak as we are. For, my darling, papa, with his handsome face and bright eyes, will never come back to us. He has ceased to care for us; and it's so dreary, dreary! But I am crying, when I promised to be good and quiet! O baby, you can never know how Dr. Bertrand has comforted me; if papa had only been like him!"

She found the baby's hand, and was holding it with clinging tenderness, when Mrs. Wilcox came up. The kind-hearted woman did not question the traces of tears she found on her patient's face, but bathed them away with fragrant water, and took her place as nurse and watcher.

Dr. Bertrand pursued his homeward way through the chilly gray air, musing on the new link that should have bound his brother to Margaret. They had heard once from the wanderer — a gay, chatty epistle, describing his voyage, the new home, and his situation, which was quite to his liking. Not a word that could be construed into regret for the past. "Don't distress yourself for me, dear Dick, best brother in the world," were its concluding words.

Richard had despatched his letter immediately, leaving

the children to write at their leisure; and now he was anxiously awaiting a reply.

More than anxiously. A sick, impatient feverishness was stealing through his veins. If he had desired a reconciliation at first, how much more now, when he had fathomed the depth of Margaret's nature, its exceeding purity, its affluent tenderness! He wanted the tie between them rightly established, in order that he might bring the fond sisters to her side, and give her a place in the household.

And then he wondered if Margaret loved his brother. Since the day on which she had so simply and truthfully confided to him the story of her brief, bright dream, no moan of desolation, no imploring prayer, had reached him. Indeed, she rarely spoke of Robert. In her first moment of motherly pride and love, she had said, tremulously, "You will write to *him* for baby's sake;" but she had no prayer for herself. A subtle pride, like minute steely points, kept guard around her heart, and forbade her to kneel where she had once been spurned.

The lights were burning brightly in his own happy home. Mabel met him with an eager caress. She did not know why he held her so tightly in his arms, kissing her again and again, and never releasing her until he stood in the library, contemplating his dressing-gown and slippers.

"I was so afraid you wouldn't come! Are you very tired? Shall I bring your dinner and a cup of fresh tea in here?"

"If you please." He glanced at her with a restless longing. O, what a comfort it would be to share his secret with her!

The children came in, uttering pathetic complaints of how much they had missed him. When the dishes were sent away, Tessy slipped into her old place on his knee, and leaned her soft, peachy cheek against his.

"It begins to snow terrifically!" exclaimed Archie; "and, Dick, for a wonder, there's but two calls on the office slate."

"But you won't go out again?" Mabel entreated, in her soft voice.

"No; I shall shelter myself in the bosom of my family for this night, unless something extremely urgent comes."

For once there did not. They sang, talked, and relapsed into contented silence. Richard put a new face among them, and smiled inwardly over its spiritual loveliness, that disarmed criticism, and made a picture finer and higher than mere physical beauty.

Margaret recovered slowly. The baby was strong, healthy, and occasionally tried his lungs in a manner that quite frightened his mother; but he was amenable to Mrs. Wilcox's magic. Richard could not think of giving up regular visits, and he was pleased with the color that fluttered in Margaret's face when he promised to come twice a week hereafter. Mrs. Wilcox was fairly absorbed in her charge, and never weary of praising the pale young mother, so like a child herself.

. Christmas passed in happy festivities. Then letters from Robert, a great thick packet, "worth waiting for," as Martin declared.

"Dear Robin," Lily said, proudly. "Isn't he a good boy to write to us all?"

Richard took his into the office for a quiet perusal. His anxiety respecting it had grown almost insupportable. He read, —

"Dear, tender-hearted Dick! It's a shame that old hag of a Mother Davis could not have let you alone. I ought to have stipulated that you shouldn't go near them, for I might have known you would fall among thieves. That girl has bewitched you! We did splendidly by them — better than they had any right to expect; and now to have her saddled upon you is unendurable. Yet you were foolishly quixotic and hasty. What a sermon you wrote, though! Did you really think I would fly on the wings of the wind and kneel at the feet of my charmer in penitential attitude?

No, Dick, that boyish folly has cost me too much already. I cannot consent to sacrifice my life to it.

"I am very sorry you thought it necessary to change her residence. Mother Davis would have managed better, and soon have taken the squeamish notions out of her. As it is, you have placed yourself in a pretty predicament. The girl has not the slightest legal claim on me, you well know. I'm not sure but she was leagued with Mother Davis to entrap me; for they thought me made of money. I feel perfectly free to marry, and bring my true wife home any time; so don't put that thing in the way, or I shall feel bound to take matters in my own hands immediately.

"I'll confess I was infatuated about Margaret at first; and the old woman's thwarting me, and holding out marriage continually, made me fool enough to run my head in a noose. But I soon grew sick of the whole affair; and I tell you truly, Dick, if I was tied to such a baby for life, I should hate the very sight of her. So consider yourself answered. I *never can and never will* marry her."

There was more in a similar strain. I think Richard could have forgiven angry denunciations better than this easy, cruel heartlessness. No regret for the pure life he had blighted! Only a boyish folly! He pressed his hands to his throbbing temples, to stay the tide of indignant blood. The great passions of life rushed through his soul like lava streams, scorching, withering his regard for his brother. He knew now what made men duellists and bitter misan-thropes. Then he paused suddenly, amazed to see whither this whirl of feeling had led him. Could he forgive? Could he love his brother, "whom he had seen"? Could he be merciful?

There was a great struggle within the man; but his better nature, or God speaking through that nature, gave him strength.

He was humbled and saddened. He prayed for patience, for wisdom, and, above all, for charity. He would have much need of them all. He must take up his burden alone. Whether rightly or wrongly, he had accepted it, and could see no escape, without bringing upon Margaret an agony of humiliation. He did not realize until now how strongly he had hoped Robert would accept his view of the matter. The keen, bitter disappointment tore his soul with anguish.

Lily tapped at the door, and asked, " May we come in, Dick?"

" Not now, dear. We'll look over the letters in the morning." How forced and hollow his voice sounded, even to himself!

By the next steamer Robert sent again. He had signed the deed relinquishing all further right to his father's property, and also enclosed a check for a hundred dollars, explaining it with these words: " I told you, Dick, that your generosity should not be forgotten by me, and I mean to keep my word. But my advice to you is, to get rid of Margaret as soon as possible. It maddens me to think what a fool you have been."

Give up Margaret! No, no. Secrecy and suffering first. " Sufficient for the day was the evil thereof." He would borrow no more trouble, but trust in God to make this crooked path straight. If *he* had sinned in not telling the *whole* truth, it was for another's sake.

" Mrs. Bertrand has been down stairs," was Mrs. Wilcox's greeting to Richard, one bright January morning. " She begins to look quite like herself. And father is delighted with the baby — he absolutely has learned to smile ;" which was a great accomplishment for such a grave-looking baby.

Richard ran up to Margaret's room. She sat in a low chair, dressed in a pretty crimson wrapper, the color lending a pinky glow to her face. Baby was perched on her knee, though it required both arms to steady him. He certainly gave promise of rare beauty — Margaret's face in a bold, decided style. He had the expression and development of a much older child; a skin of marble-like whiteness, and a high, broad forehead, with deep, soft eyes, that seemed able to penetrate futurity, and wrest from it the secrets of coming life. And now, as Richard took him from his mother, he glanced up into the manly face with mute, urgent questioning. Did he read any secret there? More than once Richard had thrilled at this strange appeal; and now, in spite of his efforts, a color rose in his face.

"So, you have been visiting?" he said gayly to Margaret, as a cover for his confusion.

"Yes, we went down to dinner yesterday, and we are going out of doors soon."

"I have half a mind to take you out in my sleigh. There's scarcely a breath of air, and it's just twelve, the warmest part of the day. Would you like it?"

"O, so much!" Her eyes were luminous.

"We will call up Mrs. Wilcox, and have her verdict. It cannot possibly injure you."

The lady came, and was of the same opinion. So baby was laid in his cradle, while Mrs. Wilcox wrapped Margaret in a thick shawl, and wound a white, fleecy cloud around her head. How like a snow-drift she looked! Richard insisted on carrying her down stairs, in spite of her blushing objections, and packed her in the sleigh, drawing the robe snugly up around her. Then at a word the horse started.

It was indeed a lovely day, with a sky cloudless as summer. The air was clear and cold, but with no bitter sharpness. The bells rang out joyful little peals, as if rejoicing in unison with her heart. She was glad she had lived, the world seemed such a bright, blessed place to her just now. They took a quiet country road, not driving very fast.

"When you are strong enough to go to church," Dr. Bertrand said, "I think baby ought to be christened. Have you chosen any name for him?"

"No, unless — if you didn't mind my calling him Richard," was her timid reply.

Richard! How sweetly musical the name fell from her

lips! It lingered in his heart long after the sound of her voice died away. And then an inexplicable feeling rose up,— not pride, not any dislike of the child; for his heart warmed towards the hapless little being,— but some subtle reason that utterly refused to be analyzed. *His* name to be the connecting link between her and Robert's child; *his* name to be murmured with caresses and endearments — to another!

"You don't like it," she said, disappointedly.

"Do you think it pretty for a baby?" he asked, with a touch of embarrassment. "I am so fond of household diminutives; and however well 'Dick' might sound for a boy, it doesn't seem just the thing for a baby. Then 'Richard' is so grand and stately!"

"That is why you never use my name," she said, musingly.

"Do I not?" and then he remembered he never had. "I like Margaret," he went on. "It has a royal ring to it, such as a princess needs; but it seems too long and queenly for every-day wear. Tennyson wedded it to sweetest music when he said,—

' O sweet, pale Margaret,
O rare, pale Margaret.' "

"Robert used to call me Maggie, and Madge," she re marked, in a low tone.

"Maggie would suit a bold, black-eyed romp, and Madge, though pretty, sounds weird and elfish. May I give you a pet name?"

"O, if you would!"

"A sweet, dainty, French and English compound — Daisy!"

She raised her eyes with that rare, beautiful sunrise glow in them, but only said,—

"Thank you."

He went on with "pale Margaret," repeating, slowly,—

"'From all things outward you have won
A tearful grace, as though you stood
Between the rainbow and the sun.'"

Presently he turned the horse, and they rode back in silence. Baby was asleep when they reached home. Dr. Bertrand leaned over the cradle, and touched by a vague sense of sorrow at the sight of Margaret's mournful face, he drew her gently towards him, and said, —

"If you like the name of Richard, let him be called that."

"I think he never will be anything but 'baby' to me. I cannot tell why, but I never fancy him a large boy, or growing up. And some little tender pet name might suit him best."

Dr. Bertrand looked intently at her as she stooped to kiss the small waxen hands. No, there was nothing like fear in those most loving eyes. Unconsciously she had touched upon a thought that had thrilled him more than once as he had gazed at the transparent, blue-veined face. What if the little darling's life should be bounded by that one dear word, baby !

"I brought you 'The Heir of Redclyffe,'" he said, wishing to change the current of his fancies. "My sisters still cry over its hero. I have seldom met with anything so lovely in the whole range of fiction as Guy Morville's brief marriage. You will like it, I know."

She thanked him gratefully. He took her hands in his a moment, and called her "Daisy," which brought the warm blood to her face.

At his next visit she spoke of the christening herself.

"Have you decided upon a name?" asked Richard, trying to shake off the feeling that annoyed him.

"Yes. We have discussed all our story heroes. Mrs. Wilcox wanted Herbert; I chose Charlie. I have a fancy his life will be quiet and peaceful. And — I wanted to ask you — if you thought me good enough — "

Her faltering voice died away in faint sweetness, and a timid color fluttered up to her forehead.

"For what?" His tone was low, and he took her hand in his.

"To be baptized with baby. If he is to be brought up a Christian child, I ought to be a Christian mother. You know I wasn't educated to think much of these things; but all my life here has been so different! And when one has been in great peril, near to death, one casts about for some anchor of sure and steadfast hope. I used to say my prayers night and morning, but I never looked upon the Saviour as a friend always near, giving strength and comfort, and helping us bear our burdens. I did pray to die at first, but Mrs. Wilcox talked so sweetly to me that I began to long for her faith. The utter desolation almost crushed my heart.

"O, it was a weary, weary time! And then the light came. I think baby helped me, too. He was so pure and sweet that I knew God loved him, and I wanted to have a share in the heaven he beheld with his beautiful, unclouded eyes. For it does seem at times as if, like St. Stephen, he saw the heavens opened."

She answered Richard's questions in her simple, reverent fashion. Her life had been so guileless, her nature so pure, that faith had little to struggle with. Old Mr. Wilcox had given her the benefit of his experience, but her baby first led her to God. In all docility she had sat down at His feet, and learned of Him.

"Mrs. Wilcox's clergyman was here yesterday," she continued. "It will soon be the Feast of the Purification; he thought it had better take place then."

"Yes, I like these festivals for spiritual birthdays. I will stand for the baby and you," he remarked, gently.

"O!" Her upraised eyes were like a noonday sunshine.

Then they went back to the baby. Was there some subtle chain of thought between them respecting this young life? It was as if they were preparing themselves for a separation. Yet Margaret remained quite unconscious of the chill her words gave him.

"I am glad his name pleases you," she said, in a gratified tone.

15 *

"Yes, I like it. But I had no right to object to 'Richard,' as I did the other day. Forgive me if I pained you." He had thoroughly conquered the feeling now.

They glanced up in each other's eyes, and were mutually satisfied. Then, just under her breath, she whispered, —

" You have written to Robert about his child ! ".

"Yes." Further answer he could not make.

" O baby ! baby ! if there was no God to help us bear this cross, we should die."

The pent-up agony of months was in that blended cry of hopeless love and pitiful despair. It was the only lament Richard had heard since the day he listened to her story — that first sad, sweet interview. And in all the time that came afterwards, he never heard another. With that pang love expired.

Margaret began her new life with touching faith and resignation. Her strength surprised even Richard. Baby throve finely, and his two little teeth were like a mine of jewels to his mother. But the far-off look never faded from his eyes. It was as if they were fixed on some unseen glory, that quite satisfied him. Mrs. Wilcox would have been better pleased with a boisterous, frolicsome child ; but Margaret liked him to sit quietly on her knee, and listen to the sad, tender talk that was ever lingering on her lips. She had no thought in life beyond him.

Yet she never drooped or grew discouraged with her lonely lot. Indeed, except for a brief while, it had never been so happy. The lovely country home, the flowers, the birds singing above her, were unfailing joys. Richard kept her supplied with choice books, and occasionally took her for a pleasant drive. Under these genial, fostering influences, the petals of girlhood blossomed sweetly, displaying the woman's heart within, pure and sacred. The inscription on its pages sank unconsciously into Richard's inmost soul.

CHAPTER XIX.

O God! I am so young, so young!
—— I am not used to bear
Hard thoughts of death.   The earth doth cover
No face from me of friend or lover;
And must the first who teaches me,
My own first-born belovéd be?
MRS. BROWNING.

THE old elm tree in Dr. Bertrand's garden waved its wide-spread branches in the summer sunshine.   Birds came and sang to it, drowsy bees hummed through the leaves, and bright-winged butterflies hovered around it.   The fragrant south wind loaded it with perfume, rifled from some far country, and the whispering river murmured forever at its feet, like a lover.   Philip Gregory and Mabel Bertrand sat in its shade, his head resting in her lap.

"What a long, delicious day!" he remarked.

"A long, lazy day!   Doesn't your conscience trouble you, 'Philip, my king'?"

"If you will repeat that beautiful poem of Miss Muloch's again, I promise not to have an atom of conscience left."

"It is infinitesimal now.   I dare not lessen it;" and her low laugh rippled musically.

"Remember how I have worked and waited for two years, and be merciful.   But I shall soon take you 'to have and to hold,' in a literal sense.   Confess, now, that the prospect is inviting!" and he glanced mischievously into the face he had crimsoned.

"It is well we are to have some useful, rational employment, or you would be ruined past redemption."

"You see I am making the most of my brief holiday. After that, a month of loneliness. Bel, you must write every day. For the remainder of my life I'll be princely generous, and excuse you."

"Will you?" Mabel fell into a fit of musing.

"Doesn't the future appear too bright, too blessed, darling? I almost tremble as I think of it. How little did I dream of this termination when I found you all in this very spot two years ago, and I a lonely wanderer! God has been so good!" His face was gravely tender, his voice full of emotion.

"'Freely ye have received,'" Mabel said.

"Yes; we will remember it in the life so soon to begin — our true life. There will be plenty of work to do. And, dearest, I am glad you have taken up my wishes so readily. While, on some accounts, a home by ourselves would be more delightful, I seem to owe Mr. Chaloner the duty of a son; and our coming will be such a pleasure to him."

"I had rather go," was the quick rejoinder. "We shall not live quite so much for ourselves."

"Bel, one would think selfishness your besetting sin, whereas I expect to take pattern by your generosity."

"There is no need; yours will be sufficient."

"You don't know." He rose up on his elbow. "Bel, I thought of pleading for marriage immediately after my ordination. And I confess it was a sacrifice to give it up."

"And so, instead, you insisted on Mr. Chaloner's taking a month's vacation, by way of penance — to you, I mean."

"He had such a fine opportunity to go with friends — and he would have been so disappointed not to chaperon you — and — several other good reasons." Philip laughed off his rising color.

> "Rebels within and foes without
> Will snatch at thy crown."

"Don't, Bel;" and his hand, passing over her lips, interrupted the lines she was repeating.

"I think I can trust you," was her quiet commendation.

"After my month's solitude, perhaps. Who but Richard, that treasure to lovers, would have thought of sending the children away, so I could have you to myself this whole fortnight?"

"The children always go to aunt Sophy's in the summer," was Mabel's demure rejoinder.

"No; Richard shall have the credit. He manages splendidly. Dear fellow! I wonder if the romance of life is all over with him. He is just the man one longs to see fondly loved by a wife, and with little children clinging to his knees. My cup of joy will not be *quite* full unless his brims over. O Bel! I'm afraid I never could have been so brave and unselfish. There comes the carriage."

Philip gave a short, boyish whistle, and waved his handkerchief. Richard caught the signal, and hastened down to them. Standing on the upper terrace, he took in the scene at a glance, and laughingly asked if the day was appointed.

"The 1st of September. Thursday, is it not?"

"I said the *last*," was Mabel's quick rejoinder.

"A most unimportant difference. Do I not deserve a slight reward for my patience, and the remarkable fortitude with which I take upon myself a month's lonely exile?"

"You do, indeed;" and Richard threw himself on the grass. "Tennyson, too;" and he picked up the book, laughingly. "First, I suppose, you said, —

> 'Come into the garden, Maud;'

And then, —

> 'Go not, happy day,
>   From the shining fields;
> Go not, happy day,
>   Till the maiden yields.'"

"Exactly! And there's nothing left for you but the part of the tragedy father, who says, 'Come to my arms, my children, and be happy.'"

"'There sounds the distant bell;'" and Mabel sprang up

in a statuesque attitude. "'I must away to the halls of my ancestors.'"

"Very creditably rendered, Miss Bertrand;" and Philip bowed low in mock politeness.

Mabel ran off, the gentlemen following slowly, arm in arm. Philip had just remarked, "We mean to keep you prisoner for the remainder of the day and evening," when Ann came down the walk.

"Here is a note for you, doctor, and the boy is waiting at the door for an answer."

He tore it open with a startling rush of apprehension, for he knew the handwriting. It contained these words : —

"DEAR DR. BERTRAND: Baby is very, very ill; please come immediately.   DAISY."

He went to the hall door, and found Frank Dawson, one of Mrs. Wilcox's neighbors. "I was to take you up, right away," the boy said.

There was no time for delay. He just turned to Philip, saying, "I have been called to a very urgent case. Tell Mabel I could not wait for dinner, and I may not be back to-night. I am sorry to disappoint you;" and he wrung his friend's hand warmly; then, gathering a few important remedies, sprang into the wagon beside the boy, and was soon out of sight. Indeed, they fairly flew along the road. Richard learned from the boy that his mother had been over to Mrs. Bertrand's, and that the baby was very sick. Another physician had been called. Frank was to be in Newark at four, exactly, as Dr. Bertrand would then be home; but he had no idea what the disease might be.

Richard scarcely needed telling. The child's teething had been accompanied by spells of languor and restlessness, but no tangible illness. Margaret's inexperience had rendered her timid and easily alarmed, and Richard could not find it in his heart to add to her fears. On his last visit she had been unusually anxious; but the baby appeared very well that day, laughing, cooing out soft, gurgling sounds, and raising his little arms to show how large he was. His mother had brought him to the gate for a last adieu, and the strange, haunting eyes followed Richard for hours afterwards. He had not expected the blow so soon.

"Faster, Frank!" he exclaimed, with a thrill of intense pain; and the horse was urged to its utmost. They passed familiar places, shady gardens, and turned the well-known corner. The cottage was before them.

Mrs. Wilcox met him at the door. Her eyes still showed traces of tears as she said, in a hurried tone, "O doctor! I'm afraid it is too late. He has changed so since noon. I think he is dying."

Dr. Bertrand went up three steps at a time, and entered the open door. Beside the bed, in a low chair, sat the young mother with her babe in her lap. She glanced up with a cry of relief, while her eyes of unquestioning faith said more plainly than language, "At a word from you, danger will fold her shadowy wings, and flee away."

Alas! sweet, tender, confident eyes. Already they began to show their vigil. When he noted the tense lines around the mouth, and the deadly pallor of the face, he knew what fears she had been striving against. He sat down beside them, and took the child's passive hand in his. The pulse was slow and feeble. Dark purplish shadows had settled under his eyes, and around the mouth were hues of ashen gray. The colorless lips were parted, showing his little pearly teeth. Only the broad forehead retained its transparency; it was deathly white, with crimson stains in the temples.

"When was he taken?" Richard asked, in an under-breath.

"You remember what I told you on Saturday about those strange attacks he had? He was so bright then; but all night he kept starting in his sleep and moaning. Sunday we put him in a warm bath, and after his nap he was so good! I took him down stairs, and he sat a long time on father Wilcox's knee, laughing and crowing; and all day Monday he appeared perfectly well, and so sweet it seemed as if my whole soul went out in love to him. Then he fretted all night again, and yesterday acted as he did before his teeth came in. First I thought I would send for you; but he grew quiet, and slept till late this morning. Mrs. Wilcox considered him better; but at ten he was taken severely, crying with sudden bursts of pain, and rolling his head. His eyes frightened me with their wildness. Mrs. Dawson went for Dr. Ward. I was afraid you might be out. He put leeches on baby's temples, and ordered baths. I'm afraid it wasn't right, for he has lain this way ever since, and doesn't appear to know even me." Drawing a long breath, she glanced up questioningly.

"It was the best thing to try." There was a death-like pause. How *could* he tell her the rest?

"Well," she returned, in a voice of assured faith, "what can I do next? You will give him something?"

"Daisy," he said, with rarest tenderness, "my dear child, we can only wait."

"How long?" Her tone showed her utter unconsciousness of the final ending.

"Let me lay him on the bed; he will be easier;" and with a little gentle authority he took up the child.

"Poor baby! Poor Charlie! Do you think he suffers much? I tried to make him drink, but he wouldn't. Do you know what it is? O, when will he be better?"

Dr. Bertrand gathered the slight, trembling figure to his heart. She was quite still, as if the rest brought a blessed sense of relief. After many seconds of silence, he said, with low, tender solemnity, —

"All pain and anguish will be over in a few hours. Charlie will soon be resting in the bosom of the Saviour. Dear, dear Daisy!"

She did not faint, or cry. Her senses were stunned, be-wildered. She stood silent in his clasp, her heart beating with great, frightened bounds, as if it would burst its prison, her eyes looking steadfastly into vacancy. Then she said, with terrible calmness, the quiet of utter incredulity, —

"You *will* save him. God has so many little children in heaven, and I have only him."

"My poor darling, human skill is of no avail. I could not have saved him yesterday; even if I could keep him a few hours longer, it would only lengthen his sufferings. Think of the blessed rest in heaven, where there is no more pain. Remember who said, 'Suffer little children to come unto me.'"

Then a wild, pathetic cry broke from the pale lips, and she struggled to throw herself beside the child. It seemed cruel to keep her there. Every pulse in Richard's frame quivered with intensest pain, and the strong arms were tender in their clasp, as if she had been a baby.

He sat down, still holding her. "Daisy, my child, listen to me." His voice was full of that deep, electric power which rarely fails to attract attention. Taking her Bible from the stand near by, in faltering tones he read that most touching of all stories, — the love and agony of the Shuna-mite woman, — ending with these words: "Did I desire a son of my lord? Did I not say, Do not deceive me?"

Some hard, dry sobs strangled in her throat, but her eyes were tearless, and her breath came in quick, painful gasps, as she said, —

"But he is my *all*. God never gave me any brothers, or sisters, or parents to love.. My life was like a desert waste till Robert came. It seemed as if God sent me the baby so I might forgive *him*. And now, to be left all desolate, to have no one to love! No, I can't bear it; let me die with my child;" and she struggled passionately.

"O Daisy, do not compel me to be cruel! I cannot bear to have his sufferings increased by your wild, unavailing

16

woe. You may sit by him and watch him if you will only
be calm. Dear child, if I could restore him, as the prophet
did! But you will not even let me help you bear it."

She ceased her frantic efforts, and answered, wearily,
" You have been so good to me always! only now — yes,
I *will* be calm."

In answer to her imploring eyes, he seated her on the side
of the bed, but still retained her hand.

" Please talk to me," she said.

He began in that low, sympathizing voice whose tender
inflections were so well calculated to soothe and enchain the
listener. He did not repeat the trite truisms about resignation ; he knew just now she could not believe them. Instead,
he talked of life and its many trials, of heaven and its
perfect rest, of God who is always wise, and sees farther
than our weak, faithless eyes. He spoke of the evil to
come, of the bitter weaknesses that beset man at his best
estate.

" O, no ! " she exclaimed, with the earnest incredulity of
love ; " it couldn't have been for him. I should have watched
over him so carefully ! I had nothing else to do, you know ;
nothing to take my love from him. I would have guarded
him so watchfully, kept him from the slightest sin."

" Perhaps God has some new duty for you. When Robert
went away, you know He sent baby to comfort you. Can you
not trust Him again ? "

" It's so hard — so hard. And then to be left alone ! "
She buried her face in her hands.

Mrs. Wilcox came up. One glance at Margaret's despairing attitude told her *all.* " Had you not better lie down,
now that the doctor is here ? " she asked, kindly.

An almost apathetical movement of the head was the only
answer. For a long while the three watched. Then she
went for some biscuits and tea. Margaret would have refused, but Richard held the cup before her, and she drank
mechanically. All this time the baby had been very quiet ;

now he began to move uneasily, and purple lines settled rapidly about his mouth.

"You had better go down with Mrs. Wilcox," Richard said, hurriedly.

The look of alarm in her eyes asked the wordless question.

"Not now," was the whispered reply.

"How long?" An irrepressible shudder tore her frame.

"Not before midnight; perhaps later. But I do not like to have you witness this."

"Please let me stay."

The convulsion came on slowly, and though not of the severest type, racked the young mother's heart with agony. Richard used all the means at his command to alleviate the little innocent's suffering. More than once he bent closely over him to hide the writhing face. When the parqxysm passed, and he lay white and rigid, Margaret's fearful cry rang through the room.

"O, he is dead! dead! My precious, precious baby!" and she flung herself on the bed beside him.

Not dead. There were feeble flutterings, faint indications of returning life.

"He may be thus for hours. Would you not rather go away?"

"O no! no! I will be quiet. But it is so terrible!" And she clung to Richard with mute agony, as if he could give her strength for this fiery trial. He had never been so deeply moved by another's woe, and he longed, with wild intensity, to be able to shield her from these pangs.

Father Wilcox came up for one last look of the beautiful boy so near heaven. He laid his trembling hand on the bowed head of the mother, and prayed that God would sustain her. Then the twilight fell softly over them, and in the midst of gray dusk the lamps were brought in. Still they watched. The convulsions returned at intervals until midnight. Slowly the little life was drifting heavenward. Tho clock told off its seconds in deathly silence. Suddenly the baby lifted his arms and stretched them out wildly, as if searching for some familiar clasp. There was a little, frightened cry as Margaret clasped him to her heart, and kissed him with the last anguish of despairing love. A great awe fell upon them. Then were the heavens opened, and the angels of God entered the golden gateway with a ransomed soul.

Richard took him from her, and laid him down, saying, brokenly, " ' I shall go to him, but he shall not return to me.' "

Her head drooped on his breast. For the first time he kissed her, and in that moment took her to his heart entirely. Her face was pale and cold, her heavy-lidded eyes closed and tearless. He remembered that after a while he summoned Mrs. Wilcox, and wrapping a shawl carefully around the passive little figure, led her down stairs. She did not even moan, or make any outward sign of grief.

The morning was breaking in the eastern skies. Clouds of opal and amethyst rayed off from the crimson spires, shooting upward from the golden chariot of day. The odorous wind sobbed tremulously through the dewy trees, as if shadowy night wept tears of pain as she trailed her garments over the hill tops, to make room for a brighter visitant. The vines on the porch shook out showers of fragrance, grateful to the weary ones who paced up and down under their blossoms, in a silence too sorrowful to be broken by words.

At length Margaret looked up, with weary, wistful eyes, and he led her back to the house, pausing in the parlor to open the shutters, and seat her on the sofa. " Wait here," he said, " while I go for a pillow."

He brought not only the pillow, but a composing draught. She drank it at his bidding, and allowed him to cover her. He glanced at the dry, glittering eyes, and continued, with quiet authority, —

" Now you must go to sleep. I shall sit here a while,

and comfort you with the promises God keeps for his children."

He took the chill hands in his, and chafed them tenderly, as he repeated verses from Holy Writ — the glowing beauty of Revelations, and the blessed promises of Isaiah. At first she listened hopelessly, then with senses sharpened by her keen suffering; and the weary look became almost grateful. Presently the wide-open eyes drooped a little, the rigid lines of pain began to relax, and sleep asserted her power; but rebellious nature gave sharp, nervous starts, and refused to be conquered. But the potent draught began to work, and the restless nerves succumbed. He watched her for a while with the tenderest pity; then pressed his lips upon the white forehead, shut out the light, and left her to a slumber he knew must last several hours.

Mrs. Wilcox had put Margaret's room in order, and washed the baby. He lay in his cradle, a sweet, natural look taking the place of pain.

" O doctor," Mrs. Wilcox exclaimed, " how *will* she endure it! He has grown into her very life. They were scarcely ever separated for an hour, and she idolized him. Those so dearly loved are always taken first."

" May it not be rather that love receives some divine presentiment of its brief stay on earth, and develops more rapidly into completeness? Dear baby! His life work is done; why it was so soon ended we cannot question. God, who took him, knows best."

" Is she asleep? "

" Yes. The slumber may be heavy, she is so completely worn out. I must go now, and will stop on my way to send an undertaker. I shall be up this afternoon to make further arrangements."

16*

CHAPTER XX.

So; closer wind that tender arm. . . . How the hot tears fall! Do not weep,
Beloved, but let your smile stay warm about me. "In the Lord they sleep."
                                        OWEN MEREDITH.

My heart still feels the weight of that remembered chain.
                                        MRS. NORTON.

RICHARD paused at the parlor door with a strange longing
to gaze once more on that face, still sweet, through all its
grief and weary vigils. He listened to the heavy breathing
of utter exhaustion, and then passed on with emotions that
utterly refused to be analyzed. He was glad to be again in
the fresh air of early morn; he had much to think of. The
future staring him in the face was not such a guest as men
love to meet.

Yet now there was no evading it. Daisy needed some
friend in this cruel strait; and who so appropriate as Mabel?
It would tend to arouse Mrs. Wilcox's suspicion if he kept
them all away at a time like this. But if he brought Mabel
there was a. painful duty before him; he *must* tell her the
truth. And then he sighed at the possibility of Daisy learning it.

When he reached home Ann was sweeping the sidewalk,
and gave him a cheerful good morning. He went directly
to the office, and throwing open the window, leaned on the
sill, inhaling the sweetness of the honeysuckles. O, how
fervently he prayed God to strengthen him for the bitter
task! He could not put away this cup.

Martin came shuffling up from the stable. He fumbled
in every pocket, and at last produced a letter.

"Good mornin', doctor. I've something here that came in last night's mail. I didn't let Miss Mabel see it, for fear. It's from California, and belike there's bad news."

A shiver thrilled Richard's heart as he saw the strange handwriting and insignia of mourning. He broke it open hastily.

"Master Robert?" Martin inquired after a long pause.

"Yes, he is dead," was the low, solemn reply. "I will tell you the particulars presently;" and falling into the nearest chair, he pressed his hands to his forehead, as if utterly unable to take in the fact. That bright, buoyant, vigorous nature; that proud, handsome face! Could it be the earth had shut it forever from human sight?

There followed an overwhelming sensation of relief. The weary, heart-corroding care, the burden that at times had seemed insupportable, rolled away. A thrill of freedom sped along his veins. Then he checked himself. *His* ease and comfort purchased at such a price! To this succeeded thoughts of Daisy. The secret that might one day blight her pure soul had been taken into wiser keeping than his. No fear of it now. God had chosen that Robert should atone for his treacherous sin by an early death. It was no longer his to bear, to pray over, and to fear. He could bring the poor, stricken child into their loving household, to take Robert's place. He could give her sisters, brothers, and a name.

He had merely glanced over the letter; now he began to read it carefully. Its contents were these:—

"SAN FRANCISCO, June 10, 18—.

"DR. BERTRAND: I suppose, my dear sir, that, by the papers of the last steamer, you received an account of the sad occurrence which resulted in the death of your brother. He died too late to allow me to write in time for the mail. No one can deplore the event more deeply than myself and Mrs. Cummings, and we offer you our warmest and most heartfelt sympathy. The newspaper paragraph was substantially correct. Mrs. Cummings had been calling on some friends quite beyond the city limits, and on her return, being rather late, had taken an unfrequented path on account of its being nearer. Here she was beset by two drunken ruffians; and I shudder to think of her possible fate, if your brother had not, attracted by her cries, rushed to her rescue. He succeeded in disabling both of the miscreants, wounding one slightly, and the other severely; but received a mortal blow himself.

"He was brought immediately to my residence, and everything medical skill could suggest, done for his recovery, but alas! in vain. He lingered three days, and expired amid the universal regret of his friends. My joy at my wife's escape is therefore tempered with keenest sorrow, that it should have been purchased at such a price. Yet I cannot refrain from congratulating you on once possessing a brother so fearless and chivalrous; endeared to a large circle of friends here; for his winning manners rendered him a favorite with almost every one he met. And I have no doubt that at home he will be equally regretted. The wretches who committed so unprovoked a murder are both in custody, and will, no doubt, pay the penalty of their crimes.

"Your brother has been buried in our finest cemetery. If you particularly desire it, I will see to sending his remains home; but if you and yours *could* decide to leave him to his final slumber in this far country, Mrs. Cummings and myself would take it as a great favor *to us*. Indeed, it is my wish to erect a monument both suitable and handsome, as a token of my appreciation of the inestimable benefit he conferred on both of us; and it will be a work of love to watch over his grave.

"You will be glad to know that his sufferings were not very intense, and also that he had every care it was possible for Mrs. Cummings to bestow. How deeply we deplore his loss, words are inadequate to express.

"If there is anything amongst his effects you desire, I shall be glad to take any trouble in forwarding it. Mrs. Cummings joins me in sympathy, regret, and the highest regard for your deceased brother.

"Hoping to hear from you as to the final disposition of his remains,

"I am, very sincerely, yours,

"E. A. CUMMINGS."

A thanksgiving surged up in Richard's heart, that his brother's death, if sudden, was in the highest degree honorable. He had expiated his sin towards one woman by the salvation of another. He forgave Robert every wrong fully and freely. The sneering allusions to Margaret had never stung any heart save his own. And he tried to believe, that in those last moments, with another world opening on his view, Robert had repented, and would fain have repaired the wrong to the poor child.

He had shrunk with intense pain from making Margaret an object of pity for any other cause than her own grief. Now, although there might be much wondering, the story could be told. Margaret could take the place in the household he had so often longed to give her. He could hardly realize that the " constant anguish of patience " was indeed ended.

Presently there was a little stir in the house. From the parlor opposite, he heard Mabel's sweet voice, as she went about her morning's work, —

> "' Then with my waking thoughts
> Bright in thy praise,
> Out of my stony griefs
> Bethel I'll raise;
> So by my woes to be
> Nearer, my God, to Thee,
> Nearer to Thee.'"

The words soothed him greatly. He called to her, and she entered with a cheerful " good morning."

He kissed her tenderly.

" What is the matter, Richard ? You look tired and ill.
Was last night unusually fatiguing ?"

He drew her down beside him, and replied in an unsteady
voice, —

" It was a night of agony. Sorrows have multiplied upon
us, my darling. I have a long, sad story to tell; but first
you must read this letter. Martin handed it to me when I
came home."

Her eyes wandered over a few lines, and were raised in
utter incredulity. Then she said, —

" It is not *true*, surely. Do you believe Robert is dead ? "

" No one would write such a letter unless the story was
beyond all question. You see it refers to papers, by the last
steamer, that we missed. You remember we wondered a
little at not hearing."

" I can't believe it. And, Richard, why do you look so
strangely ? Are there still worse tidings ? "

" Last night I watched the soul go out of Robert's little
baby. He is in heaven with the angels now ; but the poor,
stricken mother, a fair, fragile girl, scarcely older than Lily,
is crushed by her unspeakable anguish. For nearly a year
she has known herself a deserted wife, never hearing of her
husband save through me."

" I knew some fresh misfortune had occurred when he left
us so suddenly," Mabel resumed slowly; " but to be married
— to be dead — I cannot realize it at all, Richard."

" Let me tell you the story." He paused a moment for
strength, and clasped his arm fondly about her, commencing
with, " It was a hasty passion on his part, a child's love on
hers. He tired of her, and refused to support or live with
her, when the girl's adopted mother interfered. It was she
who came over here the day before he went away." He confessed his readiness to have Robert leave for California ; his
fear lest he had been the dupe of a designing woman, and
her too facile instrument; and his dislike of the whole affair.
Then he described his first interview with Margaret, the

total change in his feelings, and all those after days of pity and sympathy; her desolation, her sweetness and patience, and her absorbing love for her child. As he went through the woe of the last few hours, his voice was choked with emotion.

Mabel was weeping long before he had ended. Now she threw herself on his bosom, exclaiming through her sobs, —

"O dear, brave, generous Dick! What a burden you have borne for him! How patient you have been! how good to us all, sacrificing your own comfort and advancement everywhere! Papa could have loved us no better."

"It was what I promised *him*, dear; and I am thankful God has enabled me to perform my trust."

"I seem to forget Robert in that poor, lonely wife. If I might go to her —"

"Thank you. It was what I longed to suggest. She has no friend of her own age to comfort her. But what a sad termination for your bright holiday!"

"O Richard! when my life has been so happy and blessed, I should be worse than selfish to shut my heart from *her*. Poor Robert! O, why did he not bring her here? She must come now."

"Yes."

The breakfast bell overtook them in the midst of their planning. Philip stood ready to banter them on their seclusion; but when he saw the grave, tearful faces, he took their hands in quiet sympathy. After they were seated at the table, Richard repeated the sad history, and announced his brother's death. Philip was both surprised and shocked. He felt how utterly cruel the heart must have been that could condemn a mere child to such a destiny as Margaret's; and, in his straightforward way, he looked upon Robert's death as a direct punishment for his sin.

"You will bury the baby here?" Mabel said, as they rose.

"I had hardly thought;" and Richard's pale face flushed as he remembered the secrecy he had considered necessary, and for which there was now no occasion.

"I want him to lie in the cemetery with the rest; and if Robert should never be brought home, it will seem to be a memory of him." Mabel forced down some sobs, and continued: "Does it not appear most suitable to have the funeral from this house? It will announce the principal facts at once, and leave less room for questions."

"I believe you are right," Richard answered, thoughtfully.

"And the children must be here. It will be a better welcome for — her."

"I am fearful they could not receive the word in time."

"I will go for them," Philip said.

Mabel's gratified smile was ample reward.

Richard had some unavoidable calls on his list. While he was out Mabel wrote a brief note to Lilian and aunt Sophy, and saw Philip started on his journey. Robert's death appeared much more real when the servants came to add their sorrow. Yet her visions were of a sweet young face, desolately mourning a sadder loss than this.

It was past noon when Richard and Mabel started for Orange. The day was not oppressively warm, and the fine breeze rendered the ride a very comfortable one. Their conversation could not be otherwise than sad, yet it was tempered with many feelings besides grief. To Mabel, standing on the threshold of a new life, these events were of deep importance. Her girlhood had passed so quietly, been so blessed and satisfying, that she had scarcely dreamed of woes or wants beyond, save in the desultory manner common to young hearts. She needed not to go into the world to learn her first sad lesson. A cruel thrust had entered even that beloved home circle. And Richard had carried the cross for them all. O, could they in any after days ever recompense him!

When Mrs. Wilcox received Dr. Bertrand and his sister, her face betrayed traces of recent tears. As she ushered them into the parlor, his eye caught a glimpse of pillow and shawl. It seemed ages since he brought them there.

"Mrs. Bertrand is in her room," Mrs. Wilcox said. "She slept a long while, and was quite refreshed. But O, doctor, what can be done for the poor child? She doesn't shed a tear. Her white and stony face frightens me. It is so hard! She did not think *her* baby could die."

"I will go for her;" and Richard started.

He found Margaret standing by the partially closed window, gazing vacantly over houses and gardens bright with summer sunshine. How pitiless the cloudless sky looked! What a mockery all this beauty was!

She turned a little at his step. The weary, hopeless face chilled his heart. The heavy eyes were questioning the far depths of space for some ray of consolation; there was an urgent want in them for which human speech had no utterance. How she had changed! The complexion was gray, the whole face thin and pinched, as if weeks of suffering had passed over it.

He drew her tenderly to his heart, and kissed the forehead almost as cold as death. How natural the caress seemed! He thought it was her sorrow that rendered her so dear to him, and the sense of freedom after long restraint.

"Little sister Daisy!"

The words seemed to thrill her strangely. She nestled closer, as if fearful of losing the new place he had given her with that name. Then he went on, in a low tone, telling her how Mabel had desired to come, and what a warm, sheltered corner she should find in their household. She was to be no longer a stranger or an alien.

At any other time she must have shrunk from Mabel's stately figure and the dignity that with strangers passed for reserve. She only noticed that the voice that welcomed her had a lingering touch of Richard's sweetness in it, and the clasp enfolding her was tender and fond. She did not even glance up at the face, satisfied to take all on trust.

He judged rightly that they would make friends sooner if

left entirely to themselves; so, after a little talk with father Wilcox, bade them an affectionate good by. He had intrusted to Mabel's discretion the tidings of Robert's death, and the arrangements for the baby's burial.

That evening's paper contained the following announcements: —

" Married in New York, February 24, 18—, Robert Bertrand, of Newark, to Miss Margaret Tremaine, of the former place."

" Died, suddenly, at San Francisco, Cal., Robert, second son of the late Dr. Bertrand, of Newark.

" At Orange, July 18, Charlie, infant son of Robert, deceased, and Margaret Tremaine Bertrand, aged six months and fourteen days. The friends of the family are invited to attend his funeral on Friday, at four P. M., at the residence of his uncle, Dr. Richard A. Bertrand."

The little coffin that stood in the Bertrands' parlor that Friday afternoon was almost covered with flowers. The lovely child looked as if he were in sweetest slumber. The younger members of the family gazed with mingled awe and grief, and the neighbors were subdued by a sincere pity. It seemed more like a funeral sacred to Robert's memory than the tiny being whose birth and death had been announced in the same words. Philip read the burial service in calm, soothing tones. Mabel never left Daisy for an instant. The strain on her delicate nature had begun to tell fearfully. More than once she had lain fainting in the arms of her new-found sister; but she nerved herself for this last hour with a more than human strength. Her thick veil hid her face from curious eyes; and though an occasional convulsive shiver shook her slight frame, she made no outward demonstration.

She could not trust herself to gaze again on that dear face. If she took no formal farewell, it seemed as if her baby *must* come back. Yet he lacked neither tears nor kisses. Many regretful glances were cast on the beautifully-moulded clay. He looked too fair, too perfect, to be laid away in the darkness of the grave.

Afterwards it came to Daisy with what reverent hands Richard and Archie had sprinkled the first earth on the baby's breast, and the generous consideration with which they all received her, a stranger, whose entrance into the family had been marked with trouble from its first date. They vied with each other in kindest attentions ; but Tessy, whose face was so like Richard's, found a way to her heart immediately.

CHAPTER XXI.

One troop of duplicated Hours sped on,
And one trode out the moments lingeringly,
So distant seemed the lonely dawn from me;
But all was well.

BAYARD TAYLOR.

When fainting hearts forget their fears,
  And in the poorest life's salt cup
  Some rare wine runs, and Hope builds up
Her rainbow over memory's tears.

GERALD MASSEY.

BY common consent they all yielded Richard to Daisy. Mabel expected to see her sink entirely after the funeral; but instead she appeared quite composed. She rested on the sofa a long while, until the summer twilight waned. Tessy's little fingers found their way to hers, as they all clustered about her, talking of the days to come, when her home should be among them. Poor, weary dove! A strong hand reached out through the troublous waves, and drew her into the ark, where she might remain forevermore.

After her removal hither had been arranged, Richard mentioned the request concerning Robert, and left the decision to Daisy.

"Please don't think me cold or ungrateful," she replied, brokenly. "I am afraid I do not feel as I should about him. I forgave him all he made me suffer; but I can never, never forget his cruel neglect of baby. He might have sent one little word of love to *him*, even if he was tired of me. And I think, if he had his choice, he would not care to sleep beside baby. And perhaps it would fret him if he could know how often I should visit the spot. Am I very, very wicked?"

"No, my poor child; I do not wonder at your state of feeling. Since Mr. and Mrs. Cummings desire it so much, 1 think we had better let him remain there."

"I am glad he found friends there to love him. He was so handsome, and he could be so tender, so fond. Since he could not love me, it is a comfort to know he was never wholly desolate."

The dreary cadence of the last words pained Richard. terly forlorn she had been, he gathered more from occasional sentences, than from her manner in the s of their early acquaintance. Thank God, it was ow! He breathed the thought with fervent emo- Looking down the days to come, the slight figure of , with her soft brown hair and luminous eyes, glorified all.

ter in the evening he held a conference with Mabel, fying her with Daisy's entire assent to their arrange- ts.

"O Richard, best and dearest brother, how much you have done for us! Philip and I both think it right to put off our marriage another year, if you would like to have me at home. Some one ought to repay you."

"My darling! No, I couldn't entertain such a proposition. Not only Philip, but Mr. Chaloner also, is looking forward to a time when a bright young face shall make glad their home. I must not grow selfish when I have a new treasure added to my circle. May be no one will ever be quite as thoughtful for me as you; but it is time I was getting out of these spoiled ways."

"Selfish! I do not believe it is anywhere in you, Dick," she replied, with proud earnestness.

"Well, for my sake, you must be married at the time appointed. I don't like delayed weddings. And my bird-ling must go care-free to her new home; there will bo enough left to render me the most whimsical old bachelor you ever saw."

"No, Dick," she said, resolutely, "you deserve a better fate."

"I think then God will send it to me," was his low response.

A few days after, Philip said his last lover's good by, as he told Lily. His parting with Daisy was very tender. He had been trying to point her to the true source of all comfort, and found her gentle, humble, and child-like. It was impossible not to love her.

When he had gone, Mabel and she were inseparable. To the poor child who had never known the delights of a true home, nor the sweetness of family ties, this spot seemed a radiant heaven. It was with her grief as it had been with theirs: instead of banishing it to the relief of lonely tears, they all shared it. After a little she found herself repeating scenes that had made the brief happiness of her summer — baby endearments and answering smiles; tender mother-joys forever gone. Lingering over these fond remembrances, her heart grew warmly human again.

There was one break in her month with Mabel — a duty to be performed before Daisy could settle in her new home, and accept her new life. Richard had proposed that she and Mabel should go up to Mrs. Wilcox's for a day only; but her pleading eyes disarmed him.

"I would rather go alone," she said, quietly. "I think Mrs. Wilcox will want me to stay. She has been so kind."

"I mean you shall go up often," he returned. "But just now a visit might not be prudent."

"Please let me go." Her lip quivered like that of an entreating child.

"My dear Daisy, you shall do as you will. Only remember, you belong to *us* now."

She laid her cheek on his hand with a mute caress that was both fond and grateful.

He took her up one morning, and at an appointed day came for her. How she spent the vigil, in that room where

the baby died, he dimly guessed. What hours of anguish,
what prayers for divine grace, went up to the great white
throne, and what angels came and ministered to her, he also
fancied, for she was never out of his mind a moment.

He thought when she came down the garden path to meet
him, that lovely August afternoon, he had never seen her
look sweeter in her days of comparative content. She was
pale and thin; her lips had lost their bright coloring; but the
holy calm on her countenance fairly transfigured her. He
remembered observing just such saintly expressions in the
baby's face at times. She was glad to see him; the faint
flush in her cheek confessed it at his first words.

Mrs. Wilcox assisted her in packing. Less than a year
before, she had helped her find places for these books and
pictures, and welcomed her with motherly fondness. Now
she paused to say, amid a gush of tears, —

"O Mrs. Bertrand! I don't know what I shall do without
you!"

Father Wilcox was equally pained at relinquishing her.
She had spent hours leaning her fair head on his knee, weeping silent tears, and listening to the tremulous tones, dearer
to her than ever, for she knew he might soon be with her
lost darling. All summer he had been growing feebler, and
was looking daily for the hour when he should "depart and
be with Christ."

"Dr. Bertrand said I might come and see you often," she
exclaimed, with her farewell. "Shall it be every week?"

The old gentleman's eyes lighted with sudden joy. She
turned to Richard for approbation.

"Yes," he answered, "I will bring you up every week."

"Thank you." The tone was very sweet.

The trunks were to be sent down the next day. That
evening, after the joyful welcomes were over, there was an
animated discussion as to which room should be Daisy's.
The three girls had shared the large apartment adjoining
their sitting-room, while the smaller one was claimed by

Archie.　Besides Richard's there was only one other—
"papa's room."

"Not where papa died, or mamma either," said Lily; "and
it's delightful."

"Suppose we make a sitting-room of that," was Richard's
proposition, " and give Daisy the present one.　You will all
be nearer together then.　And I heard Archie talking quite
largely of a study; he might take one of the upper rooms,
and turn his into a sanctum."

"Capital!" exclaimed Archie, delightedly.　"You plan
admirably, Dick.　The girls are nowhere in comparison.
We will have a gay time to-morrow."

So the next day there was quite a revolution in affairs.
Archie insisted on hanging Daisy's pictures, and brought up
a little *étégère* that he declared he had heard Richard pro-
nounce a nuisance in the office.　Tessy filled her vases with
lovely flowers, and the fresh, fragrant room looked supremely
inviting.　But Daisy persuaded Mabel to share it with her
during the remainder of her stay.

The busy days that followed served to draw her from the
solitude of intense sorrow.　She was greatly interested in
the happy, honorable love before her, so different from her
own hasty wooing and ill-starred marriage.　Philip had accepted the position of assistant rector with Mr. Chaloner,
and persuaded his friend to take immediate advantage of it,
in joining a party of clerical brethren on a tour to the White
Mountains.　Lily counted up the days for Mabel. and in
spite of the grief that had fallen upon them, managed to
throw her own peculiar brightness around every one.

Mabel had too true an estimate of the love offered her to
be weakly despondent at leaving her childhood's home.　Indeed, she would have been outwardly cheerful for Richard's
sake, if her own serene nature had not sustained her.
Philip's visits had been so infrequent, that her evenings,
and a large portion of her attention, had been devoted exclusively to her brothers and sisters.　More than once she

had sighed over the prospect of leaving Richard to the keeping of one so thoughtless and eager for her own enjoyment as Lily. But God had sent this dear little Daisy, with willing hands and fondest heart, to supply her place. Young, and slight almost to childishness, there lingered about her a certain subtle power. Her intuitions were fine, and she possessed the rare intelligence which divines and harmonizes with a mood electrically. Her sense of right was so perfect that it was not possible her coming among them would be marked by any misunderstandings. Mabel was satisfied to leave her treasures in such hands.

Philip's arrival diffused a pleasant atmosphere throughout the house. Bridal gifts were inspected, packing undertaken in a very important manner; past remembrances and future hopes were blended in sad, yet happy talks. For, after all, it was no light thing to part thus, to give up all claim to the dear old home.

That the wedding should be quiet surprised no one. The day was cloudless, with a touch of summer in the air — a tender regret over the dying flowers. They were all satisfied to have no gay rejoicings. Indeed, the memory of Robert's departure, and his recent death, came up too forcibly. Lingering kisses, unbidden tears that fell softly, and fond clasping of hands, were mingled in their bridal joy. Mabel was to travel a while, and then proceed direct to Rothelan.

"Two vacant places," mused Richard, when the calls and congratulations were over. Then his eye wandered down to the *petite* figure draped in black, with satin-smooth hair, and deep, sorrowful eyes — a treasure that had come to him out of a great ruin; a pearl stranded on the shore from some convulsion of the natural order of things. He felt she was *his* in a peculiar sense.

He so far overcame his dislike of Mrs. Davis as to pay her another visit. She had accepted their separation as inevitable; indeed she was well satisfied to find her charge in good hands — hands too strong ever to relinquish her. He detailed the recent sad occurrences, and his arrangements for the future, claiming her most solemn promise never to divulge a word of that painful past.

Daisy's weekly calls on Mrs. Wilcox were a source of great interest to both. Occasionally they were extended to the whole day. Mr. Wilcox had failed rapidly, and was no longer able to sit up, except for a few moments.

" I think," she said one day to Richard, " I ought to stay, if you are willing."

He rather liked the odd, timid way she had of deferring to him. He could not refuse the pleading face, irresistible with the light of its tender brown eyes, although he said, lingeringly, —

" I am afraid you will overtask your strength."

" There isn't anything to do ; besides, Mrs. Wilcox is so very careful of me."

She was thankful ever afterwards that she went, and remained until the last sad moment.

" I don't know what I should have done without her !" was Mrs. Wilcox's exclamation. " After father grew too feeble to speak, she always understood just what he wanted. She would sit for hours smoothing his hair or holding his hands, and repeating passages of Scripture. And at the last I shall never forget the look and tone with which she said, ' Who shall separate us from the love of Christ ? ' He gave her a heavenly smile, closed his eyes, and never stirred again. She would not even unclasp his hand until he had been dead many minutes. O Dr. Bertrand, if there ever was an angel in this world, that child is one. I can't see why life had to be so hard and painful to her ; but she bears it all with the patience of a saint. There doesn't seem anything earthly about her."

Richard was not selfish, yet he felt glad no tie beyond the family held her now. She was *all* theirs.

CHAPTER XXII.

She is like a harp the winds do play upon; mark her well. She shall tell you what she dreams unwittingly, for her face is a mask — nothing but a veil, and under it you shall see her heart beat.   OLD PLAY.

LILY sat playing the Henrietta waltz, while Archie and Tessy whirled up and down the long parlor in graceful evolutions. On a low ottoman, by the window, Daisy half reclined, dividing her attention between the dancers and the gray, sullen skies. The day had been very unpromising; and now a fine rain began to fall.

"How is the weather, Daisy?" And Archie kissed his hand to her as he neared the corner.

"It rains a little," she answered, hesitatingly.

"O!" and the dancers came to a full pause. "Do you believe they will come, Lily?"

Lily glanced at her watch. "Yes," she returned, "they will be here in five minutes. It didn't rain when they started, you know, and clergymen, like doctors, are not afraid of a little storm."

"And Bel said, almost the last word, that she would surely be home at Thanksgiving!" exclaimed Archie; "so go on with the music." And they took another turn.

A carriage stopped, and before Daisy could announce it they all rushed to the hall door. There were Philip and Mabel, sure enough; the hardly three months' wife rosy and smiling, with the fondest of caresses for every one. During the first few moments they all talked and laughed in chorus.

"Now you may go up stairs," said Lily. "Daisy has

arranged her room for you, and, O Bel, Mrs. Charlton sent in a real bridal bouquet!"

The apartment was fragrant with the spicy, Oriental odor of tuberoses, and as neat as tasteful hands could render it. The three self-elected maids of honor hovered around their fair queen, assisted in removing her travelling habiliments, and were so attentive that Philip declared himself jealous, and insisted on Tessy coming to brush his hair.

"There's the doctor," said a quiet voice.

Mabel ran away from her maids, and in a moment was clasped to Richard's heart. There was only the merest space of time for conversation before the dinner bell rang.

When they entered the dining-room a general halt occurred among the three girls. Daisy's face flushed, and she glanced inquiringly at Lilian.

"O, Mabel is company now," Lily responded, with a laugh; "so, Mrs. Bertrand, you may keep your place. You see we have promoted Daisy to the head of the table, in consideration of her great age!"

"Yes, *I* have forfeited all right to the old place," was Mabel's smiling rejoinder.

"Besides," said Lily, gayly, "Philip couldn't sit at the corner of the table, and I dare say the most trivial separation would be considered cruel."

"That's only during the honeymoon, Lily," Philip exclaimed. "We have come to the second stage."

"In which Mabel cries to have her own way, I suppose," Lily retorted, saucily.

"And I, in my superior wisdom, beg her to set a good example for her sister," was Philip's rejoinder.

Lily was not to be worsted in this sort of light skirmishing; she kept them all laughing at the readiness with which she parried or subverted Philip's logic. It was a most pleasant reunion. Mabel had been a prompt and generous correspondent; but the girls were not satisfied until they had carried her off for a nice talk, in which the particulars of her bridal trip and home coming at Rothelan were described.

"It was all most delightful," she said. "Mr. Chaloner and Philip love each other like father and son; he is the dearest old man in the world. I think I like him better because he doesn't in the slightest remind me of papa. His hair is nearly all white, and his face, though wrinkled, is fair and calm; a little sad, perhaps, but so pleasant. Then the rectory is the oddest, cosiest nook in the world, standing back from the main road, up an avenue bordered by wide-spreading elms. It is rough gray stone, nearly covered with ivy. My rooms are all on the second floor. Philip's study and our sitting-room have folding doors between; then we have a large sleeping apartment, bath-room, and hosts of closets. On the opposite side of the hall are three handsome spare chambers; so you see I can accommodate you all. Mr. Chaloner has rooms down stairs just like Philip's, except that the sitting-room is used for family purposes; and there is a parlor full of lovely pictures, and a piano. Mrs. Brown is housekeeper, and Peggy, an old colored woman, comes in to help occasionally. I don't have anything to do but play and sing, and read aloud when the clergy come in tired with their labors. All the city families have gone home; so the congregation is quite small. It seems like living in an enchanted palace."

"You have certainly fallen upon the days of Haroun Alraschid. But wait a while until you are made president of the sewing and charitable societies, or some parishioner calls you up in the middle of the night to make a little broth for her sick children."

"O Lily! I think, instead, they'll all spoil me. I did make some vinegar toast one day for an old lady who is ill, and very fanciful, and she will not believe any one else can make it as good. I like most of those old-fashioned country people. We have been out to tea a great many times, and I always feel sorry I cannot eat any more; for they provide so bountifully, and always seem disappointed if you do not taste of everything."

"Bravo!" said Archie, laughing. "That last remark is worthy of Lily."

"And, Archie, one of the farmers sent me some beautiful white Spanish fowls, and Philip had a gallon of currant wine and several bushels of splendid apples given him, and hosts of little things. There are two sisters, maiden ladies, quilting me the most beautiful white spread you ever saw. They are ready to love Philip on Mr. Chaloner's account, but I hope he will prove worthy of their affection on his own."

"Very modest indeed," said Lily. "I hope they will love *Mrs.* Philip. If they fail to, we shall bring her home again."

Mabel held up her wedding-ring finger.

"Zenobia, with golden chains," laughed Lily.

"Think of a better simile; for O, Miss Lily, I shall take you into training some day. Philip has proposed that, after Christmas, you make me a nice long visit; he thinks by that time I shall have a longing for home faces. If we live until next summer, I want you all. The drives down the river are so lovely! And there are West Point, the Catskills, and ever so many places of interest."

"And I shall be so well trained that I can begin to set Tessy an example," Lily said, demurely.

Richard and Philip, having finished their cigars, joined the party. They were wonderfully happy, even to Daisy, who said little, but smiled in her pleasant fashion. It was a delightful family group.

"Are they not charming?" Lily asked of Daisy, as they were preparing for slumber. "I never saw a couple more nicely matched. Philip is attentive and affectionate, yet has that little touch of authority one likes to see in a husband; and Mabel is so sweet and deferential. They are just like story-book people. Why are you smiling?"

" I was thinking what a certain young lady said this morning concerning a husband's authority."

" O, well, these things set elegantly on Mabel, but I
could not stand them."

" Wait until your time of loving comes."

" I think I could love the hero of my choice a great deal;
but if there was a chain, I should fret at it. I should always
be trying my power with his. It would never do for him to
be 'weaker than his task,' as Carlyle says, for I couldn't
respect him; and if he was the stronger — "

" You will only think, in that day, how you can best pour
out the treasures of your heart. You will want to give continually. I think all women do."

" You are such a darling! I shall never be half as good.
But I mean to have some fun before I promise to *obey;*"
and Lily kissed her fondly.

The next day was Thanksgiving. Then followed Friday;
and on Saturday Mr. and Mrs. Gregory, as Archie styled
them, started for home. The visit had been one of thorough
enjoyment, and already the younger members of the family
began to count on the coming summer.

By the time the holidays were well over, Richard learned
the second daughter of his house and heart was likely to
prove a much greater charge than Mabel with her one ad-
mirer. She was certainly handsome. Tall, slender, with
that subtle rounding of form that renders every movement
graceful; a small, proudly-poised head, with its wealth of
golden hair, whose reflexes caught that glittering bronze
tinge painters love, drooping in silken soft ringlets; a
complexion of purest blonde, through which the varying
emotions spoke in pale pink or carnation hues; straight and
rather haughty features, and deep, dark eyes, that seemed
always changing from purple to black, or back again. The
arch of the brow was done in richest brown; the long lashes
were just tinged with gold; but above the loveliness of face,
expression held perfect sway. She was bright, dazzling,

imperious, defiant, and tender by turns. She loved with a passionate eagerness that thrilled one; yet it was seldom she seemed to strike upon a vein of affection; so she laughed, teased, was demure or tantalizing, as the whim took her. Affluent in spirits, easy and fascinating in her manners, and possessing abilities of a high order, she might have queened it in a much larger circle. Richard had disapproved of her going into society this winter, as much on account of her youth as Robert's death; yet the young people were not long in ignorance of the attraction at Dr. Bertrand's. If she could not go to parties, there were concerts and lectures, and long evenings at home, with music for an excuse.

It must be confessed she developed a decided taste for flirting. She laughed over jealous rivalries, and adroitly managed to evade ill consequences. Richard's gentle remonstrances were taken kindly, but he could see they had no effect upon her. He dreaded restriction. There was something in her eye that recalled Robert — a dangerous, luminous light, that might burst into flame, and scatter red-hot rays far and wide. It would be idle to set Daisy at managing her; indeed, utterly impossible. He did insist that they should walk together, though he made this appear as solicitude for Daisy. Yet he felt wonderfully relieved when Philip, being in New York on business, came over for Lily to accompany him home to Rothelan.

How quiet the house seemed afterwards! The parlor was deserted, and Tessy's practising the only music Richard heard. Thinking this over one evening, he proposed that Daisy should commence learning.

"When they all go away," he said, smilingly, "I shall have only you left to make the house bright, and music is one of my luxuries; I cannot give it up. I never remember a time when some one did not play and sing. I have seen mother sit, with a baby in her lap, learning a new song father had brought her. You see we have all been greatly indulged."

"O, if I could be any comfort to you, after all you have done for me!" Daisy returned, with a sudden gush of emotion. "I think sometimes I must have died, if it had not been for you;" and she shivered at the remembrance of the desolation that had yawned before her when he came.

"Yes," he said, in a gravely sweet tone, "you *can* be a comfort to me during the coming years. It appears but yesterday that the house was full of wee, toddling things; now Bel is married, and Tessy nearly ten, and in the cemetery there is more than one green grave belonging to us. It seems as if God had sent you to fill some vacant place."

She glanced up with tender, tearful eyes. In such words as his she found her dearest home welcome.

Daisy had a quick ear and much natural love for music. Richard's desire was sufficient to set her to work in good earnest. Her voice had no great power or depth; it was low, with a mournful chord running through it, specially adapting it to those old ballads of love and despair. More than once Richard had listened to her singing "Bonny Doon," as she sat at her sewing, until its infinite pathos made his heart ache, it seemed so like her own sad life. Did some dim presentiment ally her with sorrow?

Lily's letters were great sources of enjoyment. Her ready sense of the ludicrous, her droll, piquant descriptive powers, and the merry exaggeration that seemed a part of her nature, were not likely to suffer from dearth. Richard thought her fate surely followed her as he listened to the accounts of tea-drinkings given in her honor, and how the farmers' sons insisted upon bringing her home in an independent sleigh. There was a Mr. Joslyn, who soon gained sufficient courage to come to the rectory, and inquire for Miss Bertrand, and who walked home from church with her, and was quite devoted — considered, indeed, the "catch" of the village, — and Lily gravely wondered what sort of a farmer's wife she would make.

But when she had been at Rothelan about six weeks, an

extraordinary event happened, which she chronicled at length
for Daisy's perusal.   After a little ordinary chat, she began
with, —

"And now, Pet, I have a most romantic incident to relate
— quite a story-book affair, indeed. Four days ago we were
all down in the sitting-room, Mabel sewing in true matronly
fashion, dear old Mr. Chaloner, suffering from a severe cold,
pillowed on the sofa, and I reading aloud. Philip was out
making calls in Mr. Joslyn's sleigh, which that young man
had very thoughtfully sent over. All the afternoon there had
been a succession of equipages passing — dainty cutters, and
great family sleighs, freighted with the beauty and fashion of
the city. A residence some distance above here, belonging
to a wealthy New York merchant, was to be opened that
night for a grand birthday dinner and reunion. The rush
was over at last, and as it was growing dusky, I closed my
book. Mabel had just remarked on the stillness, when there
was a sudden whirr, and a horse, dashing up the carriage
road, ran the sleigh against the large sycamore, breaking it
to fragments, and hurling its occupant some distance in the
snow, while the horse, wheeling suddenly round, started off
again at a frantic rate. Mabel screamed, certain it was
Philip; but in another instant I saw the driver, who had
sprung out as the sleigh turned, and the sight of a strange
face gave me hope. We were almost paralyzed, though;
and I can't tell you what a welcome sight it was to see
Philip ride up the lane unharmed.

"He assisted the driver in bringing in the poor fellow.
Philip went for a surgeon immediately, while Mrs. Brown
applied some temporary bandages, and tried to restore him
to consciousness. I waited impatiently for Philip's return.
The gentleman appeared to suffer excruciatingly. We learned
his shoulder was dislocated, his arm broken, his head slightly
cut, and that he had sustained numerous severe bruises.
He managed to make Philip understand that he was Mrs.
Suydam's brother, and had just returned unexpectedly from

Europe. On learning his sister was here, he came up with the train, intending to surprise his friends by appearing at the party. He had some difficulty in procuring a conveyance, and was forced to accept of a rather unmanageable horse, and, as events proved, an ignorant driver.

"He would not allow any word to be sent to his sister that night; but the next morning Philip drove over for her. She was almost wild at first, and insisted on having him removed where she could be with him constantly; but the surgeon said it would be at the risk of his life. She remained until this morning, and has now gone to New York for a trusty nurse, as she considers the extra care quite dreadful for us. Indeed, the alarm did affect Mabel somewhat.

"I am installed as chief attendant, though there is nothing to do but turn my patient's head tenderly when he is tired of having it in one position, and give him a drink at rare intervals. Philip watches with him at night.

"As I am writing from my post of honor, I suppose a description of my hero will not come amiss. His name is Ulric Auchester, and for several years he has been connected with some of our first-class journals. Think of my stumbling over a genius! One can see that his sister is wonderfully proud of him. He is as tall as Philip, and much handsomer, which is saying a great deal, I am aware. His forehead is broad and high, edged with loose, jetty rings of hair, fine and soft enough for a girl. His eyes are perfect in their surroundings. I have not seen them fairly open yet, but imagine them black. For the rest, he is 'bearded like a pard,' and displays a row of white, even teeth, through a line of pale blue that will doubtless be 'ripe scarlet' some day. In short, one of the novel heroes who are proud, stern, tender, unreasonable, savage, and yet — perfection.

"And now, little Daisy-flower, I expect you will not hear anything from me except 'Mr. Auchester' for a month to come, as the surgeon declares he cannot be removed before that time. I shall give up my rustic admirers, and take to nursing for the sake of the grateful looks he bestows upon me.   Pray that I don't lose my heart, in the mean while."

Richard laughed, and then a perplexed look crossed his brow.   Daisy noticed it, and said, quickly, —

"You must not mind all Lily's nonsense.   She is so young that she thinks only of amusement; and yet she has a great deal of real good sense."

"But she is so ready to make the most of her attractions, and not in the least ignorant of her power.   What is girlish trifling now may be something serious hereafter."

"Lily is so pretty, though, that people cannot help admiring her.   She is too good to trifle with any one who really loved her."

"And you are a precious little champion," he said, with a fond smile.   "I only hope she will be as happy in the end as Mabel."

There was hardly a letter that came afterwards in which Daisy did not skip certain passages that would have increased Richard's fears.   The nurse was sent up to Rothelan; yet Lily appeared to be continually needed in the sick room.   Mr. Auchester became a favorite with the whole household.   Philip wrote letters for him, Mr. Chaloner paid him frequent visits, and his improvement was as rapid as one could expect.   But Lily was not slow in learning that she could give their guest both pleasure and pain, and she did not hesitate to vary the treatment.

Mrs. Suydam came up often, and was delighted with the care bestowed upon her brother.   Mabel, in one of her epistles, said, —

"I don't know but Lily will have her head turned by Mrs. Suydam's admiration.   Being dark herself, she thinks blonde beauty the only true loveliness.   I like her exceedingly, and she is a great favorite of Mr. Chaloner's; but it would surprise you to see how she takes to Lily.   They are very wealthy, and she goes in a great deal of society.   Her description of the party at her house was enchanting."

Richard's first thought was to send for Lily. He had an uneasy presentiment of danger that he could not banish. Daisy looked so disappointed when he broached it, and knowing the feeling was solely for Lily, he had not the courage to insist upon her recall. Surely Mabel would see if anything went amiss, and if Lily grew too much elated by the attentions of her new friends, their departure, perhaps, would work the best cure. Yet perhaps Richard was more strictly conscientious because he felt that he did not really need her at home.

CHAPTER XXIII.

So doth the shipwrecked mariner at last
Cling to the rock whereon the vessel struck.
                                    `GOETHE.

                    Henceforth
The course of life that seemed so flowery to me,
With you for guide and master,—only you,—
Becomes the sea cliff's pathway, broken short,
And ending in a ruin.
                          IDYLS OF THE KING.

DAISY ran into the library one morning to dust and put the place in order. Of late they had taken to sitting here in the evening. After she had finished, she emptied the basket of waste paper into her apron, and was gathering up the corners when a fragment in firm, elegant penmanship, caught her eye.

She knew it so well; and it gave her a pang of regret to think Robert's memory was passing so far out of his brother's heart, that he no longer cared to keep mementos of him. She fondled the paper with regretful tenderness, as she thought of him leagues away, sleeping among strangers. She had never yet brought herself to destroy one of the notes he had sent her in the old, happy days, and she scanned this with a feeling that an indignity had been offered to the dead.

What was there in it to transfix her so — to bring a white stony terror into her face? The very floor seemed sliding from under her, and voices rang in her ears, as if the whole world was crying out a fearful secret. Like characters of living flame these words danced before her eyes: " The girl has not the slightest legal claim on me, you well know;

I'm not sure but she was leagued with Mother Davis to entrap me, for they thought I was made of money. I feel perfectly free to marry, and bring my true wife home, at any time —"

There was no mistaking the person to whom this referred. Like a sudden revelation the events of her married life flashed over her — Robert's mysterious language, that she had failed to explain satisfactorily to herself; Mrs. Davis's anger at his sudden journey, and the power with which she had compelled him to make some provision for the wife he was about to desert; his utter silence concerning herself and the baby afterwards; and many deeds of Richard's, that she had allowed to pass without suspicion at the time, because occupied wholly with her child. *He* had not acknowledged her marriage publicly until after Robert's death!

She looked for some other fragment of the letter, but in vain. A sickening agony sped through every pulse. Her temples throbbed in great bounds, her breath came in painful gasps; and when, at last, she threw the papers back in the basket, and dragged herself up to her room, her very limbs seemed chilled with anguish. Who could tell her the truth? Not Mrs. Wilcox — not Richard — she could never ask him; but Mrs. Davis *must* know. Did Robert ever think *she* was leagued with that woman to entrap him!

O God! why had she not died with her baby? Why had such a beautiful life opened before her? Why had such love come to soothe her hungry, desolate heart? If not Robert's lawful wife, what right had she in this household — or to her very name? Better some far desert, or days of distasteful, wearisome toil, than this pleasant existence held on such a tenure. How could she bear the burden? How could she stay here?

Mechanically she rose, her step unsteady, her fingers trembling so that she could scarcely use them, and, as if urged by some irresistible impulse, began to dress. When the simple toilet had been languidly performed, she put on her cloak and bonnet, the thick mourning veil effectually hiding her face. Then she walked slowly down stairs, calling to Ann that she was going out for a while.

The keen, biting air of early March brought out a latent strength. She met no familiar face in her walk to the depot; and the cars were just starting. Not until she saw the houses fairly whirling past did she dare to look her spectral errand in the face. She was going to Mrs. Davis, determined to learn the whole truth. Perhaps she had been wrong in so readily giving up her first friend, and God was punishing her in this manner — sending her back to the life she had shrunk from. Crushed and humiliated, she scarcely knew whither to turn.

She had never seen Mrs. Davis since the day of their parting at Orange. Her delicate intuitions warned her that Richard preferred to have the acquaintance die out; and it was not a pleasurable one to her. She shivered a little now, as, leaving the stage, she walked through the dirty street. The house appeared dingier and coarser than ever, and the blear-eyed stragglers, entering and leaving, filled her with dismay. Taking the private entrance, she knocked at the door of the back room. Mrs. Davis opened it, starting back in astonishment.

"Land sakes! What upon earth sent you here, child? You look as if you was just raised from the dead. Do take a cheer, and thaw out a little; you look a'most froze. Be you well?"

Margaret dropped into the chair. Her torture was too tense for words at the first moment.

"Nothin's happened to you — has it? You look kind o' skeery and ghost-like in them black cloze. Dr. Bertrand nor any on em' hain't been ugly — have they?"

"No, mother." It seemed right to use the old term now. "But I came to ask you a question: why was I not Robert Bertrand's lawful wife?"

Mrs. Davis's face lighted up with an angry flush, as she

said, in a quick, excited tone, "Has that man, has Dr. Bertrand, *dared* to tell you this, after all his promises?"

Her great tenderness for Richard overcame her. Even in this agony she could not have him unjustly blamed, and she replied, with sobs that sounded in her voice only, —

"No; he has been all that is kind and noble. He does not know that I have discovered his secret, or that I came here to-day. And now I want to know all, *all*, if it should kill me dead on the spot."

There was a strange, terrible power in her eyes and voice. Mrs. Davis shrunk away, crying, —

"For Heaven's sake, Marg'ret, are you crazy?"

"No, but I think I shall be if you keep me waiting. Quick, quick! you torture me to death!"

Mrs. Davis could not resist the imperious demand. In a hesitating tone, as if she feared she was doing wrong, she supplied the missing links in Margaret's history, softening — to her honor be it said — the terrible truth she was forced to reveal.

The poor young thing listened with dry, glittering eyes, and pulses that seemed to send a liquid fire of pain through her ice-cold frame. Long after it was finished, she sat like a statue. Frightened at her calmness, Mrs. Davis spoke again, kindly.

A terrible cry broke from her white lips. She threw herself at Mrs. Davis's feet, exclaiming, hoarsely, —

"Mother, please take me back. I will be satisfied with the old life. I will tend in the shop, do anything you desire, only take me back! I am nothing to the Bertrands. I have no right to their home, their love!"

There was a sense of justice and fitness in that rough woman's heart. She said, with a blunt earnestness that was almost tender, —

"You've the *best* right there, child, and Dr. Bertrand feels so. He's a proud man, and wouldn't have done as he has, if his conscience hadn't led him just that way. He knows

Robert acted shamefully. After the baby died, he come over here and fairly swore me to secrecy. He said he'd took you home, and that you never should leave them; he won't hear to your goin'—I can tell you that!"

"I cannot stay, I cannot stay," she moaned, crouching still lower.

"Listen, child. You know this ain't any place for you. You're a sight too han'some to tend bar unless you liked the talk and fun. You don't; you've tried it enough to know. I can feel you ain't my kind. God made you nicer and finer. I don't say this because you put on airs—it's all nat'ral as the breath you draw. There ain't no company for you here. You want somethin' more than bread to eat, and you can have it at the Bertrands. They love you; they're companions for you. O Marg'ret, you'd die here."

The poor girl wrung her hands.

"Will you tell me how you found this all out?" Mrs. Davis asked, after another long pause.

Margaret related the incidents of the morning.

"If I'd 'a known *that* first, you'd never got a word out o' me. You see Dr. Bertrand's been keepin' this from everybody, and tryin' his best to make you happy. There ain't nothin' for him to find out and twit you with. If he could, he'd call Robert out of his grave, and make him marry you; and to leave him don't seem just the right kind of pay, when he's been so gen'rous. I know you ain't ungrateful, Marg'ret."

Her forced strength gave way in a flood of tears. Mrs. Davis followed up the impression, setting the truths of the case very clearly before her. If Margaret had related one unkind incident, her heart and home would have opened at once to the desolate one. But Dr. Bertrand would be deeply pained if she persisted in leaving them, and the explanation necessary for such a step could not fail to embarrass him. It was from this view that Margaret assented with shivering reluctance. She could not resolve to wound one so dear as Dr.

Bertrand, in this painful manner. For many moments she sat in deep thought.

"You'll stay and have some dinner?" Mrs. Davis said, seeing her rise as if to depart.

"No. If I must go back, it had better be immediately. I suppose it *is* best, for the present." Her tone was dreary in the extreme. It touched her listener.

"Marg'ret," she said, holding the trembling form to her heart in an almost motherly clasp, "it *is* right. He meant, all along, to make you happy. But if you *can't* stay, come here, and I'll do my best for you. You shall go to school again till you're able to teach. God knows I'm sorry for you. I hate the day Robert Bertrand came in this house."

There was a sad, clinging caress; then, gathering her cloak about her, the poor child turned to leave the room with that touch of dignity always characterizing her. The clouds were lowering, the wind fiercer than ever. Unconsciously she said to herself,—

"'My life is cold, and dark, and dreary.'"

For the first few steps her limbs almost refused to support her. It seemed as if she must sink to the earth. Rallying a little, she tried to pray for strength to take up this cross, and bear it even to the Mount of Calvary, if need be.

She was glad to reach home before Tessy. Changing her dress, she threw herself on her knees, and remained there until she heard a sweet, childish voice call,—

"Daisy, where are you?"

"In my room." She summoned all her endurance.

"Daisy, darling, how cold you are! You don't look a bit 'crimson tipped,' unless it's the end of your nose. Where have you been?"

"I went out—of an errand." It was all she could do to manage her voice.

"And you just returned in time. There's a wretched storm beginning — fine, cutting sleet. Let us go to the sitting-room, and play chess while we get nicely warm, as Dick and the dinner are not within our reach."

She felt glad to grant the child's request. Tessy was trying to learn the game systematically, without talking, and the play seemed to promise a rest. To her the pieces had heretofore appeared like human beings; but now she had no heart for the mimic warfare. And, by association, Robert's face and form rose before her — the first bright dreams she had cherished, the terrible reality. Could she endure to the end? And what would the end be?

Richard sprang up the steps with a bound. Taking in the situation, he congratulated Tessy. Another move, and the child laughingly exclaimed, "Checkmate!"

"What a bitter storm!" Daisy said, walking towards the window.

"Yes; and I'm compelled to tramp out again. I found a slate fell down stairs. My head aches, and I feel wonderfully like staying at home, and being petted."

Tessy sprang to his side, and began to administer. Then Archie entered with a merry greeting, and presently the dinner bell rang.

The grayness of the day rendered Daisy's paleness less noticeable. She rarely had any color, save when excited. Archie sustained the principal part of the conversation, having some school troubles to relate; so her silence passed unremarked. When Richard went out, they all repaired to the library, and, after it grew too dark to study, clustered together in the twilight to have a good talk, as Archie phrased it.

"What should we do without Daisy!" was Tessy's fervent exclamation. "Lily considers us a nuisance in the evening, and if she visits Bel twice a year, and stays six months each time, she won't be of much moment to us. And likely some time she'll be getting married. But, Daisy, you don't ever mean to have another lover — do you?"

"No, dear." The tone was infinitely solemn and sweet.

"I'm so glad! It will be seven years before I am as old as Lily, and it would break my heart if there wasn't some one at home to love me all that time!"

"You don't consider *me* of the slightest account," bristled up Archie.

"O, you will have to go to college pretty soon, and then you will fall in love, and be married. I'll promise to like your wife *some*, but there can never be any one quite so dear as Daisy. You're such a little darling!" and a rain of kisses covered the quiet face.

"When you are grown, Tessy, you may stay at home, and take care of Dick. I'll build a pretty house, and Daisy shall come and live with me."

"No, you won't, Master Archie! Dick will never let Daisy go away," was the confident reply.

"Daisy isn't bound to obey him!" said Archie, loftily. He had a great, boyish fondness for Daisy, and, with the romance of scarce fifteen years, thought it possible, when he grew to man's estate, to persuade her to fill the dearest position in that enchanted castle — a dream of the future.

"Would you go away, Daisy, unless Richard gave you leave?" and, with a triumphant faith, Tessy glanced up; but the twilight was pitiful, and hid the death-like face of agony. Reaching out to kiss it, the child exclaimed, in surprise, —

"Why, Daisy, you are crying! What is the matter?"

"Nothing, nothing, only —" and a convulsive sob tore up from her very heart. "I love you all so dearly, so dearly! O, how could I go away!"

"You never will," was Tessy's positive and consoling reply.

A ring at the door startled them. It was Freddy Charlton. His cousins had come from Bloomfield, and they were to have out their magic lantern. His mother would play quadrilles for them afterwards, but they wanted Tessy and Archie to complete the set. The resolute little fellow would take no denial. He even begged Mrs. Bertrand to come.

19 *

"No," Daisy replied, with a great effort at cheerfulness. "The doctor will be home presently. I shall not be lonesome in this little while."

They went rather reluctantly. Now that the restraint was removed, Daisy lowered the light, and crept shiveringly to the corner of the hearth, by the register. A bitter, dreary sense of suffering stole over her. How many times, in her short life, she had longed for love! Now it was proving itself a subtle torture. She had no claim on these generous hearts. Nay, more, she felt as if she had been forced upon them from the beginning. There was a wild desire to go away, to put such a distance between them that even visiting would be out of the question. Or if she could die!

She did not cry, or make the faintest moan; but every nerve felt sore and strained, as if she had been on the rack. She thought of her little baby with sorrowful gratitude. He was safe in heaven, as Dr. Bertrand had said that fearful night, "taken from the evil to come." Ah, how blind she had been! God, who knew best, was most kind in that terrible stroke. How could she endure the days yet to be? What must she do?

She sat in that passionless despair until she heard Richard opening the door, when she rose, and went slowly out to meet him. It was a tender fashion with Bel and Lily; of late it had fallen to her.

"The storm increases — does it not?" she asked, keeping her face well in the shade.

"Yes; it is a bitter night. I have half a mind to say neither love nor money, hardly duty, will tempt me to face it again. What a rosy, cheerful warmth there is through this house! I am so glad to be at home."

"And your headache?"

"It is no better. I have probably taken a severe cold. This March wind runs through a person like a knife, and, to use an exaggeration, 'I'm absolutely tired to death!'"

He had taken off his coat while saying this, and now,

passing his arm over Daisy's shoulder, entered the library to resume dressing-gown and slippers, and asked where the children were.

She gave the desired information.

"Haven't you been lonesome, little bird? Yet I'm rather glad of a nice quiet time, for I want you to try your skill in exorcism. You ought to have profited by Lily's instructions."

"Shall I read to you?" Her heart sank within her at thought of the effort.

"No; I want to be comforted in some other manner — as you pet up Archie occasionally. Suppose you take the corner of the sofa, and hold the pillow for me."

She arranged it to his liking; and stretching himself out indolently, he rested his head in her lap. There was a soft, pleasant light in the room; but they heard the wailing of the storm without, and the sleet crackling under the feet of the few who were compelled to be abroad. The wind moaned in the chimney like some forlorn human voice.

"How delightfully cool your hands are!" he said, passing them over his throbbing temples. "Think how lonely I should be without you, Daisy, when my girls flit from the home nest! I believe I shall keep you always."

And she had been planning how to get away! She crushed down the great rising in her heart; she tried to steady the trembling fingers that were drawn down to his mouth to be kissed, and then half buried in his soft beard, before they found their way back to his forehead. She compelled herself to listen to him — mechanically at first, but by degrees losing that numb, terrible feeling. Richard's weariness led him into a sorrowful vein; perhaps, too, the memory of an event always fresh in his mind at this season unconsciously saddened him. From his great grief they passed to hers. If Daisy's voice trembled, if her speech grew slow and faltering, it roused no wonder in his heart. He lingered tenderly over those dark days; indeed, all the days that had been precious to him from the time of their first meeting. She felt anew how he had shielded her — how he would fain have warded off every sorrow. Would there be any such merciful heart in the desert in which she longed to bury herself?

Something inexplicable fell over them both; though, perhaps, neither dreamed to what boundless realm they were slowly drifting. When he spoke of the future, blending her with every event, no fear or suspicion started in either mind. It was too early to experience any want beyond what their daily intercourse supplied. Now and then they fell into long, delicious silences, when he kissed into the soft hand a secret knowledge he had not owned to himself.

Thinking this over in her own room, his tender good night lingering like a blessing about her, and the children's kisses the guests of her pillow, the rebellious feeling of the morning died out. She no longer beat helplessly against the prison bars of fate, neither did she droop in utter despondency. Her cry still was, " All Thy waves and Thy billows are gone over me." She only realized that she could, after all, bear her trial here better than in any other place, without being able to explain what had wrought the change. She could not go away unless Richard consented. And in the dark day of her life in which he said " yes," there would remain but one place of refuge — the grave.

And so she passed the fearful ordeal, making no sign. Influenced by some unseen, unexplainable strength, that crept through every pulse, and beat off the moments by heart throbs, she ceased to struggle at length, and took up her cross in silence. It was not Dr. Bertrand's fault that in a fatal hour all disguise had slipped away. So she sat patiently down in its shadow, resolved to bide God's own time. Her soul was weak, but the most heroic could have done no more.

CHAPTER XXIV.

For love of Him who smote our lives,
  And woke the chords of joy and pain,
We said, *Sweet Christ!* — our hearts bent down,
  Like violets after rain.
                    T. B. ALDRICH.

Many a green isle there needs must be,
In the deep, wide sea of misery;
Else the mariner, worn and wan,
Never thus could journey on.
                    SHELLEY.

IT was not possible for so fragile a nature to pass through the fire unscathed. The holy children came forth with glorious bodies; but we, of a later day, bear about with us the marks of the burning. Therefore the ensuing morning found Daisy feverish, and unable to rise. At first she could not remember how she came by the fierce pain surging wildly around her heart; but presently she laid her head back on the pillow, and prayed fervently for endurance. There was much of life yet before her. She had a vague hope that some day the shadow would be lifted a little.

Tessy summoned Richard with frantic haste. He looked gravely into the sunken eyes, and noted the marks of intense suffering in every feature. If he had not seen her the morning after the baby's death, this change would have alarmed him.

"My poor, dear child," he began, tenderly, " our conversation of last night was too much for you. I don't know how I could have been so selfish and thoughtless. Your system is completely prostrated."

"No, it was not that," she returned, with trembling eagerness, pained to hear him blamed so unjustly. "I was out yesterday, and must have taken cold."

"Not in the storm, surely! Where did you go?"

"Before the storm. It was very chilly. Do not feel alarmed; I shall soon be well again;" and she partly turned her face to avoid his eyes.

Her pulse was extremely feeble. Indeed, he felt rather at loss, unless he ascribed the symptoms to some strong mental agitation. He saw that being questioned gave her pain; so he wisely forbore.

"We must have Lily home," he said. "She ought to be a grand nurse by this time."

"O, no, please don't send for her. I should be so sorry to spoil her visit!" and the languid eyes glanced up beseechingly.

He thought a moment, and then gave up his point. "You will have to take Tessy and me," he resumed.

She put her hand softly in his, as if henceforth he was to be her great rock in a weary land. Without him life would be a blank.

He came up after breakfast, and remained an hour. Perhaps, as she said, rest and quiet were all she needed. He held the baby hand long enough to count every pulse to the very finger tips. Bending over her, he pressed a kiss to the pale lips — a kiss that thrilled his manhood's blood, and left her trembling like an aspen. Familiar as their social relations had been, anything beyond the usual good night was rare between them. The little, light frost of shyness surrounding her was too dainty and sacred a thing to break rudely.

Tessy was delighted to stay at home and play nurse. It was a long, yet not tiresome day. By degrees the throbbing pain in Daisy's temples subsided, and the heartache became more endurable. She made an attempt to rise before dinner, but found herself too weak. So Tessy brought up some toast, and Richard devoted all his spare time to her.

When the lights were out, and she was trying to go to sleep, she thought, again and again, how they all loved her! With a child-like trust she committed her ways unto the Lord; and though she might never wholly resign her burden, these dear ones should not see her faint under it.

Several days elapsed before she was able to come down stairs; but after that she gained rapidly. A letter from Lily brought about an event that quite restored her. Mrs. Suydam expected to bring her brother to the city some time during the following week, and had petitioned to take Lily also. The child's heart was in both places.

"I don't exactly approve of it. I shall have to look after my family a little more closely," Richard said.

"Mabel speaks very highly of Mrs. Suydam," was Daisy's quiet rejoinder.

"The brother may make us the trouble;" and a smile lurked in the corners of his eyes. "See what it is to have a beauty who continually runs into mischief!"

"Daisy and I mean to be the comfort of your old age," Tessy said, with an assurance that sat oddly enough upon her.

"Wait until a handsome young man rescues you from drowning, or breaks his limbs in order to subdue your cruel heart. Upon the whole, I think we must see this hero. What do you say to a trip to Rothclan?"

"You are not in earnest, Dick?"

"Sober earnest, Miss Tessy. Just now I have no serious cases on hand, and the weather promises to be beautiful. Besides, I think Daisy needs some country air to bring the roses to her cheeks."

"I never saw Daisy have any roses," the child replied, thoughtfully.

"We must find a way to make them blossom. What does Daisy say to the journey?"

"It would be delightful! You are so kind;" and she gave his hand a little mute caress.

"He's a magnificent fellow — dear old Dick! He always thinks of the nicest things in the world;" and Tessy hugged him rapturously.

"Just one more mouthful of breath before my head comes off;" and he struggled, laughingly, to release himself.

"We will go on Monday, and take everybody by surprise, and bring Lily home with us the last of the week. Will that do?"

"I think Lily will like it as well as any of us," Daisy said, confidently.

Tessy went waltzing round on the tips of her toes, and finally bestowed herself in Richard's arms.

Daisy had not read much of her letter to Richard, for she was a little doubtful about the rapid proficiency Lily was making in her art. "You would smile to see me manage Mr. Auchester," she wrote. "I found out, a few days ago, that his imperial lordship had more than one weak point. At first I was very devoted. He could not even reach for a drink on account of his shoulder; and as his nurse was fond of going to the kitchen for a good gossip with Mrs. Brown, I was always at hand, and I almost believe he preferred me to the nurse. You remember the last storm? There was enough snow and sleet here to make a little sleighing, and Mr. Joslyn came over for me. He is such a steady-going young man, and belongs to a good family, who are great favorites with Bel; so she trusts me with him very willingly. The ride was tempting, and I had been rather distant of late; so I thought I would console him a trifle with the light of my presence. But you should have seen Mr. Auchester's face when I announced the fact! He said, "O, please do not go!" in such a pretty, pleading tone, that my heart almost misgave me. I could not very well break my promise, and I thought maybe a little solitude would be good for Mr. Auchester. He coaxed a while, and then was rather sulky, I fancied, and had a hundred wants. I was all amiability, and went off at last with a smiling face. Mr. Joslyn was disappointed that I would not go to tea, and spend the evening with his mother; but I had a frantic curiosity to know how Mr. Auchester endured my absence. We reached home just at dusk. I had taken off my wrappings, and was running into Bel's room to tell her of my nice ride, when nurse met me, and said, 'Please, Miss Bertrand, won't you go sit with Mr. Auchester while I make his toast and tea? He has asked for you fifty times in the last half hour.'

" I went to his room radiant, and found him decidedly waspish. He sneered a little at the ride — a sort of elegant bitterness, that he makes an admirable weapon of; and then at Mr. Joslyn, who does sometimes treat Lindley Murray rather disrespectfully. So I began to defend Mr. Joslyn, and as nurse lingered, we had a spicy *tête-à-tête*. It was such fun to see his eyes flash, and rouse him out of his customary easy nonchalance!

" After supper he sent for me to read to him. Philip had gone out. The two men admire each other extremely, and Philip spends much of his time in Mr. Auchester's room. I read a little while; but he was cross as a bear, found fault with my emphasis, my rhythm, and finally told me to put up the book. I was a little vexed at first; but when I found how everything annoyed him, I determined to have my own amusement. He wanted his pillows changed; he wanted the lamp placed so it wouldn't shine in his eyes; he wanted a drink, and twenty other things, that kept me on the stir continually; and then he had the audacity to request me to move quietly, as his nerves were not in quite so robust a state as Mr. Joslyn's! He said 'good night' in a sort of martyr fashion when I went away, and the next morning asked me — would you believe it? — if I was not sorry for neglecting him so yesterday! Since then we have had rather spicy times, and when he is very naughty I play off Mr. Joslyn against him.

"He has improved rapidly of late, and Mrs. Suydam expects to take him home next week. I think her a most charming woman. But, Daisy, she wishes me to accompany them, and I never was so puzzled in my life. I want to go, and yet I don't want to. Mabel has written to Richard, but I expect to feel disappointed whichever way he decides. Was there ever such an odd girl?"

They were all ready for their journey on Monday morning. Archie bade them good by with a rueful face, and declared he did not know how he could exist in their absence. The day was lovely, and Tessy merry as a bird. She even infected Richard with her joyous spirits. Daisy was quiet and pale, but much interested in the ride. The Hudson looked beautiful in the bright spring sunshine; its banks dotted here and there with patches of pale green, suggesting verdure; and then rising in high, frowning cliffs, broken at intervals by mysterious nooks. The girls looked steadily out of the window, and talked Irving until the conductor sang out—Rothelan.

As they supposed, they took the whole family greatly by surprise, but were none the less welcome. Daisy found herself quite an object of interest with her pale face. Lily hovered about her with fond caresses, while Tessy was soon won over to Mr. Chaloner's side. Neither Bel nor Lily had overdrawn the delights of the place.

Mr. Auchester did not make his appearance until dinner. He *was* unusually handsome, though still pale, and he carried his arm in a sling. There was nothing in him for Richard to distrust. His face was manly and honorable in the highest degree, a little imperious, perhaps, but it sat well upon him. A man so self-poised, and used to perfect control, would not be easily mastered by any feeling or passion unless strictly genuine.

He was rather quiet at first. Lily bantered him a little on being disappointed. Mr. Suydam's gardener had promised to send him some birds, but had brought chickens.

" Well," said Tessy, " you'll have to comfort yourself as the old lady I once read of did, when she boiled the hedge stake on which the crow had been sitting, by saying, ' It tastes of game, though.' "

" Extremely philosophical," laughed Mr. Auchester, " and worth remembering, when I am reduced to greater straits than this. Do you think, with your sister, that I look disappointed ?"

" Not so dreadfully," returned Tessy, slowly.

Mr. Auchester began to relate to her how he had been treated during his illness. They had put three grains of tea in two quarts of water, for fear of rendering him nervous and unmanageable, and when the nurse made his first soup, she hung a chicken's wing in the sunshine and boiled the shadow. And he had never been able to coax Lily to bring him up any nice little dish without nurse's knowledge. Tessy commiserated him greatly. There was much drollery in her nature. When they adjourned to the parlor, she and Mr. Auchester were fast friends.

As the afternoon was lovely, he sent over for Mr. Suydam's family carriage, and they all went out to ride. Daisy and he were placed on the back seat, well wrapped up, ' to keep the winds of heaven from visiting them too roughly,' Lily said. She, Tessy, and Richard faced them, Philip driving, and Mabel beside him.

Mr. Auchester made himself very agreeable, talking mostly to Daisy. In the evening he persuaded her to share the sofa with him, while the others were engrossed with music. She remembered afterwards that their conversation was principally about Lily. The next day was still more charming, as there was less restraint. Daisy's eyes and cheeks brightened with pleasurable excitement. A heart less true and honorable than Mabel's might have experienced a jealous pang at finding herself superseded in the old household place ; but she loved Daisy too dearly for such a feeling.

" I wonder if I am selfish about *you*," she said to Richard.

"So many evenings I have thought of you coming home weary in body and mind, and being comforted by Daisy's low, sweet voice, and cheered by the dear face so full of ready sympathy. I should not have dared to keep Lily so long, only I knew you had better care than she would bestow. I am so glad Robert gave her to us."

Richard remembered one night, that stood out like a star among other pleasant ones, and said, in a fervent tone, —

"She will be a treasure to us all; I am more than thankful to have her."

Mr. Auchester seemed weary, and retired quite early in the evening; Mabel was called away by a visitor, and the gentlemen went to the study for a comfortable smoke. Lily carried Daisy off to her room, and bestowing her on a corner of the lounge, said, —

"Now for a nice long talk. I have hardly seen you yet."

"Well," Daisy exclaimed, after a silence, "do you want me to begin the conversation by asking what you said to Mr. Auchester immediately after supper. It changed his mood, visibly."

"Did you think so? It was about not going home with his sister. I am so glad you all came up, and that Richard wants to take me back with him. I would like very much to go to Mrs. Suydam's; but I am sure it was *his* proposal. He rules her completely. I want him to see that he is not master of every one. How do you like him?"

"O, very, very much. Are you doing just right, Lily? for I think he admires you greatly, and if you can pain him so easily —"

"After he tells me what he means, I shall know;" and Lily laughed.

"Yet you like him?"

"Yes; that is just the word to use after a five weeks' acquaintance. But this may be with him 'pastime 'ere he goes to town;' and you see I can match him."

"I do not believe it," Daisy said, with a little crimson flush of indignation. "Or do you prefer Mr. Joslyn?"

"He isn't to be mentioned in the same week, although a good deal richer. I had to have some amusement, you know. When I first came up, he was the most eligible, and lately it has been such fun to play them off against each other!"

"But, Lily, do you think it right? Is there no danger to any one?"

"O, you grave little kitten! If I can take care of myself, *he* surely ought to be endowed with as much wisdom;" and Lily shook back her curls with a brilliant, scornful smile. "After all, it is only child's play. I dare say Mr. Auchester will forget me in a fortnight."

Daisy started at the change in the bright face. Was Lily as indifferent as she pretended? Twining her arm around the beautiful girl, she drew from her many trifling incidents that she would never have dreamed of telling Mabel. And as Daisy recalled Mr. Auchester's frank, honorable face, she felt it could not be all trifling on his part.

"And now I want to hear about yourself," Lily said. "Have you had a pleasant winter; and what made you ill? Didn't you want me just a little?"

An irrepressible shiver ran over Daisy; but quickly recovering herself, she answered, —

"Dr. Bertrand wanted to send for you; but he and Tessy were delightful nurses, and I thought Mabel needed you."

"Mr. Auchester, you mean. I did half propose going home one day, when he was rather lordly. You should have seen how it brought him down from his sublime height. O, it was grand. There comes Bel. Not a word of this to her, or you will frighten her out of her senses."

At Mabel's entrance the conversation became general. But as Daisy laid her head on the pillow that night, she smiled and sighed; smiled over the tact and ready wit Lily displayed in managing her admirers, and sighed to think what might be her fate. Dear, bright, beautiful Lily!

On Wednesday, Mr. and Mrs. Suydam came up. The lady was certainly not handsome, but taste and education rendered her charming. Easy and affable, without the slightest condescension, and really grateful to all who had befriended her brother. He was her junior by three years, the only companion of her childhood, and very dear to her. As Lily had said, his word was her law.

At first she was deeply disappointed at not being able to take Lily with her, but on second thought declared herself quite reconciled.

" We are going to give Ulric a party as soon as we can decide on the time," she said; " and I'll take my week then, Miss Lilian. So remember, you are to be in readiness."

Mr. Suydam had brought up an elegant set of books for Philip, and a handsomely bound collection of choice music for Mabel. They seemed to consider themselves largely in debt to all at the rectory.

"Indeed," Mrs. Suydam said, naively, " Ulric is enjoying himself so well, it is a pity to take him home. I'm sure no one ever had a pleasanter convalescence."

Lily granted him the favor of a walk after dinner, and Daisy was pleased to see him return in such good spirits. Mrs. Suydam's admiration was more outspoken, but his as evident.

To their departure succeeded a long, quiet evening — a regular family party, as Mabel termed it. Daisy and she harmonized as completely now as during the first month of their acquaintance; perhaps, indeed, there were more points of sympathy. She tried to persuade her to remain; but although they held a long conference on the subject, it was summarily vetoed by Tessy's appealing to Richard, who said, gravely, " Why, if Daisy desired it very much —" but the tone and the pause at the end of the sentence was all-potent.

" I have the promise of a whole month next summer," Mabel returned, confidently. " You must learn to do without her by that time."

The week was all too short, though they did manage to go to supper at Mrs. Joslyn's. There were three agreeable young ladies, who appeared to think it their bounden duty to admire Lily; but the brother was nervous and awkward, appearing to quite a disadvantage in his desire to honor every one, with Lily's eyes upon him.

The journey, the excitement, and perhaps Lily's exuberant spirits, worked a marvellous change in Daisy. The sweet, bland airs of spring, and out-of-door occupation, helping Martin tie up roses and make the garden, brought a soft bloom to her face. Now and then a musical ripple floated in with Lily's clear laugh, rendering the atmosphere of Dr. Bertrand's house joyous and soul-reviving.

Mrs. Suydam sent Lily the promised invitation, adding, "that she and her brother would drive over for her, and that she must come prepared for the desired visit. Ulric was almost well, and anticipated a great deal of pleasure. He begged the privilege of sending his regards."

"O dear!" said Lily, disconsolately; "all the people will look so elegant that I shall be completely thrown in the shade."

"Not with such a face."

"Because I look well in white muslin and blue ribbons, I suppose I must wear them all my days, comforting myself with 'beauty unadorned,' 'gilding gold, and painting the *lily.*'"

Daisy laughed.

"You do need a pretty evening dress, and a new silk," she said.

"Exactly, my dear. Yet I am afraid Richard would think me dreadfully extravagant if I asked him for a hundred dollars. Mabel was such an inexpensive treasure that my own desires shock me by contrast. I'll see how much courage I can summon up between this and bedtime."

Daisy smiled quietly to herself.

CHAPTER XXV.

Airy, fairy Lilian,
Flitting, fairy Lilian,
When I ask her if she love me,
Clasps her tiny hands above me,
  Laughing all she can;
She'll not tell me if she love me,
  Cruel little Lilian.
TENNYSON.

COMING in quite early, Richard was waylaid in the hall; but it was not the rapturous embrace of either Lilian or Tessy. The clasp of these little hands was shy and timid, the face flushed and entreating, and the rosy lips said, softly, —

"O doctor! I want to see you a moment, before any one else. I have a favor to ask."

"Professional, of course;" and there was a gay light in his eyes as his strong arm almost lifted instead of leading her to the library.

"No;" and the sudden rift of color reminded one of the break in an April sky after a shower.

"Then I will take the liberty of observing that it is not absolutely necessary to always give me my title in addressing me," he returned, gravely. "What if you vary the exercises once in a while by saying Richard? I don't suppose you will ever feel well enough acquainted to use Lily's 'dear old Dick!'"

The long lashes drooped over the downcast eyes, and the crimson became painfully deep. In that moment of silence, both remembered the only time she had ever said Richard, and that was not to *him*. He drew the fair head down on his breast, and said, with deep tenderness, —

"Child, what is it?"

"Nothing for myself."

"If Archie doesn't stop sending you of his errands —"

"He did not send me, nor any one. I wanted to ask it for Lily, she is so kind and sweet to me. Do you not think —" and she paused in her embarrassment.

"I think you are too much afraid of me, Daisy. Am I not your brother — your dearest friend?"

"It was this," — she spoke low and hurriedly; — "Lily ought to have something new and pretty to wear at Mrs. Suydam's. She is fearful you will consider her extravagant if she asks for it."

He laughed pleasantly as he replied, —

"So, that is all. Well, if people *will* admire our family beauty, we must make her elegant accordingly. Will a hundred dollars do? I don't know how much party dresses cost."

"Just what she was wishing for; and she can buy two dresses with it. You are so good!"

"Do you feel generous enough to repay me for my ready compliance?"

She said, "Richard," in a little underbreath, as if a summer zephyr had wafted the fragrance of a jasmine to him. The shyest grace fluttered like a rosy veil over her countenance. He could not resist giving her one of those rare, tender kisses.

"Little bird!" he continued presently. "Suppose we go down to New York, and find some pretty gift for Lily — a set of jewelry, for instance? Wouldn't you like to bestow this upon her?"

"It would be delightful! — only I should tell her it was not *my* gift." Daisy had long ago insisted upon Richard's taking back the money Mrs. Davis had given her. Since she had learned her true situation, she was thankful for having done this, though he kept her liberally supplied with funds.

"Well, you shall choose it, then. Can you get ready in ten minutes? We might catch the next train."

"But the dinner?"

"Lily will attend to that. As for us, there's a Mr. Taylor in New York, an exceedingly obliging man, who will serve you up a dinner at a moment's notice. See if you can dress yourself while I am brushing my hair. Not a word to Lily."

She ran off eagerly, her face one lovely glow. No interruption came as the deft fingers flew hither and thither like the quick wings of a bird. Her black dress, with its tiny neck and wrist ruffles of soft cambric, was always in order. Fastening her cloak and tying her bonnet, she stepped into the hall just as Richard emerged from his room.

He took a delighted survey of the sweet, rosy face, and said, smilingly, —

"You are a perfect fairy. I am glad the race is not quite extinct. Shall we find a coach and six out of doors? and must I bring you home before midnight?"

"Don't praise me too soon. I have not my gloves on;" and she held up her hands.

He slipped one through his arm, adding, "You can finish in the cars." Then he called, over the baluster, "Mrs. Hall!"

"Well," was the reply.

"Mrs. Bertrand and I are going out, and shall not return until evening. Do not keep dinner waiting for us."

"O Richard!" a voice cried just as he shut the door. When Lily looked out, they were turning the corner. Mrs. Hall could throw no light whatever on the subject.

The day was balmy and spring-like, the air fragrant with newly-awakened odors. Richard declared he felt unusually gay for an old man with grown-up daughters. Daisy was radiant and smiling. They soon whirled down to the city, and a convenient stage took them to Ball & Black's.

Richard seated Daisy, declaring she had an arduous task before her. The clerk began to spread out jewels. Cameos, mosaic, pearls, rubies, emeralds, and all manner of lovely, sparkling things that quite dazzled her. She looked them over with a child's eager delight, they were so beautiful.

"I think," she said, after a long pause, "there are only two things I should choose for Lily — turquoise or pearls."

"And which of those? See if your taste agrees with mine."

She studied them attentively, answering, —

"I believe I prefer the pearls."

"I am quite sure I do. Lily is so fair! How do you like this brooch with an opal in the centre?"

"It is exquisite. The changeful hues of the opal light it up like a sunrise. How Lily will admire it!"

Then they examined some bracelets. Tasteful and elegant, yet not too expensive looking for plain wear.

"We shall not find anything prettier. While the clerk is putting them up we will take a look at the pictures and bronzes on the next floor;" and giving his order, he led her up stairs.

"What lovely, lovely articles!" she said, pausing in wondering pleasure.

"It almost makes one long to be rich, doesn't it, when such elegant gold and silver services stare you in the face? And to have your house filled with arch Hebe, Ceres laden with ripe burdens, Pomona bearing her luscious fruits, and this sad-eyed Clytie, who drooped and pined in her unfortunate love, until her heart's sweetness became the heliotrope!"

"They *are* beautiful and — cold," Daisy said, slowly. "I like tender human faces and bright flowers in the place we call home. I am not quite out of conceit with *our* poverty;" and she smiled archly.

He gave the little hand a fond pressure. They were a long while examining the choice treasures that spoke of

nearly every quarter of the globe; then Richard proposed
they should go for their dinner, concluding with, —

"Afterwards we will take a tour through the Dusseldorf
Gallery.　Some of the pictures are exceedingly fine by gaslight."

Daisy thanked him with a smile.　He was in a warm,
genial mood, and rendered everything delightful to her.
Many a week could not boast of the enjoyment crowded into
those few holiday hours.

Again in the cars, she was silent, not so much from
fatigue as thought.　Richard watched the rosy face and
lovely, drooping eyes, and never guessed what was passing
in her heart.　She shivered a little at the remembrance of
her cold, bitter, terrible March journey.　Why was it the
fatal secret had not darkened her whole life?　From whence
came the light, the warmth, the sunshine?　Ah, it was love,
both human and divine, that made all so radiant; and thus
the most sorrowful of dead hopes blossomed anew by faith
in God.　It may be it will stand confessed at the last that
some of our sorest trials became the off-shoots on which
grew steadfast purposes and more noble resolves.

Lily was at the piano when they entered the house.
Richard amused himself a while with her impatient curiosity,
and then handed her the little parcel.　Opening it, she
found not only the jewels, but two fifty-dollar gold pieces.

"Dick, you are too good for anything!" she cried, clasping her arms around him.　"What little bird told you I
wanted a set of pearls and some money to spend?　This
was why you whisked Daisy off so unceremoniously."

Daisy disclaimed all honor of the proceeding, but Richard
insisted he couldn't have thought of it alone.　Lily tried on
her jewels in wildest delight.　Their delicate loveliness
harmonized admirably with her pure blonde beauty, and, if
less showy than colors, suited her better.

"I have a word more to add," said Richard.　"Don't
buy dresses too fine for my pearls."

"I'll take Daisy with me to help select them; so, if you see us flying off without a word of explanation, you will know the cause;" and she laughed saucily.

It was growing late; so they soon separated. An unspoken wish lingered in the deep eyes resting on Daisy's face.

"Good night, Richard," she said, softly, with her last kiss, while a fitful color stole into her cheeks.

Mrs. Suydam and Mr. Auchester drove over according to promise. The gentleman laughingly declared himself as good as new, and ready for another adventure. He was polished, and displayed the ease and grace refined society and careful culture invariably give. Lily was a little shy, but exquisitely charming. After Richard came in, she and Mrs. Suydam went to inspect the dresses.

The new ones had been a blue silk, chosen, she blushingly admitted to Daisy, because Mr. Auchester thought it her most appropriate color, and a white tissue dotted with miniature bouquets in rich, delicate shades. The pearls elicited Mrs. Suydam's warmest admiration. Dark, and rather brilliant looking, she shared, in common with many brunettes, a passion for blonde beauty.

Daisy superintended the preparations for lunch. She gave a little odd smile over the simple white china as she thought of the elegant services she had examined with Richard; yet the table looked very pretty when she arranged some scarlet geraniums in low vases. Was Mrs. Suydam, living in luxury, any happier than they? A quick heartbeat answered her.

Lily said her adieus with all the fondness of a warm, unrestrained heart. Her fresh, frank nature won upon Mr. Auchester. He had quick eyes to detect calculated movements, and his penetration would soon have solved the depths of insincerity. She did not know how great an interest he had in watching her just now.

Archie threw up his cap, and said they could take a world

of comfort with Daisy, now that Lily was out of the way. He told Tessy privately he shouldn't at all care if Mr. Auchester married Lily, for they could do very well without her.

The week resolved itself into ten days, before Mr. Auchester brought her back. One could readily gather from her face that her visit had been highly satisfactory. He remained to spend the evening, and had a long talk with Richard, while they smoked their cigars on the lawn. Tessy kept wide awake, to hear about the "party" afterwards.

"O, it was delightful!" Lily exclaimed, as she sat down on the edge of the bed to brush out her shining hair. "Mrs. Suydam lives in such elegant style; and they are all charming people. She treated me as if I had been her sister. But everybody is crazy about Mr. Auchester. I didn't expect to find him *quite* such a hero. People come to see him, and give dinner parties in his honor. His publishers like his book immensely. It is 'Travels and Discoveries;' for a year he was with an English scientific party. Some of the proof sheets were sent home while I was there, and we read them together. He is remarkably entertaining, for he writes just as he talks, and some of his descriptions are wondrously beautiful."

"But the party!" suggested Tessy.

"O, yes. Well, the apartments were a blaze of light and beauty — isn't that orthodox? There was a room for card playing, and all those games; a picture gallery, devoted to conversation and the like; a dancing-room, with most delicious music. Those waltzes of Strauss are perfectly enchanting. But the supper-room was magnificent. Such an abundance of lovely cut and tinted glass, and an elegant silver service, that was presented to Mr. Suydam by some Company, to say nothing of flowers in wildest profusion. Everything glittered and sparkled in the brilliant light; the wines, fruits, and jellies looked beautiful beyond description. I suppose the guests enjoyed themselves immensely; I am sure I did."

"What did you do?" the child asked.

"Danced, mostly, and when I was tired, sat still and watched the crowds of elegant people. There were many very richly dressed, but I felt as nice in my tissue and pearls as the best of them. Mr. Auchester made me a lovely bouquet, and put some flowers in my hair. He is passionately fond of flowers. It was like a glimpse of Fairy-land. I was full of enjoyment to the very brim. And Mrs. Suydam has taken me twice to the opera; and I went to one grand dinner, where numbers of the 'literati' were present; besides rides and calls, and most delightful times at home. Mr. Suydam is a very pleasant host. And now you must go to sleep, Tessy, for it's growing late."

She had a long, confidential talk with Daisy the next day, as they sat at their sewing. Daisy expressed a desire to know if Mr. Auchester improved on further acquaintance.

"I hardly know what to say about him;" and a thoughtful expression crossed Lily's face, as she went on, musingly: "he *is* splendid; he pleases, frets, amuses, and almost fascinates me. There is such a sense of power running through his low, rich, flexible voice, that it unconsciously controls every one. Mrs. Suydam takes his word for law; the children obey him immediately, and even his friends yield to his curious sway. I'm not sure that I like to be ruled in that imperial fashion! I was so vexed one morning! I was in the library, reading proofs to him, when Mrs. Suydam entered, and asked me to accompany her and the children on a drive. He merely raised his head, and said, in a cool, authoritative manner, 'She is reading to me.' Mrs. Suydam laughingly nodded her head and disappeared, and I read on. He is so quick and calm about a thing! He decides for you without giving you time to consider, and there is no going back with him. If you undertake to argue a point where he means you shall yield, he is attentive, patient, polite, but — immovable. Don't look so suspicious, Daisy; I was *real* good. Being in his sister's house, where every one set me a good example, I was as meek as you please. But I *did* want to torment him that night of the party. In the first waltz I had him for a partner; he had asked for it in the morning. I enjoyed it wonderfully. Then he brought some cream, and we went into a cosy little corner to eat it; and he asked me, as a special favor, not to waltz with any other gentleman that evening. I very foolishly promised. Some time afterwards — I had been dancing quadrilles with Mr. Suydam's nephew — the band commenced a most inspiriting waltz; but of course I refused my partner. Whom should I see come floating down the room but Mr. Auchester and a beautiful woman — some gentleman's daughter he had met abroad. My first impulse was to spring up; indeed, I hardly know what restrained me. It would have delighted me to see him flush and frown, and set his lips together in that rigid, self-commanding way. He has no superabundance of patience, I can assure you. I asked him next day why he made such a request, and he answered, in an imperious manner, 'Child, I have peculiar fancies concerning *some* women's waltzing;' and, I confess, I really did not dare to question him further."

"O Lily! don't talk so, please. It is not right to make him angry."

"My dear, he doesn't get angry now. He used to, at Rothelan. In these later times, he merely shows what he *might* do if he chose. And I believe it is natural for me to resent authority. The instant any one sets up a law, I experience a strong desire to test my strength against it. Yet I had a most satisfactory visit, and I really do love Mrs. Suydam."

Mr. Auchester made himself no stranger at the Bertrands. When he learned how fond Daisy was of gardening, he brought her many choice flowers, and interested her greatly in his descriptions of tropic vegetation, and the wonderful gardens of the old world. A fine, electric sympathy sprang up between them; they seemed to gain an intuitive knowledge

of each other's tastes and feelings. Nor was Mrs. Suydam at all inclined to relinquish her share of Lily's society.
Besides admiring the beauty of the young girl, there was
something so winsome and genial in her fresh, sunny moods,
while her ready wit rarely wounded, and never exceeded the
point of good taste.

When the time for her annual migration arrived, Mrs.
Suydam entreated Richard to allow her to take Lily to
Rothelan, but it was Mr. Auchester who supplied the argu-
ment that proved effectual.

"I don't feel at all satisfied about it," Richard said to
Daisy, as they walked up and down the garden, after the
house had settled into quiet.

"Why? I think Mr. Auchester likes Lily."

"He thinks he *loves* her;" and Richard gave a perplexed
smile.

Daisy started in pleasurable surprise. "O, I am so glad!
But it is quite sudden."

"He announced his intentions immediately after the party,
and asked my sanction. I stipulated that he should say
nothing to Lily for at least three months; but I believe his
patience is quite exhausted. The last day he was here he
begged me to consent to an engagement."

"Did you?"

"Very reluctantly. I told him what I considered the
truth — that Lily was a mere child, and likely to be dazzled
by the excitement. It is a bitter thing to make idols and
find them clay."

"You do not like him, and I do, so very much!" Daisy's
fine perception had divined this before.

"I admire him greatly. He has many estimable qualities,
and is a man of the highest honor and delicacy; yet I cannot take him cordially to my heart, as I did Philip. I have
some painful misgivings about the matter."

"In what respect?"

"Lily is fond of the widest freedom, quite conscious of

her power, impatient of control, and sometimes rather unreasonable. Mr. Auchester is keenly alive to anything that
trenches on his authority. He is exacting, rigid, and mas-
terful ; and though royally generous to those who trust him
and yield, I can fancy his being very bitter when opposed."

"I hardly think you do him justice. Besides, he loves
Lily."

"Rather, is fascinated with her. He likes her beauty, and
her free, daring nature ; but he means to tame her. Just
now he is indulgent ; he wants to accustom her to his guidance by degrees. When he gains a right to dictate, Lily
may dispute his power. 'How can two walk together
except they be agreed ? '"

" O, Lily would yield ; all women do when they love."

"Do they ?" He smiled curiously down into her face,
which answered with a crimson flush. "If Lily had fallen
irrevocably in love, I should have more hopes of her. Perhaps she prefers Mr. Auchester to any gentleman she has
ever met. Yet she may love her own will and passionate
pride better. Some very worthy women wreck their happiness on this rock. Lily is naturally restless and defiant ;
her course would be noisily persevering ; his, quietly, un-
swervingly persistent. I'm afraid she will not readily understand the kind of man she has to deal with ; and rebellion,
in such a case, would be misery."

"I believe they will make charming lovers. I cannot
allow you to pull down my ' *chateau en Espagne.*'"

"If they could always be lovers!" and Richard sighed a
little. "Neither has had the slightest discipline. Life has
been so pleasant and easy with Mr. Auchester that I am
afraid he has not acquired sufficient patience to control and
govern such a nature as Lily's."

"I am sorry you do not like him any better," Daisy said,
disappointedly.

"And yet I do enjoy his society. I think him a man of
the highest truth and honor, and generous save in this one

point — his authority. Doubtless the force and freshness of Lily's temperament please him; but she has a peculiar pertinacity, an ease and carelessness under rebuke until it becomes severe, simply because she means to have her own way in the end. Once married, with no avenue of escape, how would she endure a husband's authority, that would be carried to its utmost limit if occasion required?"

"You make him out a tyrant," Daisy said.

"No. In truth, I'm not sure but I would like to have *my* wife obey *me* — good as I am;" and Richard tried to laugh gayly, but it was only sad and retrospective. In his lost youth there flamed up the face of a woman who would give up anything save her own will. And Lily was not altogether unlike Robert. Love had failed to govern him. After a long pause, he added, "Our only hope is, that all differences may be adjusted while they are lovers, or else that they may find they are really unsuited to each other."

Daisy resolutely held to her pleasant faith. True, Lily gave it some rude shocks when she mentioned such episodes as her going to tea at Mrs. Joslyn's, and how Mr. Joslyn had attended her home, to the discomfiture of Mr. Auchester, who, on calling at the rectory, and finding her out, had come for her, missing them both. "And I kept Mr. Joslyn real late," she added; "it was such fun to see Mr. Auchester's eyes sparkle, and have him pace up and down the room like a fretted lion. He tried to scold a little, afterwards; but I acted so unconscious of having committed any offence, that he was forced to yield his point. So, you see, at the rectory I pay him for being on my good behavior at Mrs. Suydam's, which makes it about even."

Daisy withheld these confessions from Richard, and considered Mr. Auchester the most indulgent of lovers. With his declaration, Mr. Auchester had also frankly informed Lily of all that had passed between him and her brother. Her quick eye detected the advantage. It was something to govern such a man — to tease and perplex; and so Lily

hesitated a little on the bewitching boundary line. Power
and liberty were sweet things to her. She lured him on,
now by love, now by a little show of fond submission, and
presently an almost childish rush into gayeties that he could
chide, conquer, and forgive. It was his first passion; and
however cool and self-reliant he might be about other matters, the newness of this, and its absorbing power, engrossed
him entirely.

CHAPTER XXVI.

But springtide blossoms on thy lips,
And tears take sunshine from thine eyes.
COLERIDGE.

That care and trial seem at last,
  Through memory's sunset air,
Like mountain ranges overpast,
  In purple distance fair.
J. G. WHITTIER.

DAISY and Lily had changed places. It was Daisy who wrote from Rothelan, and this was part of her epistle : —

"Mabel has the sweetest little darling of a girl you ever saw, with dark violet eyes, just like yours. I wanted to write immediately, but I knew Richard would tell you, and now baby is five days old. She is very good, scarcely cries at all, and Mabel is doing splendidly. Mrs. Suydam went to New York yesterday, and bought a lovely christening robe, a perfect mass of needlework and Valenciennes lace. She is to be one godmother, and baby is to be named Alice for her, and Teresa in remembrance of your dead mother and dear little Tessy.

"Mr. Auchester accompanied Mrs. Suydam over this morning. I brought out baby, and she opened her eyes so prettily it quite amused him. He said he had thought of buying her a silver cup, but he believed he should have to get a pony instead. Lily, dear, I like him so very, very much! He will tell you Mrs. Suydam has changed her plans. On account of going West in the fall, with Mr. Suydam, she has given up Saratoga. So she and Mr. Auchester have planned a pleasant trip to the Catskills, as soon as Mabel is sufficiently recovered to travel. It is to be a real gay family party.

"Tell Richard that I am happier than I ever hoped to be. Baby Alice has come to cheer me in this saddest of all seasons. God has been very good to me."

Richard gathered from these words Daisy's earnest endeavor to overlive the memory of the past summer. He did not dream of the greater stroke that had tempered her anguish, and would forever keep her from wishing back her lost darling. It was "well" with the child, and "well" also with her, rejoicing in another's new-born hope.

How thoughtful and tireless she was! The cool touch of her fingers, the low, sweet sound of her voice, and her tender smile were invaluable in a sick room. Withal, she found time to see that Philip was not neglected, keeping everything in Mabel's fashion, from the box of cravats to the arrangement of the study table, where fresh flowers greeted him every morning.

On the anniversary of her baby's death a letter came from Richard, containing some flowers gathered from the little grave. She wondered how he could know her heart so well. Was it strange she should live over again that fearful night? How could she have borne it but for him! Not even brotherly necessity had compelled him to be so kind. All had been given from the fulness of his own grand, generous heart. It was pleasant to owe so much to his abundant tenderness.

Mabel and baby Alice throve finely. The day for the christening was appointed, and Mr. Auchester brought up Lily and the two younger ones. Tessy was wild over the baby, and begged Daisy not to grow jealous.

"For, after all," she said, in her odd, womanly fashion, "I love you with a *grown-up* love, which is much stronger. Only, Alice is so sweet, and can endure so much kissing, that it's a great comfort to have her in the family."

Mabel was taken to church for the christening. Richard,

Daisy, and Mrs. Suydam stood for the little one. It was a
solemn and comforting service to the scarcely more than
child, whose heart went back to her own baby's baptism.
He had "passed the waves of this troublesome world, and
entered the land of everlasting life." Kneeling at the font,
she prayed that she might be enabled to do her duty, not
only to this child, but to all those loved ones whom God had
given her. She had ceased to ask *why* such heavy trials
had fallen to her lot; content, and trust in a merciful Father,
were all she desired.

Mrs. Suydam and her three children and Mr. Auchester
remained to dinner at the rectory. The little ones had a
merry time on the lawn with Tessy, afterwards. Lily and
her lover strolled away, and Richard, drawing Daisy's arm
through his, led her down the shady path until they were
lost to sight.

The day was lovely. A westerly breeze blew wafts of
fragrance from the odorous pines and hemlock woods, refreshed by the late rains. Rifts of quivering sunshine flecked
the short grass at their feet, and the birds warbled from
leafy coverts. Some fine, electric sense governed each,
keeping them quiet a long while, one of those perfect pauses
of satisfied silence. Daisy was first to break it.

"I don't know how to thank you for the letter you sent
me. I wanted to answer it, only it seemed so perfect in
itself, I knew not what to say."

Her voice faltered, and the long lashes drooped over her
eyes.

"I am glad it comforted you." He took in his the little
hand that rested on his arm, as he went on, —

"How singularly the events of our lives come about!
Does it not seem as if when God was leading us through the
darkest paths, He had some pleasant valley of Elim at the
end, where we could sit down in the shade of the seventy trees
of palm, and forget our griefs?"

"Yes. The shade is so good, so grateful, after we have

been through the desert!" Then she sighed softly, for she knew all of life must be a little shady to her.

Richard had been through the desert, and borne some burdens. Not so bitter as hers, but enough to make him enjoy this restful present with the keenest pulse of his being. He could have wandered forever under these trees, holding in his heart a life so full and rich, that for the present it replied to itself in all the blessedness of hope. When she glanced shyly upward, her color deepened no more than usual, and there was the same tenderness in his voice that had come the night of the baby's death. Hitherto there had been no event in their quiet lives sufficient to rouse self-examination. Her grief still rendered her sacred in his eyes.

When they returned, they found the party gathered on the balcony, earnestly discussing some news the day's mail had brought Mrs. Suydam. The aunt and cousins, who had expected to meet her and Ulric at Saratoga, were deeply disappointed at their defection, and proposed making them a visit, if agreeable.

"They will be quite an addition to our Catskill party," said Mrs. Suydam. "Aunt Auchester is a charming woman; indeed, she was always a mother to me. Fred and Leonard are great favorites of mine, and Clara bewitches everybody, I believe. But we must make some arrangements. Dr. Bertrand, how soon will Mrs. Gregory be strong enough to travel?"

"In a fortnight or so, I think. I shall take her under my charge, you know."

"What a caravan!" laughed Lily. "Mr. and Mrs. Gregory, child, physician; three sisters and one brother to admire the baby, and uphold the mother's dignity."

"And when I add my quota," rejoined Mrs. Suydam — "an aunt, three cousins, servant, and little Isabel here, whom Tessy and Ulric have smuggled in."

Mr. Auchester stooped to kiss his favorite niece, saying, —

"You have left me out altogether."

"A great mistake," exclaimed Tessy, counting the party over on her fingers.

"I must write immediately, and learn what state and condition they are likely to be in at the Mountain House," said Mr. Auchester. "The rush will have lessened somewhat, on account of the lateness of the season. But it will suit me much better than these red-hot days. We can have such fine rambles; and there will be moonlight evenings."

"Splendid!" ejaculated Lily and Tessy in a breath.

Richard glanced at his watch, and remarked, rather regretfully, that his train would be along soon. He had a few last charges for Mabel; and while they were talking, Mr. Auchester sent Daisy and Lily for their hats, announcing that he intended to drive Dr. Bertrand to the station.

Tessy's bright face was shadowed with disappointment.

"Never mind," said Mrs. Suydam. "You shall ride home with me, and they can call for you. I must prepare my little flock for returning. What a dear, delightful day it has been! There could not be a better baby than my little namesake. I am extremely proud of her."

There followed a general dispersion. Mabel, obeying her brother's suggestion, went immediately to bed. She was a little tired and excited, but youth and a tranquil mind soon asserted their sway. Baby was laid to sleep in her snowy crib, and the young mother was not long in following so good an example.

Lily put Daisy and Richard on the back seat, as she wanted to drive. Ulric Auchester leaned lazily against the arm at his side, congratulating himself on being relieved from so much trouble.

"Richard is precious to me. I cannot have you breaking his neck," retorted Lily, saucily.

"You ought to be everlastingly grateful to me, Miss Lily, for suffering so much in your behalf. How could you have

endured the tedium of a winter in the country if I had not
been half crushed to death in order to afford you some
interest ? "

" I'm sure I don't know," returned Lily, with gravity.
" I think I *must* have been homesick. Weren't my letters to
you before that period perfect Jeremiads, Daisy ? "

" And afterwards, Mrs. Bertrand ? "

Daisy colored in spite of herself, and Lily flushed with
tell-tale warmth. Mr. Auchester enjoyed the confusion he
had created, and pinched the round arm that looked so
tempting through its white sleeve.

Though Daisy joined the badinage, her heart was not
very gay. As they paused, with the train coming down in
sight, she gave words to the thoughts of the last fifteen
minutes : —

" I am so sorry to have you go alone ! If there was only
some one to welcome you home ! "

There passed through Richard's mind a vision of the dear,
old, lonely home, and no sweet face to meet him as he
entered the hall. With rare tenderness in his voice, he
said, —

" Thank you. I shall know you are thinking of me."
Then he kissed both girls fondly, and stepped into the cars.
Another moment the train was winding round the curve,
half hidden by the foliage. Daisy's heart went down the
beautiful river-side with him. She loved them all dearly,
but she could have left the others more easily than remain
without him. She did not question her heart. Self-anatomy
was not one of her characteristics. She only felt that he
had been kind to her beyond any claim her forlorn situation
might have had upon him. Knowing her whole history, he
had freely given her a regard with no humiliating sense of
pity in it. The rest were all untried. The longer she lived
with them, the higher and keener her perceptions of honor
became. At times she shivered with a strange, intense
pain, as if she had been actually guilty, instead of deeply

unfortunate. In such moments her heart clung to Richard with hungering, despairing affection.

They chose the longest route by the river's edge on their return. Lily and Mr. Auchester kept up a gay sparring; so there was little need of her talking. At Mrs. Suydam's they took in Tessy, and by dint of slow driving they made it twilight ere they reached home.

As Mabel was asleep, Daisy went into the study, and talked a while with Mr. Chaloner. He had grown exceedingly fond of her. Indeed, she exercised a subtle influence over all she came in contact with. It was impossible not to love her.

Lily and Mr. Auchester had the balcony to themselves, where, after teasing him almost beyond endurance, she gave him some rare glimpses of her heart. Her love was such a dainty, delicious thing when she did bestow it upon him.

Their courtship was anything but a good preparation for the after life they were to spend together. Neither, perhaps, had any clear idea of the responsibility thus accepted. Lily's grace, beauty, and freshness had attracted him singularly, while yet an invalid. But for her the nurse would have had an unreasonable patient. He had never been ill a week in his life, and at such a juncture, when old friends stood ready to give a hand of cordial welcome to the young traveller, and his book needed his immediate supervision, it was provoking to waste his days in suffering brought on by another's carelessness.

At eight and twenty, with his many advantages of society, he considered himself quite an adept in reading women. Had he met Lily as the centre of some gay group, he would have been ready to suspect artifice and stratagem, because he was convinced, in his own mind, no woman of the world could be free from these vices. But Lily was so frank, so indifferent about pleasing, and enjoyed the ordinary events of life with such a thorough zest, that she invari-

ably brought sunshine into the sick room. As a background
to her picture, he beheld Mrs. Gregory, and the happy
wedded life of which he had sometimes dreamed. He liked
the deference Mrs. Gregory paid her husband, and the high-
toned affection evident in each little act, yet never paraded
obtrusively.

He imagined he could mould Lily to his will, since the
good substratum of principle was already ingrained in her
nature. There were certainly many admirable traits in her
character. And perhaps what fascinated Mr. Auchester
most was her generous submission when conquered or convinced. Although wilful in an eminent degree, there was
not a particle of sullen pride about her. He had an impatient longing to try his hand at governing the fair, high-
spirited girl while he yet lay ill in bed. And it piqued him
not a little to be compelled to sue for favors when all his
life, hitherto, he had taken them as a right.

At first, circumstances had conspired to mislead him. At
Mrs. Suydam's, when Lily had been in her most charming
mood, a slight restraint had surrounded her. And at home,
Mr. Auchester's visits had been generally by appointment;
so there was little chance for coquetry. Lily chafed at the
authority he assumed, but she was not long in learning her
own power — a dangerous knowledge for such a nature.
Richard had stipulated that there should be no positive
engagement between them, as he considered her too young
and thoughtless for so momentous a decision.

Therefore Lily queened it in an exacting, tormenting
fashion, and carried it all off with an assumption of ignorance, that he was won into forgiving even when most deeply
vexed. Yet it must be confessed he was not *quite* satisfied
with Lily's manner of loving. The hours in which she
seemed all that he could desire were rather the excep-
tions.

It might be that she had not yet come to the full time of
love, and was unable to concentrate her feelings in one

channel. He accepted the gay, impetuous child in trust for the future woman. He had a large share of both pride and persistency; and even when most tried with her, his determination for mastery over her heart never failed him. He knew if he questioned her closely about any troublesome matter, she *might* preserve an obstinate silence, but would never even hint at an untruth.

22 *

CHAPTER XXVII.

Love, thou hast pleasures, and deep hae I loved;
Love, thou hast sorrows, and sair hae I proved.
                                        BURNS.

But your red smile was too warm, Sweet,
    And your little heart too cold,
And your blue eyes too blue merely,
    For a strong, sad man to scold,
        Weep, or scorn you.
                        OWEN MEREDITH.

FOR the next ten days there was no special excitement at Rothelan. Mabel drove out frequently, and baby appeared to be in the highest state of perfection. Tessy fluctuated between it and the nursery at Mrs. Suydam's. Daisy was much with Lily, and Mr. Auchester fell into the habit of treating her as the others did — with an almost reverent tenderness. She diffused a cool and tranquil mental atmosphere wherever she went.

Mrs. Auchester and her family accepted Mrs. Suydam's invitation with evident pleasure. The day after their arrival she brought the ladies to call at the rectory. Mrs. Auchester was stout and matronly, but with girlish bloom and freshness, and a rich, cheerful voice, that found its way to one's heart immediately. Clara was barely medium height, but graceful, and not absolutely plain, though she paled beside Lily's beauty. Her arch, vivacious manner was extremely winning.

The baby was brought down for inspection. Clara amused them with droll descriptions of the only babies she had any chance to admire at home — little shining black children, dressed up in immense caps, and brought to " Missis " for a name; " except when my sister comes," she added, " who has the grace not to present herself without bringing a baby, solely to gratify my fancy."

Then she began to descant on " cousin Ulric." Both Mrs. Suydam and her brother had spent much of their young life in Virginia, with this aunt and uncle, having been early left orphans.

" You can't think how vexed I was because Ulric did not come to Saratoga. I was absolutely counting on it. And we had not seen him for five years. Now and then, some lady we met would speak of him, and half envy me my cousinship; great good it did me. But last night I gave him a lecture, I assure you."

Lily colored a little. For, after all, Mabel's objection to her becoming one of the Saratoga party had decided Mr. Auchester in remaining at home.

" He has changed so much !" Clara went on. " Do you know I felt quite afraid of him at first! He is as stately as a prince. I shall tease him out of his new-found dignity. But his book is charming. He will be spoiled by so much adulation."

" I think he bears his honors well," said Daisy.

" He's a darling," laughed Clara. " I think seriously of spending next winter in New York on his account. Fancy the sensation of being introduced as Mr. Auchester's cousin !"

Mrs. Suydam begged Lily and Daisy to accompany her home. Daisy declined, but Lily compromised by promising to come in time for supper, and spend the evening.

" You may as well begin visiting me at once," Clara exclaimed, " for if you do not I shall come to the rectory every day. Cousin Alice has said so much about you all, that I feel remarkably well acquainted."

" Clara !" said her mother, reprovingly.

" O, I haven't frightened them a bit, mamma. Perhaps it wouldn't be bad to threaten a call before breakfast."

They all laughed. "The only obstacle would be your dislike of early rising," remarked Mrs. Suydam.

Philip walked over with Lily about mid afternoon. Clara was waiting impatiently, and carried her off at once to her own room, where she made her repeat the story of Ulric's accident, and describe the party in New York. They did not come down stairs until the tea bell rang, when Lily was introduced to the gentlemen.

Leonard Auchester resembled Clara a great deal, and was still boyish at twenty. Fred, six years his senior, was much in the style of his cousin Ulric. He set about rendering himself agreeable to Lily, for Clara quite monopolized Ulric. Her gayety was contagious; and, as her sharp sallies rarely degenerated into sarcasm, every one enjoyed them.

They walked up and down the long balcony, in the summer twilight — a happy group, bright with youth and hope. Just inside the window Mrs. Suydam sat playing. Presently her fingers ran into the Olga.

"O, that sweet, delicious waltz! How it reminds me of old times, when mamma used to play it for us children! Come, Ulric!" and the next instant Clara had him whirling down the balcony to the wave-like motion.

They were passing up, when Fred exclaimed, —

"It's a shame for them to have all the enjoyment. Miss Bertrand, grant me the favor, please;" and he extended his hand.

Lily raised her eyes to Ulric with a beseeching glance. He bit his lip in vexation, then answered with one of reluctant acquiescence. Waltzing with any one besides him had been interdicted since he became her lover. Fred saw the exchange of looks, and smiled internally. He had considerable vanity, and was in the habit of appropriating the pleasant things of life, whether they were his by right or not.

They floated down the open space, fragrant with snowy stems of Madeira vines, that nodded from every column, as

if keeping time to "twinkling feet." Waltzing with Lily
was certainly the poetry of motion. The lovely face with
eyes downcast, the shining golden ringlets that fell and
floated around her, the exquisite shoulders and arms outlined through the flowing drapery, gave her a weird, Undine-
like beauty. Ulric Auchester experienced a nervous, uncomfortable sensation, akin to jealousy. He tried to strangle
it, but it proved too great for him. Could he have refused
permission without appearing ungenerous? Since he had
unwittingly set the bad example, he must abide by the result.
Yet a moment or an hour could not change Lily's allegiance.
Still, the white, slender hand drooping over Fred's shoulder
would give him a pang.

He took advantage of a half sigh from Clara to wheel her
around into a seat, and exclaim, —

"You are tired!"

"O, no, indeed! I could waltz all night. You surely are
not going to give up?"

"It's too warm for such work!" he said, decisively.

Clara found a fan, and began plying it. She paused, suddenly, to say, involuntarily, —

"How perfectly lovely Miss Bertrand is! And such
dancing! Wouldn't she bewilder the hosts at Saratoga,
or any other watering-place?"

A chill crept over Ulric, in spite of the summer night. He
tried to catch Lily's eye; he put out his foot so she must
brush past it. Both were useless. The hot, angry blood
surged to his heart in torrents, and his eyes darkened with a
new and fierce light. Never before had his passionate nature
been so profoundly stirred. The depth of jealous regard
startled even himself. By a strong effort he restrained the
feeling, and kept a calm exterior over these raging fires.
But in those brief moments he had a startling foretaste of
anguish and despair.

Lily paused at length, flushed, radiant, full of royal beauty
and brightness. Sitting down by Ulric, she disarmed him

with a trustful glance, that seemed to thank him for the indulgence he had granted. But to him she appeared just snatched from a great danger. With a total revulsion of feeling he bent his proud head a trifle, and smiled upon her. The little fingers crept caressingly over his, thrilling him with keenest enjoyment. He had hardly dreamed before how dear she was to him.

Fred sauntered towards them a little puzzled — perhaps, too, a little piqued. Mrs. Suydam sent for some cream, and in the general conversation that ensued, they planned a ride for the following morning. Clara had never visited her cousin's country house before, and was anxious to see its surroundings.

Lily and Mr. Auchester walked home. There was no moon, but the star-crowned night was none the less lovely. A faint breeze wandered through the hollows in musical monotones. He fancied he had much to say; but Lily was changeful and illusive as a butterfly, utterly ignoring the subject to which he wished to lead her. So they stood at the hall door of the rectory, he for once uncertain, and almost powerless.

"Lily," he began, rather abruptly, "I wish our engagement could be announced."

"It isn't *quite* an engagement," she returned, archly. "And you promised Richard — "

"Yes, I know." He made an impatient gesture. "Lily, you *do* love me?"

"When you are good to me — dearly, dearly;" and she stopped further questioning by her eager kisses.

A little surprised by the readiness of her caress, — for she was delicately chary in such matters, — he could only return it in silence. After some moments he said, with solemn tenderness, —

"I mean always to be good to you, my darling. If on any point I should think differently, will you not trust my wider experience, my more mature judgment?"

He could not see the half-amused expression of her face, but her silence seemed to promise faith in him.

When he had shut the gate, she ran up stairs to Daisy, in an overflow of satisfaction.

"You have enjoyed yourself," Daisy remarked, glancing at the happy girl.

"O, such a gay, delightful time! The Auchesters are charming. I believe Fred is even handsomer than — Ulric."

She uttered the name with a slight effort.

"And what else?"

"I waltzed with him, Daisy." She laughed in gay audacity.

"O Lily! — I thought — "

"Don't distress yourself, dear. His royal highness consented. Indeed, he led off by dancing with Clara, and I looked so imploringly he couldn't resist, or did not dare, before so many. I know he wanted to scold me a little on our homeward way, but for once I really managed him."

"Yet you knew he disapproved of it. O Lily, how could you?" There was a gentle reproach in both voice and eye.

"I think I ought to have my own way occasionally," Lily began, in a spoiled-child tone. "One gets tired of playing Katharine all the time to so lordly a Petruchio. It frets me to be good and obedient. I want to be equal; at least, to have my share of the power."

"After all, Lily, what difference does it make, when one is sure of being loved supremely? Are not men oftener ruled by affection than by any foolish supremacy on our part? And Mr. Auchester is older, has seen so much more of life than you."

"That's just it," returned Lily, petulantly. "He has had his fun and gay times, and I want mine. I was glad to show him to-night that his cousin thought me attractive."

"O Lily! Lily! what are you saying? Do you desire any other man's admiration while you have *his* love?"

Lily's face flushed hotly.

"I only want to convince him that there are plenty of people in the world who could have liked me."

"As if he doubted it! And if they do *like* you, Lily, what then?"

"I suppose I shall love *him* best of all, some day. Only, I keep wondering how this 'best of all love' affects one. And — I like fun. It gives me a strange satisfaction to tease him. Once in a while the chain grows too heavy, and slipping it aside, I draw in a long breath, and take a good run into some forbidden garden. After that I can endure the chain again. Did you ever feel thus?"

"No," Daisy said, slowly.

"You loved Robert *all* the time?" and Lily glanced into the soft eyes with earnest scrutiny.

"Yes, at first. I couldn't have loved any one else *then*. And if he had always been fond —"

A singular sensation compelled Daisy to pause. A suspicion flashed over her that if Robert could come back this night, it would not afford her the highest satisfaction. How had she come to realize there was a more blessed happiness in love than any she had experienced? Philip and Mabel were before her daily, to be sure, but she seemed to have gone to some other source for the knowledge.

Lily talked away her mutinous spirit, and with fond good-night kisses they went to pleasant slumbers — the one who had sorrowed so little, the one who had sorrowed so much.

The party rode over early the next morning. Mr. Auchester brought a horse for Lily, so that Daisy might share their enjoyment; but she shyly declined. He appealed to Mrs. Gregory.

"I wish she would go," Mabel said. "When my brother was up, he insisted on her taking more exercise in the open air. You haven't obeyed very well, Daisy."

"Please do," Mr. Auchester resumed. "I wish it very much." He bent his head a little, and their eyes met at the last words. Both understood intuitively. Yet it was not pleasant to be made his confidant, when all he needed was to hint a distrust of Lily, and ask from her a little watchfulness. She yielded, however, to what Lily had laughingly termed his " evil eye." It did shadow forth a curious power, difficult to dispute or refuse.

She went rather unwillingly, though she was the better for her exertion, and nothing occurred to mar their pleasure. Whether Lily felt a trifle repentant, or Fred Auchester made no effort to win her from her allegiance, could hardly be told. After a little he devoted himself to Daisy. He soon dispelled the prejudice that had risen in her mind. Indeed, he had made the art of fascination too much of a study to fail easily.

He kept a little attention to bestow upon Lily and his cousin. He fancied he should be able to determine whether there was anything deeper than friendship between them, but returned home in some doubt. Finding Mrs. Suydam alone, shortly after, he asked, carelessly, —

" Are Ulric and Miss Bertrand engaged, Alice ? "

Mrs. Suydam colored slightly, between the fear of saying too much and not enough, and answered, reluctantly, —

" Not exactly."

" I think his seclusion deserves commendation. I had no idea there was so much beauty hidden in this out of the way place. What lovely, sad eyes that little Mrs. Bertrand has ! But such a young widow — why, she could hardly have outgrown babyhood at her marriage."

Mrs. Suydam was glad to leave Ulric's affairs ; so she descanted somewhat upon Daisy's history. That there had been any cause for sorrow prior to Robert's death, had never been breathed beyond the family circle.

Clara became, as she had threatened, a frequent visitor at the rectory. She made royal friends with Tessy, and from thence up to Mr. Chaloner. When baby was awake she transformed herself into a most attentive nurse. Alice was a very satisfactory piece of babyhood, plump, white, with silky

brown hair half an inch long, and a cunning dimple in her
chin.   Every day Tessy reported progress on the baby's
eyebrows and lashes, the growth of which seemed a perfect
marvel to the child.

Mr. Auchester received word that nearly half of the Mountain House would be at the disposal of his party.   Richard
was heard from also, and the day appointed for their
journey.

Fred Auchester became deeply interested in Lily.   Ulric
watched her closely.   She would probably have rebelled but
for a counteracting influence.   This was from Fred, although
she supposed it happened naturally.   He managed that there
should be some moments and some places free from this
ceaseless vigilance.   Lily enjoyed these opportunities with
the zest of a thoughtless child.   She did not mean to be dis-
honest, she never even fancied there was anything to conceal.

Fred Auchester would not have deliberately set himself
about winning any girl's heart, not so much from a sense of
honor, as an ardent love of his own liberty.   He was accustomed to please himself first of all, without thinking much
of the manner in which it was done.   Most of the young
ladies he had met were ready enough for a flirtation.   But
Lily's simplicity and purity puzzled him a little.   She openly
laughed at his flatteries, and held herself above his familiari-
ties with a sort of regal dignity.   She fretted his vanity by
her apparent insensibility, but it made him only the more
earnest to succeed.   Consequently he manœuvred for some
hours when he could see her alone, or in the presence of
Clara, and was rather formal to her in general.

Ulric was compelled to be absent two days, as he was
invited to the city to meet some distinguished gentlemen,
among whom were two *savans*, soon going abroad.   Refusal
was out of the question, though he went reluctantly.   Lily
improved the opportunity of regaining a little of her old independence.   And so she floated down the sparkling tide
unconscious of danger.

CHAPTER XXVIII.

Alas! how love can trifle with itself!
SHAKSPEARE.

Why, then, to love and trust
Is but to lend a traitor arms wherewith
To pierce our souls.
MRS. HEMANS.

THE party at the Catskills brought with them hearts for
the most thorough enjoyment. It was to be a real holiday
for all. Even Richard laid aside his cares, and slipped
imperceptibly into a mood of indolent enjoyment. Indeed,
there was nothing else for him to do. His family seemed
inclined to dispose of themselves. Archie took to Philip
in a boyish, enthusiastic fashion, shared his walks, and was
most happy when he could command his attention for the
discussions that were the youth's delight. Tessy flitted from
baby Alice to Isabel Suydam, and occasionally strayed off
with Leonard Auchester, who appeared to consider himself
her special cavalier. The boyish element in his nature
found an outlet in these attentions. But Tessy did not
develop any flirting propensities. She gravely accepted
Leonard's escort and devotion, acknowledged flowers or
little favors with a womanly dignity that would have been
amusing but for its perfect good faith. There was no undue
forwardness to distress Mabel; so she only looked on with
a quiet smile.

Lily and Clara were inseparables, and sheltered themselves
a great deal under Mrs. Auchester's indulgent wing. Fred
and Ulric were their attendant shadows. Clara appropriated
her cousin when it suited her fancy, as she did every one

else. It was more difficult to break away from her, because she based her regard and privilege on pure cousinly grounds, and took the latter as a right.

Ulric found that in some indescribable way he had lost rather than gained with Lily. Not in regard, for in her fitful fashion she was more lavish than ever before. Yet it satisfied him less than her chary, piquant coolness. Fred's attentions could not be at all exclusive, for Lily's beauty and vivacity attracted others to her shrine. Among the lingerers at the Mountain House were several unexceptionable gentlemen, who saw in her freshness the same charm that had won Ulric Auchester months before. And this new life fed her desire for power and admiration. She seemed to ripen with a summer warmth, to dazzle with a swift, enchanting grace that stirred the pulses of those she came in contact with. Capricious, versatile, haughty, and gentle, by turns, no one could be sure of her next mood. Her fascination never palled on or satisfied any one. Ulric felt the tide too strong for him to breast, and resolved to wait and watch patiently until they came to quiet sailing.

The elders — matrons of three degrees — kept much together. Mabel had visited the mountains shortly after her arrival at Rothelan, and was quite content to miss some of the rides and walks that the girls enlarged upon so rapturously. She listened with evident pleasure to all; indeed, her apartment was considered a kind of headquarters, where every one went to report.

And Daisy? Perhaps it was not surprising that Richard should in some degree forget the others. Mabel's fond eyes had already detected the secret unconfessed to himself. Without exciting the slightest suspicion, she managed to give them much of each other's society. To Daisy it was a bright, new world, opened by the magic hand of Love. Her enjoyment rendered the mountains a fairy Alp, the falls a Niagara. The refined enthusiasm that was a part of her nature, and had met with no vent hitherto, came out now.

Her eyes deepened and filled with a tender, joyous light, the old shadow often disappearing entirely. And Richard took a strange delight in wandering alone with her — the sweet selfishness of ripening love when it longs to garner up every smile, every word, and to feel them particularly its own. What lovely, enchanting days those were! He lived in a charmed atmosphere. She felt the new life in every pulse, yet was too innocent to give it a name. And so it happened they often walked or rode happy in silence, save where the beauty of Nature in some of its wild groupings demanded words from the full soul, steeped in its perfect loveliness. They lingered in dusky hollows, where the moist odor of the trees gave out its peculiar fragrance, and the unceasing melody of the falling waters brought a dim and dreamy satisfaction, as if it was a retrospect of some past existence.

And when they chose to go nearer, to stand behind the snowy, rushing mass as it came leaping down into its bed of foam for a mere breathing space, and then whirled onward, sparkling in the brilliant sunshine, the scene was wild and enchanting. The rocky crests were dappled with pink and gray, or frost white, save where in some recess it changed suddenly to twilight gloom. Here a clump of trees stood out boldly in burnished green, or a bit of dead limb silvered with the double effect of sun and spray. The crested surge danced gayly along, breaking into richer intricacy, until the whole scene glowed in wondrous beauty. Yet what was that to the tender eyes turned full and earnestly upon him — the low voice whose sweetness found its way to his heart above the din of the roaring, dashing waters? He liked the timid yet perfect trust with which she clung to him, and dared dangers that made her tremble. Each day brought a new charm, a more delicious knowledge of the pure heart unfolding before him. He shut out the past. He wanted to think her true life dated from this happy present.

23 *

Lily was delighted with the scenery, also, and enjoyed many a pleasant ramble. But Mr. Auchester rarely had her to himself. Indeed, an intimacy with the boarders at Pine Orchard, a resort a few miles distant, soon sprang up, and called for daily drives back and forth.

Clara was not idle, nor did she allow herself to be distanced. She made a conquest quite speedily. A Mr. Vincent — grave, gentlemanly, and immensely wealthy, as Fred soon learned — became singularly attracted to the gay girl. Clara laughed over the interviews, and declared she took him into training from pure generosity; yet it must be confessed that she took unusual pains to entertain him, and that he evinced a decided preference for her society. As Lily was constantly with her, much of Mabel's oversight was necessarily relinquished.

As I said, Mr. Auchester endeavored to be patient. It was a difficult and dangerous struggle. Now and then, when Lily rushed daringly into proscribed indulgences, his eyes flashed and his voice trembled with suppressed passion. She was not wise enough to heed the signs; while he, astonished at his own endurance, rather treasured up than forgave, not so much from hardness of will as from the fact that she seemed never to think pardon necessary.

There were many delightful evenings both at the Mountain House and Pine Orchard. The last gayety of the season culminated in a hop at the former place. Special pains were taken to make the affair highly agreeable. When Tessy gained permission to spend an hour or two in the dancing-room, her joy was boundless, though sustained with spasmodic assumptions of gravity.

"And then for home," exclaimed Mr. Auchester. "Truly I shall be glad. Who would have thought we should find so much dissipation in this quiet place?"

"It's almost as good as Saratoga. I'm not sure but that I have had more real pleasure," said Clara.

"It has been charming — perfect," responded Lily. "I shall be sorry to return home."

"Is it really your idea of perfect happiness?" Mr. Au-chester asked, while his eyes forced hers to meet them.

"Perfect of its kind, certainly."

"And its kind is very satisfactory, I suppose?"

"I should be most ungrateful if it were not, after all the trouble that has been taken for my enjoyment," was Lily's adroit reply.

"I think we shall have something different presently," Mr. Auchester said, biting his lip.

"Anything for a variety," laughed the gay girl.

But when Mr. Auchester asked her to walk with him, she pleaded her dress, which must be put in order for the evening, and, with one pretence or another, gave him no opportunity to see her alone. After dinner the girls indulged in a refreshing *siesta*. Then Lily went down to the balcony, and found Fred and Archie reading.

"You are too late," Fred exclaimed, mischievously. "Mr. Gregory has taken off my august cousin. If you will allow me to try, I may perhaps be able to give you as good advice."

"I am in an admirable mood; so proceed," said Lily, archly.

"Suppose we take a little walk, then, while I collect my scattered thoughts, unless you are afraid of offending his high mightiness."

He knew it was just the sort of an insinuation to make Lily yield. He was forced to admit to himself that he had not won one victory over this charming girl, and it wounded his vanity considerably. He was not used to being thwarted in this fashion, and it increased his desire. If she would only forget every one else just a moment for him!

"You seem to stand a good deal in awe of your cousin," she said, with an arch gayety that quite took off the point of his speech. "And I am ready for the walk. Will you come, Archie?"

No. Archie was too deeply interested in his book.

Clara watched them sauntering down the path. "What a foolish child!" she said to herself. "She ought to keep her freshness for this evening."

Lily would have been very well satisfied if Archie had accompanied them. She did not intend to go far, but in the enjoyment of the walk and their gay conversation she soon forgot her prudent resolves.

Philip and Mr. Auchester returned presently. The latter lounged about uneasily until invited into Mrs. Gregory's parlor. Clara soon joined them.

"Where is Lily?" he asked.

"I saw her go off with Fred half an hour ago," she answered, with a suggestive little smile.

He generally ignored her attempts at teasing him, but just now he felt in anything but a tranquil mood. So they had a rather sharp skirmish, ending by his retreat from the field. He went immediately in search of Lily, as the best method of cooling his temper. The calmness of the past fortnight was breaking up like an ice-bound sea. Hard and jagged edges of distrust, suspicion, wounded love and pride, clashed together in his mind. What did the child mean by giving him this burden to carry? Surely she must love him in a weak, easily satisfied manner, not as he loved her. And the thought that he was not *all* to her, stung him with a keen pain.

With eager steps he sought her in familiar haunts, in vain. They must have gone some distance, then. The picture that persistently rose before him was not a pleasant one for a man in his mental state to linger over. With morbid quickness he recalled every incident since that first evening with Fred. Had they been honorable rivals, each endeavoring to win Lily, he would have regarded his cousin with a certain respect. But it was the acknowledged trifling that angered him now — that, in spite of himself, gloomed over his heart, and brought a fierce light to his eyes. The luxury of hope, the past enjoyment of bliss, and the solemn surety of a passion strengthening and deepening with every hour of his existence, turned into a tempest, and raged wildly through his soul.

Better that the fire had spent itself then, than that he, with one of those strong impulses common to self-centred men, should have smothered it. He said, with a cold, but determined mastery over himself, that he would be calm; and thus his eyes were blinded to the real crisis by the very feelings he was attempting to control.

The westward sun was sending lengthening shadows from tree and shrub, when he saw them come in sight, walking slowly, Lily apparently in her gayest mood. Some power impelled him to step aside and let them pass. Fred was carrying a bunch of scarlet salvia. When they paused at the steps, he said, —

" Here are your flowers. You will wear some to-night for my sake, and I promise to consider myself amply repaid for my trouble."

She flushed a trifle at his glance, and replied, —

" You are the perfection of cavaliers, certainly. I am obliged, and also glad to find you so easily recompensed. They *are* lovely." And she held out her hand for the bouquet.

Fred Auchester's first daring impulse was to press the dainty fingers to his lips; but he had learned a little by experience. He merely bowed, and held the hand in his some seconds longer than was necessary.

" I am all impatience for to-night !" he resumed. " The last brilliant affair of the season — isn't that *au fait?* And a crowd from Pine Orchard to help us make merry. But I think I know who will not be eclipsed."

" Your own self, for instance," returned Lily, laughing. " Such an event is not down in the almanac. There is no fear. But we must be late, for I hear the bell. Adieu!" And she glided through the hall.

" Where have you been, runaway ?" exclaimed Clara.

"Ulric went to look for you an hour ago. The young man is evidently on the 'rampage.' And, Lily, if he should ever become your lord and master, I think you would stand a fair chance of being 'brought up by hand.'"

Lily's eyes sparkled with a light compounded of pride and amusement.

"And those splendid flowers!" continued Clara. "Can't you spare me a stem or two for my adornment ? Where in the world did you find them ?"

"You may have as many as you wish," said Lily, arranging them in a vase of water.

"You had better hurry!" Mrs. Auchester exclaimed, as she entered the girls' apartment. "The supper bell will ring soon."

Lily gathered her shining curls in a net, changed her dress, and was presentable by the time the summons reached them. In the hall Mr. Auchester rose before her like a phantom, and drew her hand through his arm. Fred, coming a moment later, bit his lip in vexation.

"Where have you been ?" Ulric demanded, in a cool, stern whisper.

"Rambling, like the river in the poem, 'at my own sweet will,'" she answered, carelessly. "I must take my fill of beauty, for our stay draws to its close."

"I am thankful," was his almost involuntary announcement.

"Why? It is so lovely here!" and she glanced up with the childish abandon that had so often disarmed him. "Remember, I have not seen the whole world and all its delights. Daisy and I make Niagara, Switzerland, and the Alps out of it. I dare say, as I grow older and wiser, I shall smile over this enthusiasm; but now it is everything to me."

"Everything to you!" he repeated, with a bitter intonation. But it was lost upon her, for some one appealed to her decision in a trifling matter ; and with a suppressed sigh he held his peace, and listened to the merry badinage. All at their end of the table was complete enjoyment.

Lily might have lingered awhile with Mr. Auchester, but she pleaded dressing as an excuse for hastening away. He could not speak of the flowers without betraying a closer knowledge of their conversation than he cared to reveal just now; so, thinking if he procured some others it would keep her from wearing Fred's, he left her the more readily.

Something in his eyes and voice started a faint suspicion in Lily's mind. But she was too careless to heed it. She wanted her full liberty this night, and meant, if possible, to evade any opportunity for restriction.

Clara and she commenced the task of adorning with ready fingers. And yet, somehow, Lily dallied unconsciously. She brushed her shining hair until it was smooth as satin, and rolled off coils of golden ringlets. Early in the day she had decided on wearing white; so there was no discussion on dress. Daisy and Tessy flitted in and out, the child wide-eyed in wondering pleasure. Lily was in a generous mood, and nothing annoyed her.

"The music!" exclaimed Mrs. Auchester, as the band began their discord of tuning up, breaking now and then into snatches of inspiriting melody. "Lily, child, how slow you are! Clara is ready."

"All but my flowers. Lily promised to share her spoils with me. I should have had a knight sufficiently thoughtful to send me some sweet token of his regard. Come, divide your scarlet glory."

There was a light tap at the door, which Mrs. Auchester answered.

"Miss Lily?" It was Ulric's voice.

"Is to remain invisible full fifteen minutes longer," laughed Clara, cautiously peeping out. "What is your pleasure, my august cousin? I will undertake to convey any message to her chrysalis state."

Ulric smiled. "My pleasure and wishes, since I cannot

see her, are, that you will give her these flowers, with my regards, and ask her to wear them to-night. They are my especial favorites. And when may I have the pleasure of escorting you both to Fairy-land?"

"I'm glad you did not bring a glass slipper, for we want to stay until after midnight. These flowers are most exquisite. But some one has been before you."

"Tell her to wear these," he said, abruptly, turning away.

"I wonder where he found tuberoses?" Clara said, as she handed them to Lily. "Mrs. Kinston was frantic for some, and said she had sent everywhere. You'll have to bequeath me all the scarlet, now."

"No, indeed. I must have a little. Twist this through my curls — will you?" And taking some of the moss-buds from the edge of the bouquet, she substituted the salvia.

"That improves it," exclaimed Clara. "I don't like so much dead white."

Lily fastened another spray of salvia and a rose-bud in her dress at the throat. She did indeed look lovely. The beauty of her shoulders was enhanced, not hidden, by the dress of India mull, delicate as cambric. Her arms were bare, but clasped with Richard's gift, the pearls. The gleam of the scarlet flowers heightened the effect; yet in her secret heart she felt a little condemned for wearing them.

"You are perfect," said Clara. "You will charm every one."

"Even Mr. Vincent?"

"Poach on my manor at your peril! And now make me equally beautiful." Clara turned away her face to hide its uncomfortable warmth.

She was robed in a thin, gauzy fabric, whose black background sparkled with tiny golden wheat heads, clustered about with small, brilliant flowers. Her jewels were rubies, and with trailing stems of salvia in her hair, she looked bright and radiant.

Then they went to Mabel's room to be admired. They all felt the power of Lily's beauty. Daisy kissed her with a sudden impulse of affection.

"You do your family great credit," remarked Richard, with a bow of mock politeness.

Mabel had some charges to give concerning Tessy, who was to be allowed a brief glimpse of the gay scene, in company with Isabel Suydam. Fred Auchester made his appearance, announcing that the Pine Orchard party had arrived.

" And where's my little princess?" inquired Leonard.

The "little princess" was as grave and important as if she expected to undergo a court presentation.

Lily stood quite still until the rest had passed, for she saw Mr. Auchester waiting in the hall. They fell somewhat behind the others, and instead of bestowing a word of commendation upon her, as was his general custom, he asked, rather sharply, though in a low tone, —

" Where did you get those red flowers? I thought I sent you enough to wear."

" Thanks for yours; they are lovely. But I liked these, and Clara said they improved me greatly."

" And doubtless some one else will say it. Since you are not striving to please me, why should it matter? "

She glanced furtively at his face. It was simply impassible. It was too late for him to look hurt or annoyed. As they reached the ball-room just then, she evaded a reply.

24

CHAPTER XXIX.

Then go! the promptings of thy heart obey;
Despise the voice of reason and good counsel;
Be quite the woman, swayed by each desire,
That bridleless impels her to and fro.
                                GOETHE'S IPHIGENIA.

THE large apartment had been tastefully ornamented with evergreens and clusters of bright berries, with here and there a knot of brilliant wild flowers. The glamour of lights and music, the beautiful dresses that fluttered and settled themselves into a changeful, undulating sea, and the radiant faces, formed a most enchanting picture. To Daisy, as well as Tessy, it did seem veritable Fairy-land. She walked around with Richard, half bewildered by the sights and sounds. The waves of melody throbbing on the night air moved her strangely. The undertone of nearly all music is unconsciously sad. So she listened with a yearning heart to the violin's clear strain, the French horn blowing out deliciously tender notes, and the great clang when the heavier instruments came in grandly.

"You like it?" Richard commented, smiling down into the sweet face.

"O, so much!"

He was glad to see her thus happy. Indeed, the scene interested him not a little. Yet it seemed a long while since he had made one of such a gay company.

But when the quadrilles began, when the sea of beauty ebbed to and fro, when eyes deepened with enjoyment, she found it still more enchanting. Tessy's cup of happiness was full when Leonard led her out on the floor. And then

to have Fred, Ulric, and Archie by turns, quite completed
the little lady's delight. Before supper she and Isabel withdrew, well satisfied to go to pleasant slumbers.

Clara was quite elated by being sought out in a special
manner by Mr. Vincent. She seemed to care little for disputing triumphs with Lily, who grew more bewildering every
moment. A latent summer, warm and regal, blossomed in
her. Mr. Auchester resigned himself to what appeared inevitable. He *was* proud of Lily. He danced several times,
but only with her, and for the rest, walked with Daisy and
Richard, or watched the calm face that, amid this scene of
excitement, refreshed him like a cool shade. Some powerful feeling drew him to Daisy this night.

Quadrilles, waltzes, and promenades vied with each other
until supper was announced. Ulric would fain have persuaded Lily to retire, but she was in a most resolute mood,
so he crowded down his fast-rising displeasure. The flowers
on her breast rankled in his heart. Daisy had disappeared;
so there was nothing to soothe his chafed mind.

Again "viol, flute, and bassoon" filled the air with melody.
Again dainty feet twinkled up and down the floor, and young
hearts beat time to the happy present. Then a lull, broken
by a faint, quivering thread, that stole along like the ripple
of a forest brook; another stronger and deeper; and then a
broad, full chord of melody trembled on the air. Those who
did not care to dance listened breathlessly to the Zamora.
Several couples floated down the room, and the whole place
seemed pulsating with the wonderful rhythm. Standing opposite, Mr. Auchester saw Fred bend over Lily with an out-
stretched hand. She rose lingeringly, as if hardly resolved;
yet her eyes did not wander to his vicinity. She had no assent to require as she stepped into the charmed circle.

He watched her with curious attention. The slender
figure, the snowy dress clinging about her like a floating
cloud, the shining hair rippling over her shoulders, cheeks
of summer bloom, lips of summer ripeness, drooping eyes

with a slumberous fire prisoned in their depths, — how it all thrilled him! He thought of the night he had first seen her waltz with his cousin. Why was he not angry now? What did this cold, bland mood presage? Had she wearied him utterly with this trifling? For he seemed slowly turning into ice, or marble. The lights, the figures in the room, and the music drifted away as in a dream. Whither?

The crash of music ceased. The faint flutes blew out a lingering cadence. Fred led Lily partly around the room to a door, and into the hall. The buds in her dress had become loosened, and fell to the floor. Fred stooped for them. Ulric could see the pantomime, and his senses, electrically keen, translated it into words. Fred threw away the salvia, — it was withered, — and transferred the rose-bud to his vest. Lily held up one white hand with a playfully imploring gesture, and Ulric's eyes caught the sparkle of their betrothal ring. Fred was resolute. Lily yielded with a bewitching smile.

A moment before Ulric had thought himself all ice; now he was all fire. A blaze of jealous white heat sublimed every feature; his eyes darkened with a fierce and subtle power; his lips were compressed with bitter scorn. This was the one on whom he had lavished his manhood's proud, generous love — a foolish girl, who had no thought beyond admiration. He despised himself for being so easily blinded — he, who had always relied on his judgment — so rarely been mistaken. He hurried to them — heard Lily's false laugh. Stung to the heart, he turned at bay.

"May I ask you to finish your walk with me, Miss Bertrand?" he said, in a calm, cold tone.

Fred bowed politely and relinquished her. He gave Ulric a sharp glance, but read nothing in the impassible face.

Lily's heart beat rapidly as they walked up and down in silence. She knew he was angry by the portentous quiet, and fortified herself with arguments and excuses. At length she said, with daring recklessness, —

"What is your pleasure?"

He paused suddenly, recalled to himself, and returned, icily, —

"My pleasure is, that you decide this night to whom you owe allegiance. I am tired of this child's play. You cannot serve two masters when I am one of them!"

Every pulse of resistance within her mutinied, and she retorted scornfully, —

"Perhaps I shall not choose to serve *any* master. I confess the *rôle* of a slave is quite distasteful to me."

"Or that of a woman, either; or anything but a vain, silly child. I could have endured your wearing Fred's flowers, but that you should allow him to keep mine, as a memento of this happy evening, is too bitter. And I suppose he is ready to endow you with the love he has bestowed on every woman he has met. It is a most generous heart, truly!"

"You are unjust, ungentlemanly. He has never spoken one word of love to me!"

"Love! as if he knew its meaning!" and Ulric made a gesture of contempt. "I am done with trifling. I have borne all that it is possible for a true man to bear. I have been mistaken in you. Dr. Bertrand was quite right — we *are not* suited to each other. And since you so evidently prefer your liberty to any regard I can bestow upon you, which must necessarily abridge your power, I yield my claim."

His tone had been rapid, strong in intense bitterness. And standing in the doorway, with the light full upon him, she could see how stern and cold his face was. *She* sue to him!

"Very well."

Her voice had a prompt ring in it, that matched his own for firmness. She flashed back her curls in superb disdain.

He merely touched her hand, as he returned with her to the room, too courteous at heart to allow any one to triumph over her. The smiling faces mocked him in the blinding glare of light.　A subtle pride chained him beside her until the last bowing was over in the Lancers.　Fred kept aloof; but Leonard sauntered up, and after a few moments' conversation, exclaimed, with boyish entreaty, —

"There's that inspiriting Caledonian.　You might dance with me once more to-night, Miss Lily.　Can't she, Ulric?"

"As Miss Lily pleases," was the quiet rejoinder; and, as they took their places, he walked away.

In the hall he met Daisy.　His white, rigid face startled her.　Indeed, the control of the last few moments was avenging itself.

"What is the matter?" she asked, with sudden fear.

He paused to glance into the peaceful face, the tender, pitying eyes.　Like the rush of a wild flood his loneliness came over him, and he would have grasped at a straw. Instead, a firm bridge rose before him.　He noticed she had a shawl thrown over her shoulders, and with his first impulse, said, huskily, —

"Let us take a turn down the walk, and I will tell you. I need a friend sorely."

Indeed, his heart and brain were in a whirl of confusion. Wounded love, betrayed trust, jealousy, anger, and a sort of proud disdain, ruled him by turns.　And it seemed to him at this moment that the great want, the only blessing, of life was love.　He hungered after it with keen intensity, in spite of the grim giant of disbelief that stood ready to clutch him.

Daisy yielded to the arm placed with gentlest care partially around her.　She had been walking with Richard, who had just gone for a final glimpse of Lily and the merry revellers.　She suffered herself to be led away, thinking it would be but for a moment.

"You are so calm, so restful, Mrs. Bertrand," he said at length.　"The very atmosphere about you is peace itself. And I am weary, despairing.　My cup of life has come to the bitter dregs."

The sorrowful pathos of his voice touched her. Pausing suddenly, she read his face in the silver light. Deep lines of suffering were already written upon it, and it displayed a capability of keenest anguish.

"Lily!" was her exclamation. "In calmer moments I know she will regret this evening's gayety."

"Regret will be too late, even if it is possible for her to experience such a feeling. I have given her back the only thing she prizes — her liberty."

"O, no, no! Think a little. She is so young, so susceptible to outward impressions, and her whole life has been so free from care or discipline. And you love her — she loves you."

There was a pause of some seconds, when he resumed, in a calmer tone, —

"It seems curious, indeed it is quite unusual, for me to give confidences in this fashion; and yet I think you, Mrs. Bertrand, will understand me. It is mortifying to the pride of almost any man to confess himself mistaken as to the character of the woman he loves. But now, by the light of reason and cooler judgment, I must acknowledge Dr. Bertrand right. My passion for Lily was the first love of my manhood. Since the foolish dreams and desires of my boyish days, I have never cared to call any woman mine until now. I suppose I was blinded by her grace and beauty. And I fancied she *did* love me. It was such a luxury to quaff the first sweetness of her girlish heart! I tried to be indulgent. I yielded points my conscience disapproved of, for I knew Dr. Bertrand feared I might go to the other extreme. He said she did not know her own mind; that she was wilful, headstrong; that we were not suited to each other; and I, blind fool, rushed on all the more madly. For weeks she has shown that she cared only for promiscuous admiration. The true love of one man cannot satisfy her. It is well that I discovered the fact so soon."

"I think you are unjust to Lily. She is true and steadfast in her regards — not so fickle as she seems. If you could look into her heart this moment, you would see it filled with love for you."

"Do not try to comfort me in that manner. I am thoroughly satisfied that she *does not* care for me — at least in the only way I could accept. It is a bitter lesson, but to-morrow I shall be braver. I have shown you a bruised and wounded heart, because I know you, too, have sorrowed, and although pity from most people is unendurable, yours is sweet, sacred. Be my friend."

He took both hands in his with tender earnestness.

"Yes," she said, slowly; "I will be your friend. And your happiness, as well as Lily's, is dear to me. When I ask you to give her an opportunity to express her sorrow for this night's work, I know you will comply, difficult as it may seem;" and she looked into his face with pleading eyes.

"Daisy, it is useless."

"No; it will not be useless. Why should you two, who love one another dearly, be made forever miserable? You will find it sweet to forgive. And love is not such a frequent guest that he should be banned and barred out of one's heart."

"You take her affection for a certainty. No woman who loved could be so careless, so trifling."

"But an eager, thoughtless girl might. Lily's horror is subjugation. To avoid this, she has sought the widest liberty."

"And you know, my sweet little friend, there cannot be two kings over one kingdom. No; the dream is vain. Had she loved me truly, she would have given herself without any question. As it is, I can only regret, not alter."

A step startled them. Turning, they beheld Richard at a little distance.

"He is looking for me," Daisy exclaimed, hurriedly. "For my sake you will try — you will forgive her?"

He could not resist the imploring eyes. The pressure of the hand half promised.

Richard would have retraced his steps, but they soon came up to him.

"Truant," he said. "I fancied some of the 'little folk' had inveigled you into one of their midnight rings, and that you would henceforth be lost to mortal ken."

"Not so bad as that;" and she smiled faintly.

"I was to blame for carrying her off. It was a tempting relief to the scene within," said Mr. Auchester. Yet he did not release Daisy until they reached the steps.

She went direct to her room.· Richard noted the quiet, almost sad, face, but did not express any curiosity.

An hour after, Clara and Lily made their appearance. It was too late for conversation, and they were tired enough to go immediately to sleep. Lily's face told no tales.

They were all rather late at breakfast the next morning. Richard attended both Lily and Daisy.

Ulric bowed gravely.

"What absurd notion do you think this young man has been seized with?" asked Mrs. Suydam, after the first greetings were over.

"Repentance, after last night's dissipation," said Mr. Gregory. "I thought of prescribing a course for you all."

"Indeed, he is so little charmed by our society that he is going to New York in the first train. I am positively vexed. We shall all leave in a few days, and I am sure any business could be postponed."

"Any but mine, perhaps. It is absolutely necessary that I should go. And I think I have proved myself too fond of indulgence to return to business from choice. I *may* come back."

Daisy and Lily were the only ones who made no comments. Fred bantered his cousin a little, or rather attempted it, when a certain *hauteur* prevented further intrusion. A dim suspicion crossed Richard's mind.

There was not much time to lose after breakfast. Ulric said his adieus lightly, as he should soon meet them in the city. By an accident Lily stood quite apart, playing with a trailing vine that had fallen from its column. He went up to her quietly, standing with his back to the others, and quite hiding her. There had been a great conflict in the man's mind. But for Daisy he would not have made even this advance.

"Have you anything to say to me — Lily?" He swallowed a good deal of pride as he pronounced the name, sorely tempted as he was to call her Miss Bertrand.

It was not a tone very inviting to penitence. Lily's face flushed hotly, and her eyes fell beneath his steady gaze. She had persuaded herself that he was selfish and tyrannical. Neither did she feel sufficient need of his love to render her humble.

"Nothing." The tone was low, but he heard it distinctly.

"Very well. Perhaps it will be better to make no explanations until you return home. I will inform your brother."

She bowed indifferently. O, how sweet, how winsome, she was, even now! A word would have brought him back. She did not utter it, however, although she could not help feeling grateful that he should thus postpone the unpleasant announcement.

Daisy kept her secret. Lily filled the two succeeding days with all the pleasure that could be crowded in them. She would not think. A bright life was before her, and she resolutely determined not to shadow it by any misgiving. Love was easy to win. And yet she put something in her demeanor towards Fred that made him understand the real distance between them, and that his flatteries were as nothing in her eyes. He should not boast that she had broken her engagement on his account.

The excursion had been highly satisfactory, save to Lily and Mr. Auchester. And she proudly persuaded herself that she did not care. He fancied he felt truly thankful that the rupture had come so soon. Since she was unworthy of his love, this wound, bitter as it was, could be endured, and was to be preferred to a lifetime of unhappiness.

CHAPTER XXX.

O, Love! unconquerable in the fight. Thee shall neither any of the im-
mortals escape, nor of men, the creatures of a day.
                                        SOPHOCLES, *Trans.*

So with this.
The lines have under meanings, and the scene
Of self-forgetfulness and indecision
Breaks off, not ends.
                                        FESTUS.

ON his return to Rothelan, Richard was met by a letter
from Mr. Auchester, announcing the fact of the broken
engagement. He was too gentlemanly to indulge in any
severe animadversions on Lily's conduct, but simply stated
the case, and gave Richard full credit for his foresight and
good judgment. He allowed, in a most graceful manner,
that he had been mistaken in regard to himself, as well as
to Lily.

The thought that he had predicted it afforded Richard
small satisfaction. The spirit of Mr. Auchester's letter did
not intimate that the disagreement was at all trifling, or to
be easily overcome. He undertook to question Lily, but she
was haughty, and not disposed to discuss the subject. He
could not discern the slightest regret in her manner, and
this set him at ease with regard to her.

"I don't know what I could have been about for the last
fortnight, not to see how matters were going," he said, a
little self-reproachfully.

"No, Dick," Mabel returned, warmly, "you shall not
blame yourself for this. If I, who by right should have
been most watchful, could not gain her confidence, or

influence her, the fault is clearly her own waywardness. Mr. Auchester has acted commendably throughout, and Lily has lost a regard she may never find again. I regret that this sorrow should fall upon him; but she needs a lesson. She is too thoughtless and trifling."

Philip took the affair more seriously. Like Daisy, he felt convinced they *had* loved each other. He held Mr. Auchester in the highest esteem, and scolded Lily roundly for coquetry. Yet this did not punish her as did Richard's grave tones, and the implied condemnation in his eyes.

Philip and Mabel insisted that Lily should remain at Rothelan. Indeed, the former cherished a hope that a reconciliation might yet be effected. Mrs. Suydam had gone directly to New York with the Auchesters, from whence in a few days they were to start for Virginia, while she was to shop, and prepare for the journey with her husband.

Daisy agreed to the arrangement, for she felt Richard's home would be happier without Lily. Her tender little heart questioned itself as to whether there was anything selfish in desiring his comfort above all else.

The dear old house at Newark greeted them with a familiar welcome, as inanimate things often touch our hearts more closely than words. Daisy was soon settled in her former quiet life, after the rare holiday summer. Indeed, about ten days later, when Archie left them for a preparatory school, she found it necessary to make some effort to keep them from drifting into absolute loneliness. Yet she had never been happier. Lily's first letter was so gay and good-humored that she read it aloud to Richard.

She had been at home a fortnight, perhaps, when one evening Ann startled her by announcing that "Mr. Auchester was in the parlor, and wished to see her." Richard had gone to pass a few hours with some medical friends; so his entertainment devolved wholly upon her. With a flush on her face, and not a little nervousness at heart, she went down to him.

"I am so glad to see you!" was his first exclamation; and taking both hands in his, he held them many seconds. "Believe me that for days I have had an intense longing to see you, and hear your voice. I think I never knew weeks so long in my whole life."

She covered her embarrassment by asking after his cousins and Mrs. Suydam.

The Auchesters had left for Virginia. Mrs. Suydam had that day gone to Rothelan.

"I did not tell her until this afternoon," he said, abruptly. "We walked up Broadway, and from thence over to the depot, and had a long conversation. I extorted a promise from her not to make Mrs. Gregory miserable by her disappointment."

"Whatever pains you, must cause her sorrow," Daisy said, absently.

"More than that, I think. It has interfered with her plans for me, and she was remarkably fond of — of Lily," — he pronounced the name with an effort, — "and feels more deeply grieved, perhaps, than the actors in the drama."

His tone at the last was indifferent. A long silence fell between them.

"I kept my promise to you," he began, at length. "I did give her an opportunity of making some slight concession; but her manner then convinced me she had never truly loved me."

Daisy understood the feeling that prompted the use of pronouns. His heart was still sore, disguise it as he might. Her finest sympathies were aroused. She could not withhold them; in truth she did not wish to.

"I'm not sure but you will end by thinking me weak and cowardly," he said, with a dreary smile. "I know I ought not to linger over this episode. A brave man would tear it out of his heart at once, and go his way, making no sign. And, though hitherto in all matters I have troubled no one, it is a comfort to come to you when my restlessness becomes unendurable."

"Please believe that I want to be your friend," Daisy said, earnestly; "that I desire to share this sorrow with you, and hope —" but she had no courage to utter her hope.

"Not that I shall go back to the old love, Daisy. Every day I realize how unwise it was. I feel astonished at myself for being so easily blinded. More than once, in the past fortnight, I have paused, and asked what strange glamour enchanted the Ulric Auchester of six months ago. For then he was cool, self-reliant, penetrating, and not very apt to err in his judgments."

"Love!" Daisy answered, with a rare, sweet intonation. "And why should you be ashamed? Is not he who loves and suffers, a better man, if he bear his pain rightly, than he who dares not love for very fear?"

"Teach me how to bear it, for in your hands I seem a child."

"I don't know what I can teach you. Only, there are some dark days in every life, I think, when we seem to go down into a sepulchre of doubt, and in despair count the withered stems where we had looked for blossoms. But God's angels roll away the stone at length, and we enter the garden once more. Does He not mean that by going carefully over the path, we may learn a lesson for all time to come?"

"Mine has been learned in a sharp, bitter fashion. Experience is indeed a costly teacher. But O, the weariness, the 'aching void' that it leaves behind!"

She had passed through this fiery trial. Yet hers had been crude, unreasoning love, not possessing sufficient stamina for development. His was not so. Some electric divination told her he was struggling against the grand passion of his life; and because he could not conquer it, he shut his eyes to its full force, tried to bury it out of his sight. If he had loved less truly, he might have denied it altogether; now this was impossible.

What should she say? He would not admit the possibility

of depth or truth in Lily. On this point he was wonderfully
firm. He seemed to think he could have forgiven deliberate
coquetry more easily than this childish trifling and vacilla-
tion. And, though Daisy pleaded her cause with a sister's
earnestness, he met her arguments with simple truths, that
she could not overcome. But it was little comfort to have
Lily excused for following the inclinations of her nature,
when that very nature was proved shallow and insincere.
Yet he did not so much allege these things against Lily, as
imply them; therefore discussing the point was useless; and
not only that, but it served to strengthen him in his opinion.

It was quite late when he left her, as for some time he had
been making Richard's return an excuse for lingering. As
they stood in the hall, she realized the change that had come
over him. The glow and vivid life, that had lent such a
charm to his fine face, were fast settling into a cold and
bitter expression of weariness. Her tender pity shone out
of her sweet eyes, and spoke in her soft voice.

" Remember," he said, " you have redeemed the whole
race of women for me ; " and kissing her forehead, he was
gone. So profound was her sympathy for him that she saw
no danger in the promise of friendship she had given.

The next morning, at breakfast, Daisy mentioned Mr.
Auchester's visit. Richard smiled a little, but made no
comment.

For that, and several succeeding days, Daisy's mind was
continually busy with the lovers, as she still considered
them. She had too much delicacy to mediate unless her
services were absolutely required, and she could think of no
emergency likely to arise. She, who had done so much
patient waiting for herself, found this a hard burden to bear.

Daisy was, perhaps, more surprised by Mr. Auchester's
second visit than by the first. It was only a few days later,
and again he found her alone. Dinner had been finished,
Richard called away on sudden business, and Tessy gone
to spend a few hours with a schoolmate.

"Well," he said, when she had excused them, "I came chiefly to see you; so I am quite satisfied."

She colored with some embarrassed feeling.

"Let us go and walk in the garden," he continued. "The approaching evening is too magnificent to be spent in doors. Such a grand sunset does not always come at one's bidding."

They walked awhile, conversing pleasantly, and watching the dying day. The peculiar orange-red glow of autumn; the long, slant rays, like golden arrows tipped with flame; tree and shrub burnished in bronze; and the filmy purple dusk, that seemed like an undertone to the picture, lingering in corners and under leafy branches, gave a drowsy, shadowy light. A time for dreams or confidences, for tender talk or tenderer vows.

They seated themselves on a rustic bench, at length, their hearts steeped in the wondrous beauty of the scene. Presently Mr. Auchester said, —

"I have many things to tell you, grave little 'father confessor.' Where shall I begin?"

"With the very first." An arch smile lighted up her face as she said, "Once upon a time;" but her heart beat with unwonted emotion.

"I am going away — to Europe," was his abrupt announcement.

"O!"

Something in the voice startled him, and the unfeigned sorrow of her sweet face thrilled him with a blinding sensation, as if a new world had been opened. Thought and feeling rushed to a sudden dangerous centralization.

"Why do you go?" There was a perceptible cadence of disappointment in her tone.

"Mostly for the change, I think. I find my summer's experience has bequeathed me some bad habits — a restless, impatient dissatisfaction that I cannot dismiss or conquer; a something that tempts me to dream idle dreams, and seek vain speculations. As Alice will be away for a long while, I should certainly bore you to death. To save you from trouble, and myself from a desultory, aimless existence, I have accepted the position of private secretary to the Hon. Mr. ——, minister to Russia."

" O, I am so sorry ! " and then Daisy checked herself.

" Are you ? After all, what does it matter ? " was his moody reply.

" When shall you go ? "

" I do not know yet. Not for some weeks, I fancy. I should not have sought the opportunity, for I came home last winter quite tired of roving. Besides being somewhat acquainted with the new minister, my knowledge of the country and the language has so fitted me for the position, in his estimation, that he insists upon my taking it. The change and the active life will be a great benefit to me."

Daisy gave words to her thoughts, unconsciously.

" What *will* Lily say ? "

" My dearest friend, dismiss the subject from your mind. Nothing I could do would be of the slightest importance to her. She is perfectly free to follow her inclinations ; so am I. And since mine lead me into exile, so be it — who will care ? "

" I care," Daisy said, bravely. " This faithless, half-scornful manner pains me. It is not worthy of your manhood."

He rose and walked up and down the short path before her, his eyes downcast, his arms folded over his breast. What a singular power this child woman possessed ! Her words penetrated to the depths of his being ; roused, calmed, strengthened ; seemed to challenge the very truth of his soul — to tear away the veil from every insincere thought. How lovely she was in her pure womanhood, the honor and perfect honesty of her nature ! Surely such companionship would bestow new life ; her truth strengthen his world-weary spirit ; her love revivify the bruised and drooping tendrils of his heart, that stood sorely in need of repose, support.

He paused, glanced into the sweet face, and standing with the outward calmness of a statue, the better to sustain his self-control, he said, slowly, but with deep emphasis, —

"Listen, Daisy. I know what I am about to say will surprise you. It surprises me. And yet I shall utter it, feeling in my heart that it is a solemn truth. I love you. I think yours is rightly the nature to mate with mine. You are so restful, so patient, gentle without weakness, firm without obstinacy, and above all, so true. The feverish passion of the past summer has led me to analyze my own heart more closely. I need a woman who will take the trouble to study me a little. If I am unjust or exacting in requiring this, forgive me. O, I never thought to be such a suppliant; yet I, a proud man, sue to you willingly, cheerfully, for a little love. It is the great need of my life. One may scoff at the fact, and attempt to disbelieve it, but I think one never does wholly. It is a powerful law of a man's nature to love, to desire to be loved in return. And though you may fancy me weak and fickle, it is not so in reality. I loved an ideal in Lily; my ideal perished: what remains? Only the fact of a man's capability of regard, of love in its highest, holiest sense. And so firmly do I believe this, that I only ask you to trust me now. Give me years of probation, if you like; they will seem to me only as days in the light of my great hope. Daisy, say that you do not despise me; that in time, when I have redeemed my birthright, you will love me."

He still stood before her. Although he had not spoken rapidly, interruption on her part would have been quite impossible. Surprise at first kept her silent, then distress. What should she do? what could she say?

Do not blame him too severely. All the great passions and sacrifices of life are followed by reaction in a greater or less degree. Many a man from pique, wounded love, or honestly thinking himself mistaken in the woman he first sought, has, in a moment of disappointment, chosen her opposite. Auchester's first emotion, after the rupture with

Lily, had been extreme satisfaction. But the relief was soon followed by a yearning for some hope akin to the one he had lost. He would have been too proud to throw himself upon any woman's sympathy, even if distrust and really superior penetration had not rendered him a little suspicious. But all through his acquaintance with Lily, he had admired Daisy, and given her a high regard. The confidence, on that unfortunate evening at Catskill, established a still stronger tie between them. And now the desire of having some one to care for him when he would be far away in his new home, operated powerfully upon his feelings. In his present state her regard seemed to promise rest and peace, and it was worth an effort.

"I have offended you," he said, at length, seeing she did not speak.

"No, not offended." She motioned him to a seat beside her. Then, clasping her hands in her lap, she went on, with sad earnestness: "But I am sorry you said it. I could be your friend always, yet I cannot love you as you desire. I believe you have made a great mistake. I think you still love Lily — that she still loves you."

Her fearless manner startled him. Yet he made a little gesture of contempt as he returned, bitterly, —

"Even if you are right, what would it avail? · I cannot sue to Lily. I may have been wrong in many things, hasty at times, but God knows how patient I strove to be. I have no word to take back. Since she gave the offence and triumphed in it, does it seem likely to you that *she* will repent? Humility is not one of her characteristics. And the terms on which we stood were simply unendurable. It would make me wretched to accept them again. So you see a renewal of the engagement, without a radical change in one or both, would only bring misery. Do not think of it, Daisy; it can never be."

"Let us wait," she said, with a little sigh.

"I am willing to wait. Do not think I ask for your love

now. I only want some hope to take with me, so that the world will not be quite a desert. When time heals all wounds, and makes the tangled paths straight, I hope to prove myself worthy of you. For the present we will correspond, and you will see I can be both generous and patient. O Daisy, love has been bitter to me in the past; but I firmly believe you can make my future bright. I know you will not fail me; and in time to come I will answer for myself."

It was a cruel strait for Daisy. Her unwillingness to give pain, her deep sympathy, the thought that by refusing her friendship she effectually broke the tie between him and Lily, filled her heart with anxious and troubled emotions. More than this, she saw the great risk she ran of being misunderstood. She felt how impossible it was to love him. But she could give no satisfactory reason. It was rather one of those inevitable conclusions which force themselves upon the mind, and flash out of being all logical deductions.

He took her unresisting hand, and went on pleading his case eloquently.

" O, please don't!" she said, in a voice of pitiful entreaty. " I will be your friend; I will write, if you desire it; but more than this I cannot promise. I am sorry to give you pain, but better pain now, than disappointment in the end."

" I am content to leave the case to the future. Friendship is all I ask at present. And now shall I tell you something about my appointment?"

She caught at the change eagerly, yet unwittingly she gave him a great advantage.

Still she was troubled about the promise she had given, and, after he left her, waited some time for Richard. She fancied at the moment that she had sufficient courage to ask his opinion and advice.

CHAPTER XXXI.

How bitter a thing it is to look into happiness through another man's eyes!
                                                      As You Like It.

I cannot but remember such things were,
That were most precious to me.
                                MACBETH.

IF Daisy could have looked into Richard's heart, her light slumber would have been still more disturbed.

He had returned quite early, and not finding her in the house, sought her in the garden, as it was still light. These quiet hours with her had become an intense delight to him. Not dreaming of a visitor, he hastened down the path. A row of syringas screened the bench on which she and Mr. Auchester sat; so he caught the sound of their voices before he saw them. He could not mistake the import. Clear and decisive the words rang through his brain: "I know *you* will not fail me, and in time to come I will answer for myself." He waited in almost deathly silence for her to speak. Above the murmurous voice of the wind, above the rustle of the trees, he heard the beating of his own heart. What was her answer? Kisses, caresses, and whispered words? He turned away sick and faint, and lost what might have comforted him.

Retracing his steps mechanically, he passed through the hall, the little court-yard, and into the street, hardly noticing whither he went, so long as the place was unfrequented. He wanted to look his future in the face, for he saw clearly how it was with himself. His soul was unveiled. Instead of having buried hope and desire in the grave of a first disappointment, he found them here in their eternal freshness, their entire strength. He loved Daisy. How or when this latter passion had dawned upon him in all the solemn surety of truth, broader, deeper, richer than the other, and comprehending every want of his life, he could never tell. All minor dreams and affections had been overswept by this. Leaving behind youthful crudeness and evanescent feelings that he had once fancied must be permanent, his heart had reached the point where manhood's love caused it to throb with a pure and steady faith. This had come upon him so gradually that no struggle had occurred, no scruples had disturbed him. Sailing blindly over the summer sea of life, the deep, swift, rushing waters of a "too late" cut him off from the main land, and sent him drifting down a darker stream. Another had garnered the sweet flower he had transplanted from its ungenial soil, and caused to blossom in rare beauty. Another, who had all the world to choose from!

He was a man, and at first felt wronged, outraged. Jealousy gave a fierce tug at his heart. A certain strength and sense of power lured him on to the resolve of contesting the prize with Mr. Auchester. Surely *he* had a right to be heard. He could not give her up — his all, his second life. Every moment she grew dearer. He had never dreamed of loving in this intense manner, and every pulse quivered with the power of his emotion.

But what if Daisy loved Mr. Auchester? He remembered how from the very first she had admired and approved of him. He was eminently attractive. And Richard allowed that he had proved himself not unwise by choosing her. If *he* could win her back, if from any sense of obligation, any thought of gratitude, she gave him her regard, would it satisfy him? No, no. He spurned the thought. Love, spontaneous, above all doubt or question, must be his. This only could he place upon the throne in his heart.

And the future? He shrank from it with a pain so deep,

that, strong man as he was, he could hardly refrain from crying out that his burden was greater than he could bear. Wherein had he failed, that to him should continually be given solitary places to walk through, when his heart yearned for home joys, home faces, and tenderest tones? Every hope was swept away with this, every sweet dream that had unconsciously rendered life so bright. For when he came to disentangle the rosy web that had floated over him for months past, he found every thread was intimately connected with Daisy. How cold and gray it looked without her!

He rambled on in a vague, purposeless mood, until he heard the city clocks strike the hour of midnight. He could have prayed for the night and darkness to be eternal. Since the sweetest day of life had passed for him, what comfort could a new sunrise bring? The glory of all time had faded utterly out of his pathway.

He had said so once before, and proved — what? That a new affection could blossom over the ashes of the old. Would it be so again? Was this faculty of transferring feelings something inherent in a man's nature?

Not with such a love as this. He had come to manhood's full tide. Daisy met every want of his nature. The passion was the more absorbing, perhaps, because daily he gathered sweetness and strength from her in some subtle, indescribable manner. She gave continually out of her overflowing heart. She was peace, serenity. This was what he longed for now. Contrasting the two, his first love seemed only to have touched the surface; this penetrated the holy of holies, and became, as I have said, a part of his very life.

He came back at last to the shadow of home — the home that might have been so happy. How still and desolate! As if every leafy tree had a presentiment, as if the shadows lying so thickly around robed themselves in a deeper gloom. And going down the empty-handed years, there would at length be no happy voice to bid him welcome — no tender eyes to smile upon him. Already the chill of loneliness made itself felt in every nerve. It seemed as if a fair dead corse was lying there to confront him evermore.

Richard wrestled till daybreak. It might be that he, too, refused to let the angel go until he blessed him. At all events, he was calm, and his face had a high, saintly look, his voice an inflection of rarest sadness that startled Daisy. In order to strengthen himself, he delicately put a slight, nameless distance between them, resolved to be just to her if every step crushed his own heart.

Daisy tried to talk a little. She thought she had a great deal to say about Mr. Auchester's proposed departure, but she did not get beyond a few incidents connected with the fact. Drawing a long and desperate breath, she ventured to ask, timidly, —

"How do you suppose Lily will take it?"

"Do not distress yourself. He can never again be anything to Lily, you know," he answered, decisively.

Why should she suddenly thrill with her old fear of Richard? The solid ground seemed slipping from beneath her feet. Those past days of pain and desolation flashed over her — days when she felt he might justly be angry with her. Since then, how deep a tenderness she had discovered in that grave face! What made it cold, even to sternness, now? She wanted to grasp him, cling to him; yet some strong barrier interposed. She was pained to the heart, when at length he rose, and went out silently.

It was a long, wearisome day. No tangible grievance — only when she heard him enter the house, and then leave it without seeking her, she sat still and cold, as if stunned by some unforeseen blow. The day before she would have run down for a kiss. He noticed the omission, and fancied there was only one cause to which it could be ascribed. This gave him courage to proceed with his resolve..

Daisy made an effort to appear cheerful at dinner, and he

ably assisted her. Tessy's unclouded mood was a relief to
both. Afterwards, when she took her sewing, and sat on
the balcony, he brought an unfinished book, and read aloud.
Once he fancied she was inattentive, and said, —

"Does this weary you?"

"O, no." Then she colored, and looked embarrassed.

He kissed both girls good night before going out, and
Daisy, who had been counting on a few moments alone with
him, felt sadly disappointed.

Yet she was enabled to explain all this satisfactorily to
herself the next day, and terrible as the reality was, experienced a sense of relief. Richard had been called out quite
early in the morning, and breakfast passed without him. A
feeling of apprehension almost stifled Daisy. What had she
done to offend him? or was it possible that, in thinking
over their relative positions, his heart shrank from giving
her so much trust, so much love, and he was about to estab-
lish a new order of things?

She went to market with Mrs. Hall, and lingered in the
stores buying some pretty trifles for Tessy. During her
absence Richard had come and gone. Then she tried to
interest herself in preparations for dinner; but everything
seemed hard work.

"What an odd-looking note, to be sure," said Ann, inter-
cepting her in the hall.

Daisy glanced at it. "Why, it is a telegram for the doctor. Some one at a distance must be ill," was her exclamation.

Hearing Richard at the door, she advanced to meet him.
He smiled, but did not kiss her.

"This came for you a moment ago," she said, handing
him the missive.

He took it with an absent air, broke the seal, and at the
first glance a deep groan escaped him.

"What is it?" asked Daisy, in alarm.

He held it before her without a word. She read, —

" ROTHELAN, October 10.

" Lily has been thrown from her horse, and brought home insensible. Come immediately. We fear the worst."

It seemed so natural then that he should draw Daisy tenderly to his heart, forget his resolves, and all that he had seen and heard! She was so glad to pillow her head on its old resting-place, though she trembled violently !

" God help us all to bear it," he said, solemnly, after many minutes of silence. " It pains me to leave you alone in such anxiety, but it must be done. I will send you word at every opportunity. Our dear, bright, beautiful Lily ! O, I pray fervently it may not be as Philip expects !" Then looking at his watch, he continued : " I have scarcely another second to lose."

He did not release her, however, but walked into the office with his arm over her shoulder. As for her, she seemed to realize, in some indistinct way, that the storm brooding over them had at length broken. It may be that she hardly understood Lily's imminent danger. And yet hers was no selfish sentiment. It only seemed as if for the last twenty-four hours they had expected some terrible event to occur, and its coming had brought a positive relief. The shock restored Richard to his former self, and that was all she could ask at present. His farewell was necessarily brief, and though sad, its tenderness comforted her inexpressibly.

When she came to explain the matter to Tessy, she felt it much more keenly. Her voice was choked with sobs. The dinner, the dessert of cream that she had taken so much pains with, passed almost untasted. Tessy clung to her in wildest apprehension, and the two mingled their tears together.

" Mr. Auchester !" Ann announced, on her return from answering the door bell.

Daisy bathed her face and added a few feminine touches

to her dress, kissed Tessy fondly, and taking the telegram in her hand, crossed to the parlor.

Mr. Auchester rose to greet her with a cordial smile.

"What has occurred?" he asked suddenly, remarking her paleness and agitation.

She could not trust her voice, and merely handed him the note. Neither did she look up to watch the effect it produced.

There was first one of those almost deathly silences. Then he uttered a despairing cry, whose wild pathos unnerved her.

"My God! Lily dying! dead, perhaps! Never, never again to see her in this life!"

A sickening agony, a constriction of throat, of muscles, of very heart, seemed strangling him, and obeying a vehement impulse, he paced the floor hurriedly. Daisy saw that he was moved by the strongest emotion that could possess and conquer a man. It had conquered him. He had met the truth face to face in his path, and he was far too honorable to thrust it aside. The mortification it might cause did not now disturb him. It was the most passionate, tenderest regret, akin to that of Mary when she said, "Lord, if thou hadst been here, my brother had not died." If he had been there, if he had not relinquished the right of watching over Lily, of guiding in some degree her pleasures, her varying, impetuous moods, there would now remain the kindred right of going to her. Instead, he was barred out. His only privilege would be gazing on her cold, waxen face, when the sweet lips had passed the shore of speech. He knew now how beyond everything he had loved her.

He came back to Daisy presently, his face rigid and ashy pale. "I don't know what to say," he began, in a husky tone; "indeed, there is nothing I can say in extenuation of my conduct. For the last fortnight I have been wilfully, perversely blind. And yet, although I have forfeited your respect, I ask, as a favor, that you will believe it was from

) petty spite or pique that I sought to forget my attachment
Lily in another. For the time, I honestly believed I had
eased to care for her. Only some sudden blow like this
ould have startled me into the truth. I have been worse
than weak — wicked."

" No, no," she interrupted; " I absolve you from all wrong
intention. I read you better than you know yourself, and
am now, and for all time, your friend."

" Daisy, you are an angel! All that is true, and noble,
and pure in womanhood, centres in you. I, who have hitherto been so proud of my strength, my resolves, my cool
judgment, stand humbled and rebuked before you. O, how
can I ever atone ? "

" No atonement is needed," she said, simply. " It was a
mistake."

" I thank God, from the depth of my heart, that you did
not give me your love when I pleaded for it. If to the rest
was added a consciousness that I had betrayed your kind
heart, my burden would be bitter indeed. This exhibition
of irrepressible feeling cannot have surprised you more than
it surprises myself."

He took both hands in his, and looked directly into her
eyes — calm, pitying, not the eyes of love or disappointment. His face crimsoned from a sense of shame. She
ended his embarrassment by saying, frankly, —

" I shall not go back from my promise, neither can I
allow you. Whatever may be the issue in Lily's case, our
friendship remains a fact."

He shivered with dread at the terrible vision haunting
him. When he could command his voice, he answered, —

" Thank you. I do not deserve this consideration at your
hands, but how deeply I appreciate it no words of mine can
explain. I have suffered much in the past month, and there
may be a keener pang in store for me. To think of Lily
bright and happy without me, can be borne; but to know
she is lying in the cold grave, shut away from the home and

26 *

friends she delighted in, mouldering in unconsciousness, while the whole earth is beautiful and joyous, is terrible."

"God may deal tenderly with us," she returned, a confident faith lingering in her tones. She could not believe Lily would die. Whether it was because of the suddenness of the event, so difficult for the mind to take in, or a higher and more triumphant faith, she scarcely knew. As Mr. Auchester listened, he felt comforted, strengthened. His regard for her grew into reverence.

Another day passed, and another. Lily was still alive, but unconscious. A third with the same dreadful suspense, the same agonizing fear. O, what prayers went up to heaven for the dear girl, so precious to them all, in spite of her waywardness. Mr. Auchester came every day to hear. Still, he did not indulge in any fallacious hope in regard to Lily. In truth, if he could have at that moment knelt beside her, and asked back her love, it may be that he would not have done it. Forgiveness, tenderness, sympathy, these would have been his offerings; but love once outraged and trampled upon, held its own way with a kind of royal pride.

At length came a gleam of hope. The daily telegrams had been necessarily brief; so a letter was quite a luxury to Daisy. There had been, in the first hours of restored consciousness, imminent danger of fever; but, this happily averted, Richard spoke hopefully of the case. Mabel was quite worn down with anxiety; and as he expected to return the next day, he asked Daisy to come up in the morning, and remain, until some further improvement took place, with Lily. Mrs. Hall or Martin would accompany her to New York.

Lily had been riding with Mr. Joslyn on the morning of the accident. Her horse, usually gentle enough, had started suddenly, reared, and thrown her at the instant. The smooth surface of the rock on which her head had struck produced outwardly a severe bruise, and internally an injury, from which the gravest consequences were at first apprehended. As Richard spoke of the hopeless days and nights they had all endured, when Lily's life seemed hanging on the slenderest thread, Daisy's heart throbbed with the deepest emotion.

The tidings were grateful to Mr. Auchester. During his evening call, Daisy gave him the letter to read, and delicately busied herself with some trifle, that she might not observe how it affected him.

"If you will allow me the pleasure of escorting you in the morning, I shall be most happy," he said, when he had finished.

Daisy signified her willingness.

"Poor Lily!" and he sighed. "May she be wiser and happier in time to come. I suppose you have no idea how long you may remain at Rothelan?"

"Some weeks, doubtless. You see Dr. Bertrand does not anticipate a very rapid recovery."

"Will you write to me occasionally, Daisy? I have no other mode of hearing."

"With pleasure;" and Daisy's face brightened.

He remarked it. "Don't misunderstand me, please," he began, gravely. "While I confess to you that I cannot at present dismiss all interest in Lily,—do not care to, in fact,— you must accept the situation as it is. I shall go to Europe shortly. Thus sundered by the ocean as well as our own wills, it is hardly likely that we shall ever meet again. It must be my continual study to forget. I am glad human nature is so constituted."

"O Ulric!" she exclaimed,—almost the first time she had used his Christian name,—"you tempt me to make my favor conditional. Why should you and Lily, who *could* be so happy together, shadow each other's lives in this fashion?"

"I am not convinced that we could render each other happy," he returned, coldly.

"And yet you love Lily?"

"The time has passed when I could deny such a thing to you, my sweet questioner. But my love is not all that is needed for complete happiness."

"And if Lily repented, regretted that painful past, loved you — what then?"

His eyes drooped under her fearless gaze.

"Daisy, you are wild!" he said, vehemently. "Your love for us both leads you astray."

"No, it is rather your blindness. If one word from Lily can restore peace, will you not grant her another opportunity? O, I beseech you, for her sake, for your own!"

He was deeply moved by her earnestness.

"Lily will not say even that one word. Forgive me, Daisy, if I cannot bring my mind to sue where I have been trifled with, not once, but many times."

"I shall never ask you to sue to her. She gave the offence, and unless she repents truly, I have no desire to see you take up the old life. But in the days that are to come, when Lily will have long hours for remembrance, her heart may soften. She may discover how much she did love, how much she still loves you. She may be ready to make any concession."

"Well?"

"May I send for you then, if she wishes it?"

"Daisy!" His voice had a quivering sound, as if it came over a sob.

"You will grant me this," she pleaded. "Your happiness is so dear to me that I think you may trust me not to ship-wreck it. I shall have better opportunities than any one else of learning the state of Lily's heart. I ask you only to accept your own happiness."

"O, child," he said, "you hardly know what you are undertaking. I cannot believe. It will never, never be."

"But if it should come! If in those hours of solitude Lily's heart should send up a yearning prayer for what she has so heedlessly cast away, you will be pitiful, you will answer!"

There was a long silence. His breath came rapidly. His whole frame trembled in the powerful contest. The clinched fingers, white and almost bloodless, indented deeply into his hand ; yet he felt no pain.

" Daisy," he said, at length, in a slow, faltering voice, " you have conquered. I put my heart, my very life in your keeping. I dare not hope, but I *will* wait. Yet remember, it must be Lily's desire solely. 'No influence must be brought to bear upon her. If of her own free will she expresses sorrow, regrets the past, and can so far put aside pride as to acknowledge this to me, I will come. If not, do not grieve unnecessarily for me. I shall bear all the rest with the courage of a man, and never again pain you by an unworthy weakness. O, my darling friend, how much you have been to me ! "

They clasped hands silently at their parting. And on the morrow his deferential tenderness had in it the highest respect, the most perfect confidence. Daisy little guessed, when she left him at the New York depot, how long he stood watching after the cars were in motion.

CHAPTER XXXII.

There are inscriptions on our hearts which are never to be seen except at
dead low tide.   BULWER.

I thought I held in my hot hand my life crushed up: I could have tost
The crumpled riddle from me, and laughed loud to think what I had lost.
A bitter strength was in my mind ; like Samson, when she scorned him — blind.
                                                    OWEN MEREDITH.

IT was a lovely autumn day, and Daisy found no incident
to disturb her journey.   She had hardly risen from her seat
when they arrived at the station, before she caught sight of
Richard's face, as it passed the car window.   And then she
was welcomed with a smile that said so much.

"You asked Martin to bring you to the depot, I hope?"
he said, as he was handing her into the carriage.

"No, for a better attendant offered.   How is Lily?"

"Very comfortable.   If fever doesn't set in, she will do
nicely.   But the anxiety has told a good deal upon. Bel,
though I suppose baby made it worse for her.   Alice has
thriven beautifully.   I am so glad you could come."

"You have all been so kind to me that it is a pleasure to
find myself useful."

It was gratitude that spoke then, he thought, and a desire
to render favor for favor.   Then they talked of the accident,
and how it had fared with Lily.   Richard was pleased to see
her looking so bright and well, and though the old pang
smote his heart, he put it resolutely away, and was cheerful.
She, glad to find him so like the Richard she best loved, and
not being pained by coldness, forgot the brief hours that had
been so terrible to her.

Mabel's welcome was fond and sisterly. Baby Alice had grown almost out of recollection, but soon made friends. The change in Lily was greater than Daisy had dreamed of. At the first glance she did indeed seem dead. Besides the gray pallor, her face had a wan, pinched look; the lips, always so brilliant and laughing, were rigid and ashen-hued; and every feature contracted, as if with intense suffering.

There would not be much to do: To sit and watch that no change might take place without due observation, give her a little nourishment or medicine, keep the room dark and quiet, were all the instructions Daisy received. Except that for herself she was to spend two hours out of doors every day, and be occasionally relieved by Mabel, so the confinement should not become tiresome.

She could not decide at first whether Lily recognized her or not. The poor child slept almost continually, or looked about with vacant, staring eyes, and seldom uttered a word. Daisy was, if possible, more shocked than by the announcement of the accident. Richard left them that afternoon, promising to be up in a few days, or if any change for the worse occurred, he was to be sent for immediately.

For a week there was not much perceptible improvement in Lily. Yet nature was silently and powerfully awakening the dormant strength and energy. She began to talk a little, evince a desire for certain dishes of food, and show her pleasure when any one entered the room. Richard made them all joyful by pronouncing her recovery certain. Daisy, watchful and tranquil, kept her place without a sign of fatigue. Once in three or four days she wrote to Mr. Auchester; but the subject so near both hearts was never touched upon.

When her amendment became positive, Lily's youth and good constitution made it rapid. They were astonished to see how she gained daily. The deathly paleness vanished; her eyes grew lustrous; the old dazzling smile came back; and little petulances, so like Lily, announced a return of her proper self.

Mr. Joslyn was most devoted. Choice fruits were sent over, such as could only have been obtained by a journey to the city, Daisy well knew. Rarest flowers, calls, not only from him, but from his mother and sisters, who evinced the warmest interest in Lily. It gave Daisy a strange, painful presentiment. She learned from Mabel that he had been Lily's constant attendant since her return from the Catskills.

"It has troubled me much," Mabel said; "but Philip judged wisely, that thwarting her would only make her the more resolute, and perhaps lead her to accept Mr. Joslyn. He insists that she really loves Mr. Auchester."

Daisy experienced a sudden impulse to confide her secret to Mabel. But she knew that under some circumstances it ought never to pass her lips, and refrained.

And then one day an unaccountable change came over Lily. She appeared well as usual in the morning, but by noon had grown strangely restless. Daisy questioned her gently, but received most unsatisfactory replies, and for the remainder of the day, Lily bestowed the merest monosyllables upon her attendant. There was, withal, a visible impatience, mixed with a sort of sullen resolve to bear alone whatever oppressed her. It pained Daisy, and gave her no little uneasiness, when she found that Lily had a fever for several hours, and not the slightest desire for her supper.

"If you would try some of these grapes," suggested Daisy; "or a piece of the pine-apple, which is a great rarity at this season."

"I wish you would take it all away," said Lily, fretfully. "I'm not worth that trouble to any one. And if you'll stay down stairs, and let me be quiet, I think I can go to sleep."

Poor Daisy! For the last two hours she had been reading, and scarcely stirred, lest Lily might feel herself watched. But in spite of the quiet, even at nine in the evening, Lily's voice had a wakeful sound, and her eyes were heavy, with purple shadows underneath. Something had gone wrong. Daisy vainly tried to find a cause for offence.

Richard came up the next morning. After asking Lily a few questions, he sought Daisy.

"Were there any visitors in yesterday to see Lily?" he inquired.

"No."

"She sat up too long, or talked too much. I find her feverish, and in a very irritable state."

"Not from either of those causes," replied Daisy. "She only sat up once yesterday, — hardly an hour, — and was unusually quiet. Yet I noticed she had some fever."

"Strange!" was Richard's grave remark. "She has the appearance of being strongly excited or annoyed. Has she worried about anything?"

"Not outwardly. I tried to learn the cause of her disquietude, but in vain."

"See if you can win it from her. I am afraid it will retard her recovery."

Then their eyes met, and both colored with a conscious knowledge, though each was wrong as to the cause in the other.

"Never mind," he continued, hurriedly. "Don't distress yourself. If Lily will indulge in unreasonable moods without the slightest cause, she ought to bear the penalty alone. I am sorry for her, but the fault is not in the slightest degree yours. Have Bel and the baby up here frequently, and don't seem to notice her."

Even if Daisy had been so minded, she could have learned nothing from Lily, who was, if possible, more reticent, and certainly more miserable, every hour. Her fever increased.

Late on the following day Mr. Joslyn brought a beautiful bouquet. He kept Daisy for some time in the hall, talking to her. As soon as released, she ran up stairs.

"Are they not lovely?" and she held them before Lily. "A Cape jasmine, and some orange blossoms. Will the odor be too strong if I leave them in here a while?"

"I don't want them! Take them away! And I wish —

27

Mr. Joslyn wouldn't bring any more," said Lily, with flushed face and contracted brow.

"Well," was Daisy's quiet rejoinder. Placing them in the adjoining apartment, she lingered a while. When she returned Lily was in tears.

"Have I distressed you?" she asked, in a tender tone.

"No."

Lily winked away the tears resolutely, and crowded down a great sob, that seemed like a ball of fire in her throat. Then she suddenly turned her face, and said, in a half-smothered, passionate manner, —

"O, I don't know what to do! I am so wretched! Why couldn't I have died in that fearful time! They had no hope for me, and I shouldn't have suffered any pang of separation. But to live this dreary, dreary life!"

"Why should it be dreary, Lily?"

"I can't reason; I never could. I only know it *is*."

"When you are well enough to go out, you will feel differently about it."

"I don't want to go out. If I could stay here forever, and see no one but you, and Bel, and Richard, it wouldn't be so hard!"

"Dear Lily, God has seen fit to bring you through a great peril, and surely He will send nothing that will not be for your good."

"Do you believe *He* sends everything? Doesn't it seem rather as if He sometimes let people go plunging into all sorts of wrong and trouble, until 'they stick fast in the mire, where no ground is'? And then everything becomes so dreary, so dreary!"

"They cried unto the Lord, in the days of the Psalmist."

"If that was all, I could find it in my heart to cry continually. But I don't know how to turn in this world. Everywhere a face meets me. I cannot hide away from it. And because I have been so wrong, and find myself all tangled up in such a web, — if I could go out of life quietly —"

Daisy's heart beat with high hope. She made an effort to steady her voice, and said, slowly, —

"God has some work for you still to do — some happiness for you yet to enjoy. With Him all things are possible."

"But I can't undo anything. I was so wild, so utterly thoughtless! I don't know what possessed me, unless it was an evil spirit. But I did not mean — " and her voice failed through weeping.

Daisy kissed her tenderly.

"Has Mr. Joslyn been here every day?" she asked, at length.

"Yes."

Daisy hesitated a little, not feeling quite sure of her ground.

"He sent the flowers. I heard him talking to you. And he has sent many things. O, I wish I had never seen him!".

Daisy scarcely knew what comment to make.

"What has he said about the accident?"

"He feels sadly distressed. He told me, one morning, he knew the blame ought all to rest upon him. No one rejoices more at your recovery."

"He is so good! But it wasn't his fault. May I tell you, Daisy? Perhaps I shall feel better after I have talked it over. I don't know how I came to tell him that the affair with — with Mr. Auchester was ended. Instead of keeping him away, I let him come. I thought I could prevent his caring very much about me. But I suspect *that* had begun long before. I did stop him several times from saying anything pointed, and tried to act so that he would see the intimacy, on my part, was for mere pleasure. The morning of our ride he was real serious. I evaded him carelessly; but presently he laid his hand on my horse's neck, and said, determinedly, 'Miss Lily, I won't be put off in this fashion any longer! You shall tell me —' I knew what was coming, and hit Bess a hard cut with the whip. She started violently. I thought I had the reins in my hand — I don't know how it ever came, but it was a fragment of my dress instead. I tried to grasp the bridle, but Bess threw me like a flash. I suppose she was as much frightened as I. If the rock had not been there, I might have escaped serious injury. As it is, I have made you all a great deal of trouble."

"And you do not love Mr. Joslyn," Daisy said, greatly relieved.

"Love him? O, no! I sometimes wish I did. He is so generous, so warm-hearted! He hasn't a mean or selfish thought, and his wife would reign a very queen. I am afraid they all like me too well. I did resolve, a few days ago, to — please him, but I cannot;" and Lily shivered violently.

"Why?" Daisy was observing her narrowly.

"Because I *cannot* make myself love him. Is it not curious that the heart should decide against a person who is in every respect worthy, who would take pleasure in devoting to one his whole life? Why not love one good man as well as another? Yet I know I should make him wretched."

"O, it would be wrong, wicked, to hold out hope to him," Daisy exclaimed, vehemently.

"I know it. For even if I promised, I don't think I ever *could* marry him. But to disappoint him so bitterly! And yet I suppose I must get well, and go through with it all — tell him how little I meant, how selfish and heartless I have been. It seems as if good and honorable people will despise me henceforth. I hate myself! It is all 'blackness of darkness.'"

"'So when they cried unto the Lord in their trouble, he delivered them out of their distress,'" repeated Daisy.

"What a comfort you are! After all, it is best to meet the result of one's wrong-doing fairly and without evasion. And I have been very wrong."

"Dear Lily, when we have confessed this, God will give us strength for the rest, and peace, and happiness."

"No; I shall never be happy again. I don't mean on account of any one particular event," — and Lily colored violently, — " but life changes so much. Every bright thing fades away, and leaves you only a cold, gray shadow. Maybe it is the autumn and the mournful winds that make me feel so dreary; but I know there can never be another spring to my life."

"There is a ripe and glowing summer yet to come. One shadow can never stretch through all time."

"I think I must be content to sit in the shade, without spring or sunshine. Forgive me, darling, for all the trouble I have caused you. I will try and be a better girl."

Lily turned away her face, and Daisy felt it would be unwise to continue the conversation. Although she expressed no special regret for the lost love, Daisy gathered that it was still strong upon her. She had little fear of the final result. And now that the ice had been broken, she could gradually lead Lily to a better state of mind. There was a visible improvement in her on the following morning. She went out to the sitting-room, admired Mr. Joslyn's flowers, and seemed resolved to be rarely good-humored with everything. But though she discussed the gentleman freely, and regretted her behavior towards him with sincere earnestness, she seemed resolutely resolved to date her unhappiness no farther back than that. She did not shun any mention of their stay at the Catskills, but refrained from alluding to the relation that had existed between herself and Mr. Auchester. In vain Daisy tried to lead the conversation to this point. She fully understood the delicacy of her position, that while attempting to mediate between them, she must in no wise compromise Mr. Auchester's sensitive pride.

Accident brought about the result at last. Lily was gaining rapidly again. Richard desired her to be very careful, for the least over-exertion brought on a most distressing headache and a recurrence of the fever. Lily was really

27 *

glad to be excused from visitors; in her present mood she wanted no one but Daisy. She walked about her two rooms, but had not yet ventured down stairs at the commencement of the fourth week.

She was dressed in a pretty wrapper, and lying on the lounge in the sitting-room, still pale and somewhat thin, but not, as she expressed it, "altogether frightful." Daisy had curled her hair, which Philip declared the greatest improvement that could have been made. After reading aloud to her the psalms for the day, Daisy took up a little dress she was embroidering for Alice, and to please Lily, sang some old ballads. This morning it was "Lord Jamie Douglas." She noted the scornful yet approving smile that crossed Lily's face at the verse, —

> "I whispered in at my lord's window,
> Yet never a word would he answer me.
> Fare ye well, then, Jamie Douglas;
> I care as little as ye care for me."

But at the last, where true love triumphs over all, Lily turned away her face, and presently fell into a light slumber.

Daisy bethought herself of a letter to Mr. Auchester that she had been prevented from writing the day before. Opening her desk that stood on the table, she went rapidly over two pages. Then she began to wonder whether she should ever be able to send him the fruit of her faith in Lily. All this time he had waited patiently, asking no questions; but soon his departure would put it out of her power to do anything for them. Indeed, *could* she do anything?

Lily stirred, opened her eyes, and closed them again. The girls were at opposite sides of the room, the little wood fire on the hearth shining out between them. The atmosphere without was soft, mellow, and hazy, the sun partially obscured by drifting clouds, only breaking forth now and then, with a rosy orange hue.

Lily's tone was more careless than curious as she asked, —

"What are you writing?"

"A letter," answered Daisy, with a slight flush and hesitation.

"How odd! Is it to Dick? I expect he misses you sadly."

"No; it is to Mr. Auchester."

Lily gave a violent start, and flushed redly.

"He is going to Europe shortly," Daisy went on, keeping her voice steadier than the throbbing at her heart. "He has accepted a governmental appointment, and will be absent three years at least."

"You have seen him," Lily assumed, faintly.

"Yes; he had been over twice before the day of the accident, and after that came regularly. He was very anxious about you, and asked me to write as frequently as I could."

"Shall you write to him while he is abroad?"

"Perhaps." Daisy made an effort to keep her face tranquil.

There was a long, long pause. Daisy bit the end of her pen-holder, and considered what to say next.

Lily spoke. Her voice was low, as if there had been a great struggle, and she was hardly sure of it.

"I can think how it will end. I am glad you will both be happy. You are the only woman in the world good enough for him."

"O Lily! you are quite mistaken. There can never be any sentiment warmer than friendship between us."

"Why, Daisy? Is it quite impossible for you to love again?"

"You do not consider whether Mr. Auchester's affection can be transferred at a moment's notice."

"There would be nothing to transfer," she answered, bitterly. "His fancy for me has perished. I question whether it ever amounted to positive love."

"Lily!"

"Yes,"— Lily raised herself a trifle in her excitement,—

"he thought he loved me, but events proved he had a much higher regard for his own will."

"And you!"

"I couldn't endure being tyrannized over like a baby."

"And so. you bestow this tyrant on me?" Daisy could not forbear smiling.

"I mean—" and Lily flushed hotly—"I don't know that I can make you understand; but Mr. Auchester *is* a really superior man—grand in many things, capable of loving with devoted earnestness. He would make some woman entirely happy. I want to do him full justice. But all the sharp points in our natures were forever coming in contact. And so you can see how he needed some one better and nobler, who would study to please him—to whom his wishes would be positive delights. I'm not sure but he would be very indulgent in that case. Instead of derogating from this woman, I acknowledge she would be very much my superior."

"I question if he would love her as well. It is not, after all, so much what is fit for us as what satisfies us; and I think, in the majority of cases, one's own heart decides rightly. But if you understood so perfectly what was needed, why did you not conform more to his will?"

"Because it isn't in me. I can't be good. I shall always be a trouble to myself and every one else. I shall always rush through brambles and thorns for something that looks bright beyond, and find it only a Dead-Sea apple."

"Yes, if you depend solely on yourself. But God means we shall look to him in the great straits of life, ask him for strength. He stands ready to lead us out of by and forbidden places."

Lily's eyes filled with tears. "You are so sweet," she said; "so good. And yet somehow God gave you a great deal of sorrow. Isn't it so all through life? Don't the fragrance and beauty drop out just as one reaches forth a hand to gather the flowers, and one finds withered leaves instead?   And to go on weary, waiting, hungering for what will never come!"

Daisy smiled over the perversity and inconsequent reasoning.   She knew there were many places on the green and sunny shore of peace that Lily dared not linger over, but glided lightly by, as one does on broken ice, and that her heart was longing for the ark from whence it had flown.

"Lily," she said, "why do you not go back, and confess you have been wrong?   You had in your hand all that any woman can have; you blindly threw it away.   You taxed Mr. Auchester's love, and faith, and patience to the utmost, and in one fatal moment it gave way.   Is it wise to sit over the ruins, and make them stumbling blocks for all the future years?   You cannot deny to yourself that you loved him. And in some solitary hours, in some spasm of the better nature struggling within you, your heart will refuse the pottage, and cry out for its lost birthright."

" You think me altogether to blame," replied Lily, warmly. "He was often unjust and unreasonable for a mere trifle. And if he knew me at all, he must have known that in my heart I cared for no one but him.   Was it pleasant, think you, to be continually watched and suspected? taken to task for a word or a laugh? Ulric Auchester's jealousy is a very tiger."

" You must confess, Lily, he bore many things patiently. What proof did you ever give him of your love? How could he trust, when he knew the beacon liked to dazzle with false lights? When you showered favors, that he had sued for, on newer faces, and gave him some little fragment, why should he have been content? You are sorry that your heedlessness has caused and will cause Mr. Joslyn so much suffering; but have you no thought for the man who had a right to build all his future on your love? Think, Lily, he should have been your prince — your pride and joy. Do you believe, if you had loved as he desired, he would have proved distrustful?"

Lily was silent. The voice that she had never been wholly able to stifle smote her heart bitterly.

"Well," said she, wearily, "it is all over. No matter whose the fault, it is done, past recall. The sooner we forget, the better for both."

"No; there is a wiser course."

"What?" Lily glanced up eagerly. Their eyes met, and she read it all without a word. Burying her face in the pillow, her whole frame shook with the effort she made to repress her emotion. She murmured, brokenly, —

"No; I couldn't, I couldn't, Daisy. And then he doesn't care for me now. It is right and just that he should despise me. He will find some one better."

"I think the woman a man loves truly is always the best to him. And if her love proved stronger than her pride; if sorrow was deeper than anger; if she was brave enough to repent, confess — "

"Daisy, he wouldn't forgive me! He spoke to me the morning he went away. I saw his will in his eyes, and his resolve to be complete master, if anything. It roused all the defiant blood in my nature — made me wild. I couldn't have felt sorry then if his glance had killed me. O, you little know him if you think he would ever humble himself that much again! His pride is a very giant!"

"Lily!" — the voice was solemnly tender, — "I have only to write one word in my letter; I have only to say, 'Come,' and he will be here to listen — to forgive, if you ask it."

Lily choked down her sobs. Now and then one bitter, burning cry tore its way up, and was smothered by sternest resolution. A cold shiver seemed freezing her. Happiness within her reach! Love at her very door — and such love! The weary desolation of the future, that so terrified her when she glanced out upon its midnight blackness, exchanged for peace, for blissful rest!

"What did he say?" Her voice quivered with anguish.

" My darling, what he said to me is a matter of confidence between us alone, which I cannot betray. I can only tell you that if you want him he will come. And there is but one condition."

She went on with her letter. Lily's face was hidden; but Daisy saw the convulsive movements, heard the sobs. She wondered how she could write so calmly when her heart throbbed with a wild tumult of hope and fear.

" Lily," she asked, presently, " shall I send ? "

Lily's heart beat audibly. Without moving, she said, low and huskily, —

" No."

Then Daisy folded her letter, sealed it, and took it down to be sent with Philip's. When she returned, she raised the tearful face, and kissed it again and again.

" My dearest," she said, " since you have decided, you must be brave to bear the cross you have assumed. For your own sake, for all our sakes, you must not make yourself ill and miserable. There are many happy days yet in store."

Happy ! What a mockery it seemed ! This man, who should have been the crown and glory of her life, learning slowly to forget her — to think her unworthy, incapable of high and generous regard ! How the thought stung her ! She *did* love him. How his nobleness shamed her ! Never, never to see him again ! never to be held to his heart ! to hear his voice, and yet to live !

CHAPTER XXXIII.

Come back with me to the first of all;
  Let us learn and love it over again —
Let us forget and then recall,
  Break the rosary in a pearly rain,
And gather what we let fall.
                    ROBERT BROWNING.

IT would be difficult to describe the mood that led Lily to reject this last overture of Mr. Auchester's. There was a little wounded feeling that Daisy should have been so preferred in his confidence, and that she should refuse to repeat what had passed between them. Yet when Lily came to reconsider this point, she blushed for her unworthy thoughts.

Pride was still strong within her. Could she make the thorough acknowledgment he would demand? Her nature was strongly self-centred — one of those which refuse utterly at first to be purified by suffering; which, when evasion is no longer possible, bear on in stoical silence and contempt. It seemed to her now that Mr. Auchester might have taken some kinder way to win her back, — as if the grandest and kindest thing in the whole world was not the simple truth.

A sense of shame had much to do with her resolution. Looking over the past summer, she could not find any place where *he* had given the provocation. As Daisy said, she had tried his patience until it resolved itself into distrust of her love. She had been wayward, trifling, fond of power, eager for admiration, when, if his would have sufficed, she might have had it in lavish abundance. How many times she had put him off with a little, cold caress, when he had been ready to lay his whole heart at her feet. Not because she did not love him — indeed, she could hardly understand the madness now. He was not a humble man, like Mr. Joslyn. He would grant favors, but he *could not* be ruled or forced into any step. His manhood, so glorious in its power and integrity, could be depended upon to the uttermost. She had always admired this resolute strength, even when most earnestly contesting it. Yet how could she confess herself altogether in the wrong, and have him smile over her with the stately consciousness of right!

Daisy watched the conflict with a sort of breathless calm — just as we sit still in the luminous light of some great hope, knowing it is ours, yet hardly daring to believe. With a girl less true and sound at heart than Lily, she might have had some doubts, or even if solitude had not been so strongly in Mr. Auchester's favor. It seemed cruel to stand aloof from the struggle; yet she knew if Lily fought this battle alone, and conquered self effectually, it would be the beginning of a new life for her. One by one the strongholds behind which she had intrenched herself were giving way. She grew more uniformly gentle, and by degrees came to a higher standard of thought and belief. Her affection had in it a vein of sad, yearning tenderness, that one can scarcely refrain from answering with tears.

A mental contest of this kind could not pass without leaving some marks of the fire. Philip began to grow extremely anxious.

"I cannot bear to see her so wan and sad-eyed. This lovely Indian-summer weather would brace her up, and bring some roses to her cheeks. I have half a mind to take her out, without waiting for Richard's fiat."

Lily looked wistfully through the golden air, over the hills, to the purple river, and then said, almost sadly, —

"Not to-day."

"But I'm afraid you'll never get well and blooming. I should like to see the old riotous spirit once more."

" No," she returned, softly; " help me to pray for a better one. First, ' the kingdom of God.'"

" ' And all these things shall be added unto you,'" he continued, reverently. " My dear child, God often leads us through dark paths, that we may see only the great light surrounding Him. And if we follow, even with fear and trembling, He will accept. But we must do what He bids, suffer what He lays upon us, never doubting but that it will be for the best. We must not question what might have been, or what will be; but only believe, take up the cross in our way, and find rest in its shadow."

Daisy wheeled her chair up to the window, and stood with her arm around her, a few moments after Philip had left the room.

Lily was thinking of the cross in her way, that she had stumbled over so many times during the past few days. God meant she should be very happy. If she missed the great joy, it would be only through her own perversity.

" Daisy!" The voice was faint — a mere breath, as she whispered, — " Do you think he would come — would forgive?"

How the words thrilled her! She could hardly repress a wild cry of joy.

" My darling, I *know* he would."

The fair face buried itself on her shoulder. There was a low, quivering, but distinct sound — the shy entreaty of a child, —

" Will you ask him to come?"

Daisy kissed her for the answer she could not give. She hardly knew how full of tears her own eyes were until she heard Lily's sobs. Smiling through them, she ran away.

Lily sat in the silence of a great joy, too happy to think. Her crown of thorns had blossomed into roses. She trembled in every pulse, she drew her breath gaspingly, and yet she was no longer miserable. The dear old world glittered and was full of rejoicing; the sky above shone as in other

days. Involuntarily there went through her heart the
words,—

> "And yet, perchance — O Heaven! such thing might be,
> As that one giant joy should come to me,
> Eclipsing common joys."

Daisy lingered a moment in the hall, to regain her composure. Then she went to the study. Mr. Chaloner sat
reading a paper.

"You are going to New York?" she said.

"Yes, in the next train. Can I do anything for you?"

"A great favor, if you will."

She drew some paper towards her, and took up Philip's
pen. Her greatest trial for the past week had been to
refrain from prematurely startling Mr. Auchester. But she
had the gift of rare, exceeding silence. Now she hardly
knew what she wrote; but it was enough to send the shadows of unhappiness trooping to their darksome abode.

"If you will call at the Metropolitan and leave this note;
or better still, see Mr. Auchester. He might like to send an
answer."

"With pleasure." And Mr. Chaloner gave her one of
those courtly bows to which his white hair seemed to add a
peculiar grace.

Philip drove around at that instant. A moment later her
messenger of peace was on its way.

Then she returned to Lily. Both girls flushed with
unwonted embarrassment. Lily's eyes still shone with tears.

"My darling!" Daisy exclaimed, "you deserve much
praise for your courage. I wanted to help you, but I had
been put under bonds."

"I feel weak and cowardly enough. My heart faints
within me at the thought of meeting him, and yet I long to.
I am glad it cannot be until to-morrow."

Daisy started, but held her peace, and allowed Lily to
believe the letter was going by mail. But in her inmost
soul she felt that the day and evening would not pass without
bringing Mr. Auchester.

"He won't think it unwomanly — will he? He is so particular on some points."

"Since he gave the permission, you shall not render yourself miserable with vain surmises. What else could have been done?"

"If I were only better! But when I think of all that has occurred since, I am afraid he can never love me again. It is right that he should know."

"Yes. But he has never ceased to love you; so there is no need of beginning again. Do not conjure up mountains of unnecessary trouble. Rather wait on the Lord, and he will bring it to pass."

Sound, healthy vitality was a component part of Lily's temperament. Repentant she might be, but not morbid. So resilient a nature works its own cure. Her spirits began to rise visibly, for the battle was ended. Never in all her life would she have to fight such a contest over again.

Daisy read to her a long while. After dinner she bestowed her on the lounge, administered a composing draught, closed the shutters, and gave her strict injunctions to go immediately to sleep. Her strained nerves relaxed, yielded to the pleasant influence, and she soon fell into a tranquil slumber.

A peaceful air seemed brooding over the house. The drone of bees, the chirp of late insects, and the song of birds, had a lazy, monotonous sound, brimmed with the deliciousness of languor. The spicy air was full of golden films, the tree tops shone in crimson and gold, and wherever Daisy's eyes fell, a glowing picture of still life presented itself. You could not connect it with motion. She always remembered this day with wondrous vividness.

Baby Alice was in a quiet mood also. She lay on a pillow on the floor, — while Mabel sewed, — now and then turning her wondering eyes gravely to her father, who looked up from his book to chirrup to her occasionally.

Daisy knew some explanation was needed before Mr.

Auchester made his appearance. Both Philip and Mabel had delicately refrained from questioning her about the letters. Seizing this golden opportunity, she bespoke Philip's attention, and related her story, excepting the episode concerning herself, that events had proved manifestly untrue.

Philip listened in astonishment.

"My dear Daisy!" he exclaimed, "you are a most courageous little body. You have certainly bearded the lion in his den, and come off more than conqueror. That you should have found the way to Lily's heart, actually made her take the first step towards a reconciliation, surprises me beyond measure."

"I could not have done it but for her love. That was my most powerful ally."

"I was sure of it," rejoined Philip, triumphantly. "I knew Lily must have a heart — it's a distinctive Bertrand feature. As for Ulric Auchester, he's a splendid fellow, and deserves a better wife; but I'm thankful he has fallen to Lily's share. I only hope he will keep her in better order than heretofore. She used to vex me last summer. If he had used a ' high hand,' as people say, he would have saved himself much trouble."

Mabel laughed. "We have all tried at managing Lily, and Daisy has succeeded the best of any. In the depths of my heart I am glad she is to fall into such good keeping. She would drive a weak man to distraction, and make herself miserable. Such a nature is best governed by a superior will."

"I question if Lily has not more thoroughly subdued herself than any one would have been able to subdue her," said Daisy.

"Auchester will take good care that the volcano doesn't break out again, I think. Daisy, there is no possible adjective that can be bestowed on you to do you justice. Who would have thought, a month ago, that we could all be so happy?" And Philip caught up Alice, half smothered her with kisses, and held her out at arm's length.

" My little daughter," he continued, with amusing gravity, " if you grow up half as beautiful, and are half as great a flirt, as your aunt Lily, you shall be soundly whipped and sent to bed without your supper ! "

Alice gave a smile that portended she might grow up as pretty.

Lily slept for three hours. Daisy brushed her hair and put on a dress, announcing her intention of asking Philip and Mabel up to tea.

" I certainly feel well enough to go down," said Lily. " May I to-morrow ? "

" If you wish," was the rejoinder.

The supper was a decided success. Lily received her visitors in great state. She looked bright and charming, and was in excellent spirits.

" Tessy ought to be here," remarked Philip. " She enjoys anything like this wonderfully, for her grave face is only a mask that covers a fund of inexhaustible drollery. I expect she matronizes Richard in an astonishing degree. You will find him perfection when you return, Daisy."

" As if he had not always been perfection in Daisy's eyes !" responded Lily, archly.

A torrent of brilliant blood rushed to Daisy's face. She could not give the slightest reason for it, and to banish it, joined the laugh against herself. It was well she did not notice the freemasonry of glance between husband and wife, or she might have blushed again.

Philip rose and made a speech in his most grandiloquent style, regretting that it was necessary for him to leave the delightful group, but he really was compelled to go to the station after Mr. Chaloner.

The housekeeper carried away the dishes. Lily sat on the lounge, having a good romp with baby Alice. Mabel and Daisy tried to talk unconcernedly. But when the sound of carriage wheels broke upon them, Daisy's heart gave a great bound. Three men alighted, and there was no mistaking that tall, handsome third, although the purple dusk was falling fast.

"Come, my little lady;" and Mabel took her baby in her arms. "It's bedtime; so you must make believe kiss aunt Lily, and go."

"O dear'!" said Lily, ruefully. "Don't send me to bed, please. I slept through seven distinct spheres this afternoon, and feel in a most royal state. I have half a mind to go down and surprise Mr. Chaloner."

"Daisy!" called Philip.

Mabel made a pretence of baby "good nights" to cover the retreat. Daisy almost ran over Mr. Chaloner in the hall. He caught her in his arms.

"Did I bring you home the proper reply?" he asked. "But your smile answers. Is there to be peace in the household?"

"I believe so."

"Thank God, for Lily's sake. And Mr. Auchester is worthy of the highest happiness."

She entered the open drawing-room door. Both her hands were taken in an earnest clasp.

"O Daisy!" Mr. Auchester began, in a voice so full and rich that she listened, unconsciously entranced. "How can I believe it! 'Her own wish,' you said, 'after days of struggling.' What a will the child has! I have read your letter times without number to-day. My precious, precious friend! Your clear vision and brave heart have saved me pangs of untold anguish. Can I see her soon? Every moment seems an age!"

"Yes," Daisy answered, with a tremulous laugh, "if you will only release my hands, so that I can go and prepare her. She fancied that the letter went by mail, and doesn't expect you until to-morrow."

"You would be a perfect treasure to a stage manager for surprises!" he returned, gayly. "You need not put a girdle round the earth in forty minutes, but bring me to happiness in less time than that, I pray you."

She was gone.　Mabel, on the stairs, gave her a squeeze and kiss.　She went straight on to Lily, and then stood still in perfect bewilderment.

"Let me go down stairs," pleaded Lily.

"No."　She drew a long breath, and struggled for composure.

"What is the matter, Daisy?"　Lily glanced in her face with startled eyes.

"I have word from Mr. Auchester."

"O Daisy!" and she uttered a wild cry.　"Will he come? No, don't tell me he will not; it would kill me now."

"My dearest, he is here!　The note went with Mr. Chaloner.　Be calm, for I cannot send him up until I am sure of you."

"Here!　Let me think a moment.　I seem blind, and drowned in happiness!　The long, dreary night is to end, the everlasting day has come!　O Daisy! is it all true, *true?*　How good God has been to me!　And how good you have been!"

She sat still, quite exhausted.　Presently, in a tone that was calm from excess of joy, she said,—

"Go for him, Daisy."

He was in the hall, and sprang up stairs the instant he heard the door open.　Daisy beckoned him in, and passed out herself.　The room was in a glow of orange and purple twilight, through which the fire sent arrows of gleaming flame.　His eye took in the drooping figure, the shining curls, the sweet face.

"Lily!" he said, softly; and yet it was the man's involuntary authority that spoke.

A cry, sad, sweet, touching in its utter humility, faltered up through quivering sobs.

"O Ulric! let me come back to my old place in your heart.　Do what you will, only love me a little!"

"Always, my darling!　Please God, nothing shall ever again come between us."

"Never again!" and she lingered over the words with exceeding tenderness, as if they were sweet to say.

And then they were content to remain silent through moments of bliss, so pure, so exquisite, that no pen is worthy to describe them. The true level of both lives had been reached. For them there could be no more doubt, no more coldness. They grew into one heart, one life, as all true love must,— she rejoicing to be his, he rejoicing to be hers. He raised the dear face, and kissed away the tears sweeter to him

> " Than all the smiles in Christendom."

Daisy gave the lovers all the time she dared. She sat in Mabel's room, dreamy and quiet. Both hearts were too full for any talk on the subject so dear and precious, and all others seemed out of place. She allowed two hours to elapse before she went up and tapped lightly at the door.

"Come in," said Mr. Auchester. What a cheerful ring there was in the voice!

"A most unwelcome visitor, I know;" and Daisy crossed over to be encircled by an arm slender and soft from the one side, strong and manly from the other. "Doubtless you have not the remotest idea how much time has passed. If you have not smoothed out all the crooked paths, I quite despair of you. Being Lily's keeper for the time, I shall have to invite you to relinquish your charge."

"O, not quite yet, please."

"Don't make me cruel," said Daisy. "I shall have to give an account to Dr. Bertrand, and wish to present Lily in good order. She has had enough excitement for the present."

"We have been talking of — of our future lives," continued Mr. Auchester; and it seemed such a sacred thing to touch upon, that his voice fell to a tender pathos. "And Lily agrees with me that a marriage will be best. She is quite willing to trust my love in all things. But it must be so soon — and will Dr. Bertrand consent? What do you think about it ?"

Daisy started. Lily to go away — for years, perhaps. Then, as her mind took in the whole matter, she answered, slowly, —

"I think he will. I believe it is right and best."

"Bravo !" and he gave her hand a little squeeze.

"I suspect," Lily said, dryly, "that if you asked Richard for the roc's egg, Aladdin's lamp, or the key to the northwest passage, he would give them to you straightway. Ulric, you see, is a little afraid of him."

"If you think I mean to set Daisy at any more hard work, you are mistaken. And I shouldn't feel surprised if he delivered you over to my keeping without a word."

"Out of pity, because you will have so many afterwards," annoted Lily, saucily.

He laughed. "Daisy has trained you so well that the prospect does not alarm me. And since we owe our happiness to her, I suppose I must learn how sweet it is to obey."

He rose with his arm still around Lily.

"It is *best*," Daisy replied, with a bright smile.

"But I mean to have her all day to-morrow. I give you fair warning."

"I shall resign my commission, I think. Dr. Bertrand will surely come."

There was a little more tender talk between the lovers, lingering good-night kisses, and Ulric turned away reluctantly.

"Don't you keep Daisy very long," he said. "Think how many weeks I have been without the sight of a dear, familiar face, and be merciful. I want a nice talk with her."

"Ask what you will. I am in a princely, generous mood."

He came back for another kiss.

When the door was closed, Lily took Daisy's face between her hands, and looked for many seconds in the deep, untroubled eyes.

"Daisy," she began, "Ulric told me all, *all* — what you had never even let me suspect."

"It was not fair," Daisy said, struggling to get beyond the reach of the watchful gaze.

"Yes it was fair and right. His nobleness made it so. And, Daisy, we should scorn to have one thought in our hearts that we dared not tell each other. And I hardly feel right about accepting my happiness until you assure me —"

"O, Lily, Lily! foolish child! Not but that he is grand enough for any woman to love — only somehow God seems to take care of these things in his own way."

"You are so simply, almost severely, heroic, one might say, that one hardly knows what sacrifice you are not capable of. But O, Daisy, if it had been another woman — a woman who loved him! I shudder to think of it. Yet I could never, never have blamed him! He was much better to me all the time than I deserved."

"It couldn't have been another woman, Lily. Do not think of anything so terrible. It wasn't with him 'the stern necessity of loving,' but simply 'blind contact.' We had been thrown together so familiarly, and that fateful night we met by merest accident. After he had once opened his heart to me, it was so easy to go on. It was not the desperate clutching at straws that led him astray afterwards, but the sense of desolation, the longing for some balm to apply to his wound. With the world, I dare say he was as proud and self-contained as your inmost heart could desire."

"He does love you, Daisy. I can hardly explain it, but I am happier in the fact."

"I want to be to both as the dearest of sisters."

"As you will be, my darling, forevermore."

Presently she began again : —

"O Daisy! how could I have lived but for you! When I think of his true, priceless love, his patience, his peerless honor, I stand quite still, quite still, abashed, and feel like saying with another joyful woman, 'He raised me by love upon the pedestal of his own high thoughts, and I stood there, with downcast eyes, worthy of his love, for he had made me so.' Life is too short to repay him. And so you need not fear I shall ever hew out broken cisterns for myself again. I feel safe, secure, triumphant in his love. It is my whole world from henceforth, my glory, my crown of highest womanhood. At last I have come to my inheritance!"

How lovely she looked! Was this really Lily? Daisy felt bewildered.

"O my darling!" Lily said, with her good-night kiss, "it is such a blessed, blessed thing to be happy! If it was not for God watching over me continually, I should feel afraid to be alone with it, lest its glory should strike me blind. How do people live who never have this light dawn upon them, but wander continually through cold and dark? God help them! And now go to *him*, Daisy. I couldn't be selfish this night, of all nights in my life."

CHAPTER XXXIV.

And love; because we then are happiest.
We shall lack nothing having love; and we,
We must be happy everywhere — we two!
For spiritual life is great and clear,
And self-continuous as a changeless sea.

Come to the light, love!   Let me look on thee!
Let me make sure I have thee. Is it thou?
Is this thy hand? Are these thy velvet lips —
Thy lips so lovable?

FESTUS.

DAISY went as one in a trance.   It seemed to her as if,
somehow, she was not quite ignorant of this great joy.   Had
Robert brought it, with his handsome face, his winning voice,
his eyes, that could be so deep and tender?   No.   Had any
stray glance fallen in that brief episode with Ulric Auchester?   O! a thousand times, no.   Where then?   She trembled and dared go no farther.

A fragrant waft of *Habaneros* drifted from the balcony.
She stole out shyly, as she caught sight of Mabel's dress.
She would rather have sat down in the deserted study, and
dreamed.   But one of life's first lessons to Daisy Bertrand
had been the grandest part of St. Paul's eighteen-century-
old definition of charity.   *Seeketh not her own.*   It was more
this than any personal energy that gave her the influence
every one yielded to without questioning, even enjoying the
gentle sway.   There was no central point of *self* with her.
She did daily and hourly for others just what her hands found
to do; not in a rigid, duty fashion, but with vital human
pleasure.   And now she went out on the balcony, because
she knew Mr. Auchester was there and wanted to see her.

29

"O, is that you, Daisy?" He rose and threw away his cigar. "Are you too tired to walk a little way?"

"I am not tired at all."

"Get a shawl, then. I must begin to copy Dr. Bertrand, for carefulness."

"Here is mine;" and Bel wrapped her up in shawl and Nubia, for the autumn nights were rather chilly. Being thus dispossessed, she entered the house; but Philip remained to finish his cigar.

Mr. Auchester and Daisy walked down the path silently. He began, at length, by a commonplace.

"What a lovely night!"

"Yes. In every respect."

"I suppose you think everything is lovely to me at this present moment. Indeed, I'm not sure but it is so. For happiness seems to be the best kind of glasses yet invented. I have so much to say to you, and yet I hardly know where to begin."

"At the very last," said Daisy, archly. "The subject will read the same both ways."

"Yes." He drew her closer to him, and in a low voice, that was not quite steady, went on: "From your hands I take my happiness. I cannot find words to thank you. I shall show you best by guarding it sacredly in all time to come. It is such a great and solemn thing to take a loving woman and say, as Robert Browning did, — 'This woman's heart, and soul, and brain are mine;' and her sweet, pure life, forever. I seem in these last few hours to have grown out of and above my olden self. It has dropped down like a discarded garment. Entering this new and complete world, I tremble, yet I feel strong. You have opened this sphere to me, Daisy; you have brought me out of the tangled wilderness into the house Beautiful."

"O, no," she rejoined, softly. "You saw it all yourself, long before."

"'Through a glass, darkly.' I should have gone on blind

and dumb, until some fatal day of awakening. How many times in the last few weeks I have hated and despised myself for that unintentional falsehood to you, God only knows. It has been a rankling thorn, a keen, stinging mortification. Yet to-night I feel thankful that a higher power allowed me to stumble as I did. It has shown me my weakness, or rather my false strength. It has brought me down to the level of the most childish thing Lily ever did. And I am glad to be there. She shall not shame me in any noble confession; and O, Daisy! what a royal heart the child has! She has startled me to-night by depths and heights such as one dreams of, but rarely realizes. And the past summer, nay, all my life, I have had a tendency to an egotistical and perhaps selfish indulgence of personal will. It has been necessary for me to command a good deal, and I have slipped into it imperceptibly. Yet this experience will prove a valuable lesson to me. I shall not again act without considering what the result may be. God mercifully shielded you from any bitter consequences of my impetuous words. And having been under the cloud and through the sea, we shall enjoy our good land of promise with a deeper zest. Let me say, again and again, that under God it is your gift."

"I am so glad you are happy! It is not a new love, but the dear old one, strengthened, purified."

"You are right. I feel now that my affection for Lily is, and ever will be, the one great love of my life. And her happiness shall be my study, my chief delight. Not that I have ceased to believe a man should be master of his own household; but his authority and dignity are to be tempered by the regard he must ever sustain towards the woman who fills that dearest of all positions — wife. And relying on a better strength than my own, I hope to deal wisely and justly, not only with her, but also with myself."

"'Who giveth liberally, and upbraideth not,'" subjoined Daisy.

And then they lapsed into silence. Under this silvery

light both hearts unconsciously went back two months, to another glorious night. How changed! What were tree, and shrub, and moonlight then? Of all women in the world, she would be next to Lily in his estimation and regard. A weak man may shun a woman to whom he has in some hour of extreme bitterness betrayed himself; but a noble man never, unless she proves unworthy of his confidence.

A bright morning dawned upon Rothelan. Lily was going down to breakfast—a great event. She felt her head swim a little on the stairs, yet the fond arm around her steadied not only her swaying figure, but the palpitant motions of her heart. She felt the touch of that protecting hand through all her nerves; a master hand it was, but it no longer roused her mutinous blood. She was glad to have it there; for now, strange even to her own heart, liberty was no longer sweet.

Mr. Chaloner read the morning prayer for the household. Lily's heart throbbed with deepest emotion at the sentence in the general thanksgiving, "We bless Thee for our creation, preservation, and all the blessings of this life."

O, how manifold they had been to her! There must be one continual hymn of praise swelling up from her heart for these many mercies. She began to understand what the apostle meant, when he said, "In everything give thanks." Henceforth it was to be not only duty, but delight.

Some time after breakfast Mr. Auchester took Lily out for a short drive. She returned radiant, though she confessed to feeling a little tired. He arranged the pillows on the sofa in the drawing-room for her, and sitting down, talked over the time when they first met, and she had done these little favors for him. And he made her smile, as well as blush, as he spoke of the many times he had felt tempted to catch the pretty white hand and kiss it rapturously.

She was profoundly thankful that, with all her folly and wilfulness, she had never fallen into the habit of allowing caresses from others. Even Fred, with all his audacity, had stood a trifle aloof. And though there were many things to regret, there were few to actually blush over, with her lover's eyes upon her.

She took the first occasion to mention one incident of the ride to Daisy. They had met Mr. Joslyn. And so the perplexing subject was likely to settle itself without any further difficulty.

She began to develop the possibilities of a magnificent woman. Her very face seemed to acquire, in the dawn of this ripening love, the steadiness and resolve it had heretofore lacked. A bewildering glimpse of sweetness flashed ever and anon out of the deep eyes, or the curves of the mouth, which was rapidly assuming its olden scarlet. She began to realize, with a tender seriousness, what this visit was doing for her. Giving Mr. Auchester the right, and he taking it every hour, of being *first* with her. In the summer he used to say, pleadingly, ' O Lily, will you not?" now he simply said, "You will," as if the matter was beyond doubt or questioning.

Quite late in the afternoon, as Daisy sat alone by the study window, sewing, a familiar form turned into the path. She ran to the door without waiting a summons, her face aglow with pleasure. All day she had been on the watch for Richard, resolved, if possible, to have the first interview.

"Well, how are the household?" he asked, smilingly.

He did not stoop to kiss her, for he could not bring his feelings to the calm basis of fraternal affection. She remarked it, and it gave her a sense of pain.

"Doing splendidly! to use a Lily-*ism*. Philip has taken Bel and the baby out, Mr. Chaloner has gone to visit some parishioners, and — "

"Why not go up stairs at once, then?" he asked, as she drew him towards the study door.

"Because — no one is there. I have so much to tell you."

"Lily!" — and his countenance expressed alarm.

"She came down stairs to-day. You will think her perfectly well when you see her. I have been trying a new cure, and succeeded admirably. So sit down and prepare yourself for a good long talk."

He seated himself, a little amused at her manner. She drew a footstool close to his side, and appropriating it, rested her arm upon his knee.

"We have been so happy, so very happy! It seems like a dream, or a page out of a fairy book. Mr. Auchester came last night — I sent for him."

Richard might have seen it all at once, as she thought he would. Instead, he braced himself for the blow with that mechanical stoicism we use in the great straits of life, when every faculty is stunned. He looked steadily beyond Daisy's face, at the corner of the table. He remembered for years afterwards the peculiar conformation of the black scroll-work and clusters of flowers on the crimson ground of the cover; and a Church Journal that overhung the edge, so nicely balanced that he almost expected to see it fall to the floor with a breath. The blood curdled at his heart, and impelled him to shiver with icy coldness; but he resisted stoutly.

She saw his face turning pale. That he could misunderstand her, appeared so utterly impossible that it never crossed her mind. She could only explain it as displeasure against Mr. Auchester.

"O Richard," she cried, "please don't be angry! I know you do not think it for the best; but Lily loved him so, and he was willing to come — to forget all the past. It seems so right, so just, to me. Why should two people, who love one another dearly, be kept forever apart, and miserable, for lack of a few words?"

"What was it you said?"

Richard pressed his hand to his forehead, and shut his eyes, for the whole room whirled round with lightning rapidity, and he could no longer think. Was it not Daisy? Surely he had not heard correctly.

"Lily and Mr. Auchester —" but Daisy's voice sounded far away, fathoms deep under the sea.

She was greatly distressed. With a grave, almost tearful earnestness of tone, she made another beginning.

" I am sorry that you cannot approve. It might not have
been quite right to take the matter in my hands, but it had
to be done then, if at all. When you see their perfect happiness, I think you will forgive me."

" Their happiness," he repeated, in a confused, absent
way. " Lily's and Mr. Auchester's ? "

" Yes."

He placed his arm around her with a sudden, ungoverna-
ble impulse. He gazed into her eyes until the crimson tide
of her heart flashed up and drowned the white out of brow
and cheek. His again! O, it was too strange, too sweet;
incredible! The very glory of assurance blinded him.

Presently he made a strong effort to calm himself, and
asked, —

" What about Lily ? "

" It was all my doing. Are you very angry ? "

" Angry with you ? O child, Daisy, as if such a thing
could ever be! Tell me the whole story."

She told it simply, as if she had been a third person, yet
withal so beautifully, that he listened as to a romance ; all
the while thinking how wondrously she understood human
love, and human hearts.

She brought her story down to the present moment, ending with, " They are in the drawing-room."

" Let me think a moment. And they have really resolved
to be good children. Daisy, how dared you meddle with a
man like Mr. Auchester ? And am I to go in and give consent for the second time ? "

" Yes," with a happy smile. " But O, Dr. Bertrand — "

" What ? " he interrupted, with an amused look.

" Richard," she corrected, bashfully, " there is another
thing I want you to do for *my* sake."

" Anything for your sake. On that ground you may
dictate terms like a tyrant."

"Then," joyfully, "I mean to have just my own way. And it's about the marriage. Mr. Auchester doesn't wish to give up going to Europe, and he *does* want to take Lily with him. I think it much better than a long engagement."

"Amen to that," said Richard. "Truth to tell, I'm afraid Lily wouldn't be quite safe all that while. And if they do love each other, — as now there seems no question about it, — I think the wisest course would be marriage, even at this hasty rate."

"O Richard, you have made me so happy!" Then she clasped her arms around his neck, and kissed him of her own sweet accord.

He held the little arms in their place for many seconds, and gave back kisses uncounted. He wanted to tell her the perfect rapture in his heart, but he could find no words.

"And you are not displeased?" she murmured, her face all hidden by his.

"O, no, no. How could I be, when you have restored Lily to happiness? Love is such a dear, precious treasure! I am afraid I made a little mistake in the beginning. What I intended for carefulness, Lily construed into license. Perhaps the wisest course would have been to have relinquished all authority in the affair, and delivered her at once into Mr. Auchester's keeping. But it's so hard always to do the best thing for the circumstances. Lily needed a mother's thoughtful care;" and he sighed a little.

Daisy went off to announce Richard. Obeying Mr. Auchester's invitation to enter, she caught, in his full, rich voice, the last lines of Coleridge's Love, —

> "I calmed her fears, and she was calm,
> And told her love with virgin pride;
> And thus I won my Genevieve,
> My own sweet, smiling bride."

"After the poets, Daisy," he said, glancing up.

"And after Daisy, the doctor," she returned — "a suggestive alliteration."

"Dear old Dick! is he here?" and springing up, Lily ran into the hall, to be clasped to a heart whose warmth and fondness no fault could ever destroy.

"O Dick!" she began, in a voice that sounded as if it came through waves of tears; and what she could not say was lost in kisses.

"I know *all*, my darling. God sent Daisy to be an angel to us. She always finds the shortest path out to the light."

"Yes. And I am so happy! I believe I never knew what happiness was until last night. And, Richard, will you — I mean — the trouble was all my fault, and he —"

"Shall have his dear, naughty girl, with my blessing, Lily. But one doesn't need two such lessons in a life. I can trust *you* henceforward?" And he glanced deeply into her eyes.

They filled with tears. "Yes," she answered, quite humbly.

"Now for Ulric."

Lily was delighted to hear him use Mr. Auchester's Christian name. There had always been a fine, indescribable formality between the two.

The gentleman answered for himself, by advancing to meet them. A warm color suffused his noble face, as, reaching out his hand, he said, in a tone that clearly asked a favor, —

"Dr. Bertrand, will you not give me a brother's place in your heart, as well as your household?"

"Willingly, joyfully;" and the two hands rested in a clasp cordially fraternal.

"If you can trust me, I hope to redeem the past."

"And I think Lily understands better what she is doing than she did six months ago. We have all made some mistakes about it — except Daisy."

They entered the room again. The manner in which Lily clung to Richard touched him deeply. The conversation unconsciously fell into a sweet, half sorrowful strain.

Afterwards Richard and Mr. Auchester discussed the subject by themselves, and arrived at a most amicable conclusion.

"I am sorry to go away, on some accounts," Ulric said, "and if the position was offered to me now for the first time, should hardly accept it. But, besides being a personal friend of Hon. Mr. ——, the opportunity is really too fine to be thrown up without just cause. Since Lily is willing to go, and has a great desire to travel, I think I can make it very pleasant for her."

"It will also be better for you to begin your life away from old associations," Richard replied; and thus consent was given for a marriage at their earliest convenience.

"Auchester *is* a fine fellow," he admitted to Daisy, afterwards. "I believe I never did him quite justice before."

Mr. Auchester concluded to go to New York that evening with Richard. He explained to Lily that there must of necessity be a great deal to do.

"And I'll write to Alice this very night, and hurry her home."

"O, that would be too bad!" exclaimed Lily.

"She would rather come, I know. She would never forgive us if we went on by ourselves. Besides, she is a capital judge of all feminine matters, and will know just where to begin, to make the affair come out straight. You are not strong yet, and I can't have you worried with the thousand and one things that belong to a wedding."

"How wise you are!" Lily rejoined, mischievously.

"Yes; or, at least, determined. So you have nothing to do but get well and rosy as fast as possible. I shall be up every day or evening until you are strong enough to go home."

"I think I could do it now. Or shall I try to-morrow?"

"Not until Alice returns. Remember how tired you were this morning, and the headaches. I want to show Richard what excellent care I can take of you. And now be a good child, and obey every word of Daisy's. I appoint her my vicegerent."

Lily said good by. Yet somehow it came very hard.

"What if I should never see him again, Daisy?" she said, solemnly, trying to keep back some foolish tears. "People die suddenly, you know —"

"Since you have both been so near the grave, and lived, I think you can trust God for the rest."

"I will," she answered, rebuked for her momentary distrust.

She went to bed quite early, and soon fell asleep. The excitement and exertion had not injured her any, they all perceived on the following morning. She tried to sew a little, and succeeded very well.

"I will not be sick a day longer," she said, in a resolute tone. "It is clearly indulging in laziness."

CHAPTER XXXV.

Mine to the core of the heart, my beauty!
Mine — all mine, and for love, not duty;
Love given willingly, full, and free;
Love for love's sake, as I love thee.
　Duty, a servant, keeps the key;
But Love, the master, goes in and out
Of his goodly chambers, with song and shout,
　Constant and happy, merry and free!
MISS MULOCK.

As Mr. Auchester expected, his sister hastened home, leaving her tour unfinished. She could not wait a day, but went immediately to Rothelan to see Lily, and express her delight. Still she was greatly disappointed to think Ulric was again going abroad. She could not resist saying, —

"I did so hope he would settle down somewhere in quiet, and behave like a reasonable citizen of the United States."

"I am afraid it is my fault," began Lily, penitently. "If I had not —"

"Well, we will forgive you, since you are to pay for the mistake by years of exile. I am more than glad to have it end even this way, since you have learned how necessary you are to each other's happiness. But Ulric wants to start just as early in December as he can. So you will have only about three weeks in which to prepare."

"Three weeks!" said Lily, in dismay. "Why, I believe Bel was a whole year making wedding clothes."

"The sooner the better, my dear, for it will grow colder every day. It is a bad season for a sea voyage, too; but since Ulric is so resolutely bent on going, the best thing seems to be to go as soon as possible. He quoted Mr.

Rochester to me not an hour before I started : ' Fine clothes, and all that, are not worth a fillip.' Still you must have a few, I think."

"I don't know what can be done in that little while," Mabel said.

"O, you'll see how much I can accomplish. I mean to be real industrious after this long idleness," rejoined Lily.

Mrs. Suydam laughed.

"If you could have heard half the charges Ulric gave me, you would not count on doing very much. 'Don't worry her with troublesome details,' said he ; 'for as soon as she comes home, I shall take her under my wing, and you will hardly catch sight of her.' "

"Somebody must go out shopping, and all that."

"Ulric may possibly grant you permission to shop, but it wouldn't surprise me if he bought out a dry-goods' store at auction, and sent it home to you."

This time it was Lily who laughed. "We will see," she said.

And they did see. The next day Richard took Daisy and Lily home. Mrs. Suydam and her brother came over to dinner, and afterwards they proceeded to make arrangements. Ulric insisted that Lily was not strong enough to be burdened with so onerous a duty, and that Alice should take charge of the *trousseau*, leaving only the selecting and approval to Lily. Richard allowed her *carte blanche* in the matter, glad to have Lily so relieved. Mrs. Suydam's wide experience of fashionable life rendered her competent for the undertaking. Her energy, and the cheerful manner in which she went about everything, were good to behold.

So the next day there was a grand shopping excursion, which included Daisy, Lily, Mrs. Suydam, and, part of the time, Mr. Auchester. After a peculiarly lovely shade of blue silk had been selected, his interest flagged, however. Mrs. Suydam possessed rare delicacy and good judgment. She thought they could find all they needed at Stewart's ;

and therefore Lily was not dragged about the city. While she and Daisy went through various departments for minor but still necessary articles, the lovers discussed the relative beauty of white satin and white silk.

"I believe I like those soft, heavy silks best," Mr. Auchester said. "I don't know which is the more suitable, but I do not ever want to see you in anything stiff, that gives you a dressed-up look. I dislike it."

"We'll have the silk, then," was Lily's decision.

Mrs. Suydam did not think it necessary to purchase more than Lily needed at present, for the sake of mere show. Her gift was an elegant velvet cloak, at which the child was surprised and overjoyed. The whole affair was concluded satisfactorily, only Lily whispered to Daisy, "It doesn't seem as if I had half enough; but then Mrs. Suydam never makes a parade over anything; so I suppose it's all right." When she had the dresses fitted, Ulric concluded their number was legion.

Mrs. Suydam carried her point about another matter. She wanted the wedding to take place from her house, and in Trinity Church.

"Ulric said I was not to insist upon it," she explained to Lily, "because he had to hasten the time in such an unceremonious manner. But as you are to leave immediately, this will be the only compliment he can pay his friends. He spoke of it first himself, but he was afraid you would not quite approve."

Lily thought it made no difference to her, so long as Philip performed the ceremony. Richard would rather have given his birdling his blessing in her dear old home, but he acquiesced, for he could see that it would be more convenient. And then Mrs. Suydam had taken so much trouble — was still giving her whole attention to dress-makers and little details that would have puzzled Lily sorely. Daisy, Mrs. Hall, and the sewing machine made brisk work of it at home. There was a continual going back and forth from

city to city. Mr. Auchester was Lily's relentless shadow.
He would not listen to such a thing as her sewing, although
she declared if she was so idle the marriage would have to
be delayed another month.

Lily's languid state indisposed her for any vigorous mental exertion; and so Ulric found his little rebel very tracta-
ble. She was quite content to leave the guidance of her
bark in more experienced hands, and drift gently down the
stream in measureless content. Yet besides this there were
principle and regard. She had reached that point of affection when to inflict pain on one beloved gives the heart a
pang. Satisfied to be entirely happy, supremacy of will
tortured her no more with its illusive importance.

Finding no longer a swift current of opposition to his
wishes, Ulric Auchester grew unconsciously gentle. As a
commander resolved upon besieging a fortress, he was stern
and uncompromising; but after the capitulation, one found
him the most clement and considerate of conquerors. Relying fearlessly upon his generosity, Lily found she gained
more from him than in the early and unsatisfactory days of
their engagement.

"Only," she said, laughingly, to Daisy, "he doesn't want
me to be too good. He told me a story last night about
Count and Countess Somebody,—I've forgotten the name,
—who were so very amiable and unselfish that each insisted
on giving up any point under consideration, and was so intent upon doing just what the other wished, that the result
was, they could never agree upon pleasures, or journeys, or
the commonest events of every-day life. Finally they both
became angry over so much goodness, quarrelled, and
parted—an event we desire to avoid, as it would be exces-
sively inconvenient when we are in Russian wilds."

"Siberia is not far off," suggested Daisy, with a mirthful
gleam in her eyes.

"Daisy, you do not more than half believe in me. I
suppose it does seem odd to you that I should find something

better in the world than my own 'sweet will;' but it is even so. And the matter that once appeared so difficult to me, has resolved itself into the simplest of all elements. I just begin to learn what a pleasure it is to yield. I suspect I have given you all trouble enough, heretofore."

Daisy could not forbear kissing the sweet mouth, so ready with its concessions.

Lily astonished Mr. Auchester one day by asking if they could not as well embark at Boston.

"Certainly; but why?" and he looked surprised.

"I'll tell *you* why, though you must help me keep it a secret. We all went to see Robert off — poor, dear Robin, who never came back. It will remind them so much of that. I want everything to be gay and happy up to the latest moment. It will be sad enough when it is all over. And therefore I want it as little like that parting as we can possibly make it."

Tears were glittering in her eyes. Touched by her thoughtfulness, he replied, —

"My darling, it shall be as you wish. I think it a better arrangement."

So he announced that he intended to take Lily to Boston, to show her the city.

"It will not do for her to go abroad without having seen a little of her native land. I only wish there was time for a more extended tour."

No one questioned or made any comments. And after that, Mr. Auchester kept himself and Lily in the most brilliant spirits. Everything went on auspiciously. November was remarkably pleasant; and although it was rather lowering and cold the last of the month, December came in brightly. Mrs. Suydam was untiring, yet never displayed a sign of fatigue or trouble. When the dresses were done, she packed them, — at least, all those Lily would not be likely to want soon. Having travelled much herself, she knew just what was needed, and the best disposition to make of every article. And last of all the wedding dress was finished; the

veil and wreath came home, and some elegant presents were
sent in that quite astounded Lily. Nothing remained but
the ceremony.

"If it will only be clear!" she said, as she laid her head
on the pillow in her own room at home — the last time she
was to be there as Lily Bertrand! Whether she should ever
come again, God only knew. She trembled at the thought
of her new life, yet she could not wish it different. Love
with her was at full tide. Fear was cast out. She cried
humbly to God that his presence might go with her to
strengthen and support.

The morning was most beautiful — a clear, crisp air; a
sky of the peculiar frosty blue, seen only on the finest of
winter days; and a sun whose splendor had never been exceeded. Lily was wild with delight. Before breakfast she
ran from room to room, saying good by to nooks and corners that held for her dear memories, both pleasant and sad.
Here mamma's face seemed to gleam out — a sweet, yet indistinct vision, something that brought a waft of heaven and
the angels. And dear, dear papa! She drew a long, quivering breath. He had carried them up stairs on his broad
shoulders, played hide-and-seek with them through rooms
and halls. Here they had all laughed with him on that fatal
evening. In the room below they had kissed him for the
last time — the last time! and then her tears fell fast indeed. A little distance above here, in the cemetery, he lay
asleep, waiting for the dawn of the resurrection; beside
him, baby Charlie — a dream, a strand of Daisy's life woven
in with theirs. Here they had laughed and frolicked with
Robert; here Mabel's quiet girlhood had passed, blessed with
all that makes life so rich to enjoy. And her own! O, the
dear old home! the happy household, dividing, straying off
into the keeping of others!

She came to the table with a smiling countenance. Her
resolute will stood her in good stead this day. She kept
them all merry by the force of her own gay spirits, fully

resolved to have her day shadowed by no gloom. Archie
had returned the night before. After the meal they started
for New York.

Mr. Auchester met them at the ferry with the family carriage. As they were riding up, he glanced at his watch, and
whispered to Lily, "It is ten. Only three hours more;"
which called a bright color to her face.

At Mrs. Suydam's they were greeted by the Rothelan
household. Little Alice dressed in her beautiful christening
robe to do honor to aunt Lily's bridal; Bel, sweet and fair,
in her lavender-colored silk; Philip, in a sort of merry
mood, amusing himself by quoting Katharine and Petruchio
to the blushing couple.

There was no break or awkwardness anywhere. Everybody's apparel, to gloves and handkerchief, was in the most
perfect order, and readily found. There was no bustle, no
disorder, and plenty of time. Indeed, too much, Mr. Auchester thought. The moments lingered unconscionably.

At length the dressing began. Lily's hair, always so
beautiful, needed no more artistic hands than Daisy's. The
golden ringlets rippled in their silken sheen and softness like
a summer sunbeam. And then came the lovely white silk,
with its ample, flowing skirt and train, its point lace; the
veil, whose filmy folds seemed like a soft cloud, toning down
her dazzling radiance, and shutting within the purity and
beauty of girlhood. A wreath of orange blossoms and starry
jasmine crowned her.

There had previously been a little discussion about Daisy.
Since her baby's death she had worn mourning steadily.
Richard, in his perplexity, had applied to Mrs. Suydam.

"A deep purple silk will be the prettiest and most suitable for her," the lady answered readily. "There will be
nothing in the color to disturb her. I think she will not
object."

The dress had been a gift from Richard. Mrs. Suydam
managed the rest. A tiny ruche of illusion at the neck and

wrists, and Daisy was lovely indeed — a pleasing contrast to the tall, elegant women fluttering about the apartment.

Lily went down to the library to be inspected by Mr. Auchester and Richard. She flushed a little as she thought of the night of the party, when Ulric first twined flowers in her hair, and asked her not to waltz with any one but him.

Both gentlemen gazed at her in admiration. Indeed, it was impossible to do otherwise.

"The carriages!" announced Tessy, running through the hall, bright and childish in her pink silk, and important with the thought of holding Lily's bouquet during the ceremony.

Lily put her hands upon Richard's shoulders. Her lips moved, but no sound came; her eyes sparkled with something beside their own lustrousness.

"I know all," he said, gently. "And whatever of pain there may have been in the past, I want you to remember, when you are far away in your new home, that you have given me much joy, much comfort. And in our dear father's place, whose duties I have often failed to perform rightly, I say, God bless you, my darling, forevermore. May His face shine upon you continually."

"O Dick! tender and true. Papa could have been no more patient — could have loved me no better."

He kissed away the tears ready to fall.

The whole party came trooping down the wide stairs. Mr. Suydam gave orders in his courteous fashion, saw that the ladies were well wrapped in shawls, and marshalled them to the carriages. A niece of his, hardly second to Lily in beauty, was to be bridesmaid.

"It's a shame to cover up so much white glory," Ulric said, with a laugh; "but it won't do to run the risk of having you shiver with the cold, or look like a ghost."

They then started. The midday sunshine transfigured the winter scene, and imparted a certain warmth to the atmosphere. Arriving at the church, the party lingered a few seconds to disrobe, and pass under Mrs. Suydam's watchful eye.

Ulric bent over Lily until cheek and lip touched.

"The last kiss of girlhood," he said.

It brought a bright flush to her face, whose rosy hue hardly died away during the ceremony. She was amazed to find herself so tranquil, listening, answering with solemn joy, being given away by Richard, and feeling the ring as it slipped to its place on her finger — her golden chain, the signet of another's proprietorship.

Their pride in Lily was certainly very pardonable. She was indeed most exquisitely beautiful as she stood there, calm, unconscious of self, yet so thoroughly human and womanly. Mrs. Suydam was glad to show her to her own and Ulric's friends, dowered in her own right with a peerless loveliness no gold could ever buy. And the crowd who gazed felt its wondrous power.

Ulric and Lily knelt to receive the blessing, while the rest stood. After this Mr. Chaloner's hands were folded over both heads, and his voice, ripe to tremulousness with age, repeated that most beautiful and tender of all benedictions: "The Lord bless thee and keep thee; the Lord make his face to shine upon thee, and be gracious unto thee; the Lord lift up his countenance upon thee, and give thee peace, both now and evermore."

Before they rose Ulric kissed her. Her husband's first kiss! Lilian Bertrand's seventeen years of girlhood were ended; Lilian Auchester's new life begun. They walked slowly out of church in a spirit of great calm and happiness, — she trustful, clinging; he with a certain manly grandeur and dignity that enhanced the beauty of his face and figure.

Mrs. Suydam, with her characteristic delicacy, had forborne to invite even her most intimate friends to the house. Her own as well as her husband's hospitality was of that high order which never leaves a sense of obligation. And on this last day she gave up the house to them with so cordial a sweetness that each one felt entirely at home. So there was a joyous season of kisses and congratulations after their return. All wanted a special look at Lily, and she had to stand with Mr. Auchester as she did in the church.

"After all," said Tessy, gravely, glancing at Lily, "I think he is fully as handsome as you;" which frankness was greeted with a peal of laughter.

"Bravo!" returned Ulric. "That is the first compliment I have had, after all my efforts to render myself elegant as possible. Tessy, if his High Mightiness, Count Petropoloswatoski is still unmarried, I will whisper a private word in his ear, and save him for you."

"I won't have such a name!" was the child's energetic rejoinder.

A summons to luncheon interrupted them. Lily took off her veil, and went to the table in her wedding dress, to the great delight of everybody. They had a grand, enjoyable time. Mr. Suydam, as host, was admirable. He drank Lily's health, and showered upon them both wishes grave, gay, and not a few whose comicality elicited much mirth. From the ladies Ulric came in for his full share.

A little time to don travelling attire, to interchange a few of those tender, sisterly words so hard to utter when the heart is full to overflowing. Yet they could hardly realize that Lily was going away for years. It seemed as if in a few weeks she *must* come back to them.

A good by to Ann, Martin, and Mrs. Hall, who had come over to witness the wedding. The rest went to the depot at Twenty-seventh Street. And there Ulric found a crowd of literary friends, who had stolen a march upon him — friends who shook hands in a heartfelt fashion, breathed wishes that would linger like benisons when the blue ocean rolled between them. They glanced at the bride, in her dress of rich, warm brown, not less elegant or graceful than when in church, her beautiful face framed in with white and scarlet, her golden ringlets gleaming with every movement. Her smiles and responses were enchanting. And both were blessed with a "God speed" from generous hearts.

Lily nodded from the car window, bright and radiant, as they steamed slowly out of the depot. But the face she turned to her husband was flooded with a rain of tears.

"And now," exclaimed Philip, when they had returned to the house, "nothing remains but for us to drink *skal* to each other, and depart in peace. Dear, winsome Lily! How we shall all miss her! And yet it is a marriage after my own heart. The right man and the right woman, in spite of trouble and perplexity. Richard, my dear fellow, your family is thinning out."

"Yes." Both look and tone were a trifle sorrowful.

"And since we have lost our beautiful Lily," said Mr. Suydam, "I shall lay claim upon this little girl. The children are wild to have her visit them, and I'll promise no dangerous young man shall fall in her way."

"Not quite yet, I hope," subjoined Richard, amused at the idea of such an event in connection with Tessy.

Daisy and Bel enjoyed a little feminine cry up stairs. Then, much against Mrs. Suydam's entreaties, they began to prepare for a departure.

"It has been such a delightful day!" said Mabel. "And you have made it doubly enjoyable to us all."

"Lily is worthy of, and welcome to, all that I have done. But it is so unsatisfactory to have them go off in this style! I am afraid in a few days we shall begin to consider it a dream. And this certainly is the best baby in the world," she continued, tying cloak and hood upon Alice. "When she grows up we will have another bonnie wedding with a fair lassie."

The most heartfelt adieus were exchanged, and promises of visits not few nor far between.

"I think, Dick," Archie proposed, "that I had better go right on to school. Then to-morrow will not be a broken day."

Richard acquiesced.

"I'm coming home Christmas to have a good time with

you, Daisy ; " and he kissed her with boyish fervor. " Tessy, child, good by."

" It was such a nice wedding!" Tessy said, as they sat over their late supper. " So much prettier than Bel's! If ever I get married, I shall be dressed in white silk."

Richard bestowed upon her a quiet smile.

Lily found time during her two days in Boston to write a letter home. It was dated by hours. Every time she came in from a ride or walk she had a few lines to add. The Mall and Mount Auburn were despoiled of much of their glory at this season; but she went to the top of Bunker Hill Monument, and to many other interesting places. And Ulric was charming beyond any description she could give.

Richard was glad to have her take up life in this earnest fashion. She had been home so little, of late, that her absence did not seem at all strange. The household had not been much disturbed by these few weeks of pleasant confusion, and soon resolved itself into its former native quiet. Tessy went to school, and being a great favorite with her young friends, was full of engagements. Daisy studied music perseveringly, and attended to Richard's comfort.

CHAPTER XXXVI.

"Come! If you come not, I can wait;
  My faith, like life, is long;
My will not little, my hope much;
  The patient are the strong.

Yet come, ah, come! The years run fast,
  And hearths grow swiftly cold —
Hearts, too; but while blood beats in mine,
  It holds you, and will hold.

And so before you it lies bare :
  Take it, or let it lie :
It is an honest heart, — and yours
  To all eternity."

A week later, perhaps, Richard came home one evening and found Daisy alone in the library, her work-basket on the table, and some trifle of sewing in her hand.

"This is nice and cosy," he said, with a cheerful smile — "to sit under one's own vine and fig tree, — or roof tree, if you prefer, seeing the quotation sounds summery, — and know there is to be no more marrying or giving in marriage for a month, at least."

"I think your rejoicing rather premature;" and Daisy looked amused. "Not an hour ago I had my consent, or at least approval, asked."

"By whom, indeed?" His face expressed his astonishment.

"It is quite a story; so you may as well sit down and listen. Our applicant is Mrs. Hall."

His quick perception remarked the *our* in her sentence.

"Mrs. Hall! Well, I am surprised! Not but that she is a worthy woman, and deserves to be happy."

" Yes, *deserves* to be happy. She is good and kind. A very excellent gentleman, I believe, who lost his wife several years ago, has persuaded her to fill the place. He has two daughters, one of whom married last winter, and removed to Chicago. The other has kept house for her father since; but she longs to visit her sister, and the sister is anxious to have her. Mrs. Hall had promised to marry him in the spring, but this younger girl, Carrie, is all impatience to go West, and begs her father to hasten his marriage. There seems no good reason why Mrs. Hall should refuse. He owns a pleasant little cottage, and has a home all ready for her — is a steady, an industrious man. I fancy Mrs. Hall thinks more of him than she cares to show."

" Well, really! Of course there is but one thing to say. Only, how shall *we* replace her? I am afraid it can never be done."

" That is just what I want to talk about, Richard; " and the thoughtful little face was turned from the needle-work to him. " As Mrs. Hall says, nearly everything is so different from what it was when she first came here. The children were little, and needed much attention, and the sewing occupied a great deal of her time. Now the sewing-machine makes that easy work; Archie will be home very little hereafter; there are only Tessy, you, and I — a small family. Cares are greatly lessened, and Mrs. Hall seems to think we can dispense with *her* very well. Ann is an excellent cook and manager, and Martin so willing to do anything out of his special province; so I want you to — to —"

Daisy blushed, and became confused. Something in the eyes, bent so earnestly upon her, caused the blood to rush in quick tides to and from her heart.

" The case is stated very systematically. What shall I do ? "

" I want to be housekeeper," she said, bravely. " I don't seem to have much to do, and, like Ann, I'm afraid I shall soon begin to grumble at the lack of work. I want something to busy my mind about, and give me a pleasant interest. I dislike to feel so idle and useless."

Richard came around behind her chair. He had intended to wait weeks longer before he spoke of his love, for in the last few days he had realized how utterly ignorant she was of any deeper than brotherly feeling on his part. He meant to unfold it by degrees, to draw from her little tokens of regard, so that, when the time came, she might know her own heart. But how few plans of life ever *can* be put into execution! He felt he must speak now.

"Will it not be too fatiguing? I cannot have your mind all occupied with cares and duties to the exclusion of myself. You see I have not arrived at the perfection of unselfishness."

"O, no. I shouldn't do very much. And it would never take my evenings, for dinner is out of the way so early. I think Mrs. Hall would be better satisfied if we did not need any one immediately, for in her heart there is a little idea of a divided duty. She has devoted herself to your welfare for such a long while. At all events, let me try this winter. I have grown so well and strong now, that you need not be at all afraid."

"Your eloquence persuades me to try the experiment."

"O, thank you! thank you, a thousand times!" Her tone was joyous. "You have done so much for me, that I long to repay you a little."

Bending over her from above, he took the sweet face in his hands.

"My darling," he said, in that full tone one falls into insensibly, in the great moments of life, when one is thrilling with the radiance of hope,—happiness. "My darling, you *can* repay me, and I *want* to be repaid."

She struggled to free herself. Her breath came rapidly, and in a sort of blind, confused way, she murmured,—

"Can I? How can I?"

There was a few seconds' silence. He wanted to look on

the beaded cup before he raised it to his lips — the sparkling wine of life! Then he said, softly and simply, for the grandest truths require but few words, —

"There is a better and dearer position for you to fill, my little Daisy. I love you. I want you to be my wife."

"O Richard!" The cry was bitter, heart-breaking. "O, what made you say it? What made you love me? I can never, never marry you!"

He started aghast.

"Think a moment, Daisy. Why can you not? Have I been too hasty?"

"No, it is not that. But I cannot marry you. It almost kills me to pain you, but the truth is best."

Her voice was wonderfully, fearfully calm; cold it sounded to him. He was stunned — hurt and faint to the very heart's core. Such a living, burning, despairing anguish as rushed over him, he had never experienced, even when he fancied her lost forever. Her tone seemed to cut him off from hope still more than her words.

"O, if you had only let me die long ago, Richard! I think you kept me alive, and this seems like such bitter ingratitude; but it is not. Why did God let me live to wound you, my best, my kindest friend!"

He tried to recover himself a little. He was still weak, like a man who has been drifting about many days in mid-ocean, under a scorching sun, waiting for some friendly sail to come and rescue him. But her pathetic cry touched him to the quick.

"No," he returned, "you shall not wish yourself dead for the sake of any pain you have given me. I will be strong and bear it. Yet tell me —"

"No, I cannot; don't ask it. I am surely, surely right."

He tried to think of some cause. In that moment there seemed only one — that she had loved Robert more than he suspected; that she *did not* love him, and was too honorable to mislead in the slightest degree.

"O Richard, Richard, forgive me!" With that cry she found her way to his arms, and nestled there like a stricken, shivering bird. "If you knew how it breaks my own heart to pain you, you would pity me a little. I will stay here; I will never go away unless you wish it. I will do all I may for your happiness; but that one thing I can never do."

Unconsciously she had appealed to his strongest feeling — generosity. Why should he torture her by vain questions? She appeared so positive, so resolved. If she *could not* love him, why not accept his fate like a man? for every pang he caused her to suffer inflicted double pain upon himself. He would always keep her; and, though no tenderer tie might come between them, hers would be the one face by his hearth. O, no, it was not quite desolation.

"Forgive me, forgive me," she pleaded.

"I do. God above knows how sincerely."

"Thank you." It was a penitent, half-inarticulate murmur.

"Daisy, you will stay here always?"

He called her by the dear name he had given her, causing her heart to thrill with thankfulness.

"Yes, always, always; unless you send me away."

"I shall never send you away."

The voice was so sweet, so sorrowful! All the man's tenderness, all his grand, true love spoke in it.

"O," she said, brokenly, "you are so good!"

The wet face touched his. The sweet mouth lingered of its own accord. What passed into her kisses that they should so stir his very soul? The effect on him was electrical. He was too bewildered to stir or speak. Could it be possible she did love, and was still ignorant of it? He could not believe her lost to him. There was some mistake.

Presently — how, neither could ever have told — they took their seats quietly, she pretending to sew, he pretending to read. Ann came for some orders, which she gave in a comparatively calm tone; Tessy returned from a neighbor's; they all said good night, in the ordinary manner, and dispersed.

Richard lowered the light, and resting his elbow on the table, dropped his forehead on his hand, and fell into a reverie. His heart gave a great bound as he remembered Daisy had not once said she did not love him. Was it some imaginary duty, or vow to Robert, that bound her? He looked the matter dispassionately in the face. She was willing to remain; nay, she evidently seemed to desire it. His regard was so precious to her, that she had pleaded for it. He knew better now than at any time in his past life what love really was, and he understood a woman's nature more clearly. Daisy bore him a deep, tender affection, so akin to love that he hardly knew how to make a distinction. If it were only haste on his part, and surprise on hers, the matter could easily be remedied. Or some duty she fancied she owed the dead — he would learn what it might be, and prove to her that God did not require any such sacrifice. He could with a word release her from all bonds; but he must suffer many tortures indeed before subjecting her to so cruel a humiliation. That she knew or suspected the truth, Richard never imagined.

Well, he would wait. His patience had been taxed so many times that he resigned himself now with scarcely a sigh. If she *did* love him, she could not altogether hide it. She would not be able always to evade the close watch he meant to keep. Some word, some glance, would betray her. He did not wholly despair.

Tessy had pleaded so to be Daisy's room-mate, that during these cold nights the two shared the same bed. And Tessy, innocent child, talked in her pleasant, confidential fashion, said her prayers reverently, and burrowed under the soft comfortables, curling herself up in a ball to await Daisy's advent, the golden-crowned head alone being visible on the pillow.

Daisy tried to read a little, but the words had no meaning, and fell on her brain like lead. She took some geranium leaves out of her hair — they were beginning to droop.

31 *

Richard had twined them in the soft braids just before dinner. Her fingers trembled over them caressingly; then she opened her prayer book, and laid them in with touching tenderness.

"Daisy, hurry to bed. I'm almost asleep."

It was a very sleepy tone.

She knelt down to pray. It seemed as if she had so much to ask for; yet all she could say was, "God be merciful to me — give me strength and courage to save *him*." Then there was a long break. No matter what else she said, these sad-toned refrains came in continually. Now and then a tear fell, but she did not really weep. Her wet face grew cold; her whole frame began to shiver irrepressibly. She realized that a sudden chill might lead to sickness, and she could not again endure being questioned by Richard; so she crept into bed. Tessy was soundly asleep. With the friendly darkness around her, self-control relaxed a little, but she never sobbed audibly.

It was her extreme humility that led her to save Richard from what she considered a false step — one he would surely regret in coming time. At his first word of love, the whole history of her married life rushed over her with one of those vivid lightning glances that pierce to the very depths of the soul. He dared not, *could not*, acknowledge her marriage until after Robert's death. What if Robert had *not* died! The thought was too terrible. One other circumstance fortified her mind strongly, and indeed *had*, all the evening. She had acquitted Richard hundreds of times for the pain he gave her in not wishing the baby to be called by his name. But this had always seemed the strongest proof to her that in his heart he felt and recognized the peculiarities of her position. There was no anger mingled with this. It was right he should do so; and now, when he was carelessly forgetting it, she would save him.

Save him from what?

And then, as if the clouds had been opened, a sudden revelation overpowered her. All this time she had been counting on a mere abstract fact — her duty in a certain view of life. She had not considered the one great love at all. This glimpse of her heart terrified her. When or how this new passion had dawned upon her, she could not tell; but she knew it was Richard's love that had made all these later months so delicious, and — her love for him. This was the glamour that had dazzled her eyes. And now what must she do? If it was right an hour ago not to burden him with a half-blighted life, it was right now. Richard was worthy of the noblest woman in the land.

And if in time he met and loved this most noble woman?

She placed her hand over her mouth, so that she might not be constrained to cry aloud in her anguish. Her eyes throbbed and burned like balls of fire; her heart beat in high, surging waves; but her hands were icy cold. Yes, she loved him. And sitting at his table, being his companion through long, quiet evenings, interesting herself in all matters pertaining to his household, yet knowing the one place she could never fill, would be martyrdom. She had a dim presentiment that the struggle would be too great for her, and she must succumb. Yet the end seemed death; and it would be hard to leave such a bright, happy world.

She heard the clock strike every hour of the night. Most of the time she lay with wide-open eyes, peering through the darkness for a ray of hope. Once or twice, in childhood's restless love, Tessy flung her soft arms around Daisy's neck. She kissed the dear face, so like Richard's. Then visions of Lily floated by, — the time she had said, " It is such a blessed, blessed thing to be happy! " — the time she had stood at the altar — and the last sight of her sweet face. After a while morning dawned.

Six months ago Daisy would have betrayed her vigil. She was a trifle pale, and her eyes had a certain weariness; but it was noticeable only to the keenest observer. Richard saw it, but let it pass without comment. The breakfast hour was made cheerful by Tessy's animated description of her last evening's entertainment. Then the child had a hunt for her books. Richard was waiting in the hall, for he always drove her to school in the morning. She ran back to kiss Daisy.

"Good by," said Richard, through the half-open door.

Daisy swallowed a great sob, and rose from the table with unsteady steps. She had no *right* to complain of the withholding of any caress. But she knew, by the experience of those two unforgotten days before Lily's accident, how terribly his coldness could punish her. And, by the same sign, she knew how much she cared for him. She began to consider whether she was really right, and found her firm faith of the night before wavering.

Mrs. Hall had been made happy by an evidence of Richard's interest and approval, and she asked Daisy to go out with her to select her wedding dress. This done, they called on Miss Carrie Bentley, and found her a pleasant as well as pretty girl.

"She doesn't seem to dread a step-mother very much," Daisy said, afterwards, with a smile.

"O, no. And when she is at home, I shall try to make it agreeable for her. Mr. Bentley is fond of his children, and I should be very sorry to come between, and create bad feeling. But I think everything will be right."

Richard was in and out through the day, as often happened when he did not have to visit patients at a great distance. Daisy's evident discomposure touched him, and, it must be confessed, gave him a secret thrill of joy. But just at dusk, as he was called away by a sudden summons, the weary face, with its downcast eyes, moved him to pity. He took her hand in his, but checked the rising impulse towards a warmer demonstration.

"Daisy," he began, quietly, "since we have resolved to accept the old life, let us take it up bravely, and be as happy as we were before."

"Yes." She uttered the word mechanically, her whole soul protesting against the impossibility.

" Kiss me, child. There, we are friends for all time —
are we not? Mistakes are not irremediable. Kindest good
night."

His manner threw her completely off her guard. She felt
pained at the incongruity of his lightheartedness. Not a breath
escaped him. He was in that mood of subtle penetration,
when one feels empowered to translate the most hidden
secret. So he went out into the cool night with a heart
throbbing from a sense of pleasure, rather than pain.

On the whole, Daisy was more at ease after this day.
Richard began to manage the case from his premises, appearing blind to the momentary weaknesses that overtook her.
Mrs. Hall's approaching marriage interested her. The wedding was quite a contrast to Lily's. Mrs. Hall went to church
in her plain brown silk dress, and after evening prayers were
ended, stood up with Mr. Bentley and said her vows. Then
he took her to the new home, where a few friends were waiting to congratulate and make her welcome.

Richard had accepted Philip Gregory's invitation to spend
Christmas at Rothelan. Under any other circumstances he
would have preferred remaining at home, but he deemed the
change advantageous to Daisy. He fancied she was beginning to droop a little. Tessy and Archie were more than
delighted. Richard went up with them, and enjoyed the
pleasant festival, but as he could not stay, came a week later,
and brought them home.

The next excitement was a long, closely-written letter
from Lily. She gave a most amusing account of her sea-
sickness, and one storm they had encountered. They were
likely to spend the coldest part of the winter in Germany,
and had already fallen in with some of Mr. Auchester's
friends. It was the old, gay Lily in every line. But when
she came to Ulric's care and tenderness, Daisy could hardly
refrain from tears. These things had a new meaning for her.

And now their days were indeed rounded by outward calm
and quiet. The joyous old house took on an almost lonesome

air. "'Deed, Mrs. Bertrand," said Ann, one day, "it's a pity there are no more childers to grow up after Miss Tessy. It's a bad trick they have of making men and women. A house isn't half so pleasant when there's no one to pet and scold."

Daisy, who had hitherto been self-reliant to a wonderful degree for so gentle a nature, began to grow strangely distrustful. She had not the courage to go over the events of that painful evening again, and tried to satisfy herself with the commendation that she had at least acted honorably. But a point she had not then considered came up to trouble her. If Richard, knowing all her past life, had loved her, and asked her to be his, was it right for her to condemn him to unhappiness?

She found it quite impossible to take up the old thread of life, and go on satisfactorily. Knowledge had come in the place of innocent unconsciousness, and knowledge is not necessarily joy. It cast a sombre, reflective shadow. She rarely felt at ease. Sometimes for an hour she forgot the burden; but when she raised her eyes, it confronted her. Thus it came to pass that the solitary talks with Richard were no longer a delight. A nameless fear crept around her, lest in some unguarded moment she should do wrong, since she could no longer tell what was right. She took Tessy for an intimate companion. A third person had come to be a relief between her and her best friend.

Richard grew stronger and more resolved each day. That Daisy was restless and disturbed, he could see plainly. That she tried to hide her heart from his scrutiny, he could also divine; but he ceased to fear. When he again besieged the fortress, he intended it should capitulate unconditionally. He evinced no impatience; love was becoming too really grand for that.

The auspicious moment came at last. Tessy had put on her choice pink silk in great state for a birthday party of one of her schoolmates. While Daisy sewed some blonde edging on her blossom-tinted gloves, she fluttered around in childish delight. Richard and Daisy went out to see her safely bestowed in the carriage.

"I want to stay a good long while. Be sure not to send Martin until *after* the clock has struck one," she said.

Richard smiled in amusement. Then he shut the door, and they walked together into the library. For a wonder, Daisy made no excuse to hasten away. His easy chair stood before the table, and sitting down in it, he still kept his arm around her waist.

She was in an absent mood, and let things go by without any thought. She did not even observe the silence, that lasted several moments. He fancied the face was paler and thinner; certainly it was sorrowful.

"Daisy!" A slight turn of his arm brought her to a seat upon his knee.

Roused from her abstraction, she glanced up. The eyes that met hers were tranquil, but determined — not to be easily evaded.

"Daisy," — and the tone was so natural that she scarcely started, — "I want to ask you a few questions. Nearly two months ago we discussed a matter that gave us both much pain. Yet, in thinking it over, I find that I want it settled in a more satisfactory manner. Do you love me, Daisy, as women do those who are always to be first and best? Is it Yes, or No?"

She was bewildered for an instant. She tried to turn her eyes away, but he transfixed them by some subtle magnetism. Her face flushed slowly.

"I think it is Yes," he went on. "Since that night I have read much of what you have been trying to hide from me. And now, Daisy, as love is clear, what is it that stands between us and happiness?"

"O, please —" There was a world of entreaty in her voice, and her face began to droop. He allowed it to fall upon his shoulder. Then he continued: —

" But I *do not* please. You have chanced upon a very tyrant this time. I cannot allow you to make us both miserable. I think you will not want to, when all is understood. That night I was hasty to speak, and as hasty in giving up. But I believe I hold all your happiness in my hands, even as you do mine. Speak, Daisy; is it not so? I cannot take silence this time."

To keep him from raising her face, she said, faintly, "Yes." And then the secret of her heart was told.

" There was some trouble I have never been able to quite understand. Was it because you loved, or fancied you had loved, another?"

" No."

" Whatever we may have thought in those early days, we have learned since that the true love of our lives was its later blossom, not its first; or, at least, that it is not quite impossible to love again. You will tell me what the difficulty was?"

He felt her shiver in his arms, yet she did not offer to stir or go away.

"I believe I know all the events of your life. There is not one that could in the slightest degree alter my love for you. Can you say the same for me? And if there should be any word or deed whereby I have pained you, Heaven knows I repent it sorely."

She knew his love was of the unchangeable. Beating against the tide was simply useless; she must soon be overborne by the current, swept away from her fancied moorings, and compelled to face this broad, calm ocean. What matter? She was weary of struggling, and repose seemed good. She had only to reach out her hand to her guide.

" You have always been kind — noble."

" That is not sufficient, Daisy. Something is still left unsaid. I love you well enough to trust you with every thought of my life. I want you to do the same. Truth and confidence are the only basis on which we can rest."

She made a great effort at calmness in this extremity which it was impossible to evade, nay, absolutely wrong.

"Richard," — the voice was faint and slow, and came up through tears, — "you said you knew *all*. And if it had been Mabel, or Lily, whose life — "

"What do you mean?" There was no longer composure, but alarm. He had never fancied her hesitancy proceeded from anything deeper than a little sensitive pride; surely, that fatal secret was locked safely in his own heart.

"I mean that I know just what you did for me, — gave me a home and a name, when I could not have claimed either."

She felt the arm around her tremble with strong emotion.

"Good heavens, Daisy! But it is quite impossible! Child, let me look into your face! What terrible thing have you dreamed?"

She was the calmer now. The shadow of fear fell away when the brightness of his love shone upon it. The cross she had so blindly borne fell into fragments. Her hand found its way down to his, and clasped itself among willing fingers.

"I believe you never meant me to know it, you shielded me so carefully. But in an evil hour — "

He was all fire and energy. His voice trembled with suppressed anger.

"Did that wretch dare, after all her solemn promises to me — "

"No one dared. O Richard, let me bear my own fault. I learned it by accident. It was so wrong."

"Daisy," — his voice was husky and broken, — "tell me the truth, child."

She repeated the story — her finding the torn scraps of Robert's letter, her journey to New York, her resolve to go away, and her utter inability so to do. More than once she faltered, and was compelled to pause, thankful that her face was hidden from him.

"My poor child! To endure it in silence so long! Why

did you not come to me — trust me? Is not my love sufficient for you now?"

That sweet tone conquered the last remnant of pride, or
distrust, or whatever it might have been, making a gulf between them. She had been shielded, not so much by a
sense of duty, as by the irresistible power of love. It was
all clear now.

"Richard," she confessed, with most touching humility,
"I was wrong that night. I am yours, if my life, if my
love, can atone — "

"O Daisy! sweetest flower of the world, won at last! —
at last my own!"

There was a silence of tender tears, tender kisses.

By degrees they gained courage to talk over the past.
Just as one recalls a half-forgotten song some chance word
has suggested, line by line, until it all comes back, Richard
traversed the days, until he thought he must have loved her
first when she came upon him that morning in Mrs. Davis's
room. To him she had never been Robert's wife. She
understood now that it was more from a sense of tender
exclusiveness, almost jealousy, and *not* dislike, that he had
spoken when she had proposed the baby's name. He told
her, of his own accord, how he had taken himself to task
afterwards. And all the incidents of her life, to the episode
with Mr. Auchester, which, terrible as it seemed at first,
had led to such happy results, betrayed how she had always
been, in his heart, —

> "best,
> Loveliest without compare."

She listened as if in a dream. Was there indeed so
blessed a thing in store for her as this tender, ever-present
love! With every word of his she realized it more truly.
And she was thankful to give him what he prized so dearly
— her whole heart. The shadows of the past fell away.
This later love, purified by suffering, grown strong amid
long, dreary vigils and many tears, stood boldly forth now,
and was crowned with a holy, ever-enduring faith.

Tessy came home flushed and happy. Daisy stole shyly away from her lover. Yes, it had come to that!

There were no differences, no misunderstandings. They went their way peacefully, growing more deeply into each other's hearts with every passing hour. She felt she belonged to him in a peculiar sense, and he re-read his dream of love — this time the blossom of truth, and constancy, and manhood. They could not take life in Lily's joyous, riotous fashion, but they were none the less happy.

Mabel was their only confidant until the bridal day was appointed. That was for early June — a quiet affair, with the same folded hands to bless her that had blessed Lily. She took upon herself her true name — Daisy Bertrand, Richard's wife! It gave her a feeling of sweet, solemn awe.

Afterwards a grand holiday. Not Europe, as Richard had once dreamed; not with the woman who had filled out that picture; but over wonderful lakes and wonderful rivers, through cities that had risen as if by the command of the fabled genii; over broad, smiling prairie lands, back again to Niagara, to the St. Lawrence with its crown of beauty — the Thousand Isles. How happy they were! how content!

Last of all, home. She crossed the threshold, as a blessed wife, whose portals she had passed for the first time with her dead baby. She clung to her husband's arm, and glanced up into his grave face, and the royal smile that illumined it was her welcome.

"The beloved of the Lord shall dwell in safety by him, and the Lord shall cover him all the day long."

CHAPTER XXXVII.

That more and more a providence
  Of love is understood,
Making the springs of time and sense
  Sweet with eternal good; —

That all the jarring notes of life
  Seem blending in a psalm,
And all the angles of its strife
  Slow rounding into calm.

And so the shadows fall apart,
  And so the west winds play;
And all the windows of my heart
  I open to the day.
                              J. G. WHITTIER.

Do you care for any more? Great joy, like great grief, is sufficient unto itself, and needs no translator. Therefore the clasp of happy years must always be Carlyle's "golden silence." Yet joy does not come to every one. Wan and trembling hands reach out for it often but too vainly. Hungry eyes entreat for it with that wordless pathos nothing save the coffin lid can shut out — go blindly down through life, groping for what has dropped out of their cup. God pity them! Do not such worn and weary souls need a heaven far beyond what happy ones require?

But of the peaceful years that came to the Bertrands there is not much to say. No shadows, few fears. A steady going on to the life eternal. Days as perfect as ever come to any one.

Will you look at one more picture — a June day in the old garden under the elm tree? Did you ever pause and examine an elm tree that has grown very old? It has long, stout arms reaching out hither and thither. When these were younger and shorter, they brought the foliage together with a peculiar density. The sunlight was sifted through in golden grains. For thirty or forty years, mayhap, no new branches have grown, only slender little twigs, waving things that droop like moss, and flutter to the faintest breeze. The long, brown arms are all covered. A cluster of leaves hangs out here and there on so fine a stem that it seems suspended in mid air, or simply painted against the blue sky. And the branches growing farther apart every year, with no new ones to fill up the interstices, the sunshine falls through in streams. If we could all be sunnier at the last!

The family are gathered there, except one who "is not" —one to whom Daisy even has learned to give a tender place in memory. The picture is more perfect without him. Alas, that we should say so of any one who has ever been one of a happy home circle!

Richard Bertrand is ten years older than when his dying father commended these children to his care. His face is still grave, for all its happiness, but so sweet, so full of unutterable kindliness blossoming out with steady beauty! Behind him, Daisy, who will never outgrow that look of later childhood. Separate her from the rest, and she might sit for a study of dawning girlhood. But her children are here. Aubrey, who will never be called Richard, though that is his name as well, because she keeps it for only one in the world. There is something in his face suggestive of the Charlie who early fell asleep in Christ. It used to trouble her at first with a tender, motherly pain. But this Lily, trying to balance herself on her small feet, while her father steadies her with his hand, is the perfect embodiment of laughing babyhood — a little romp, a mischief, a darling plague. And beside her uncle, whose favorite she is, stands Alice Gregory, bidding fair to emulate in looks, at least, the Lily of past times. Below them, at a little distance,

Philip and Mabel. In her lap she has the latest born of her household, pink and white perfection; while her sturdy boy, two years the junior of Alice, tumbles over Archie's shoulder, now and then achieving a fall on the soft grass. They are a little older, but Mabel is still as fair and sweet. Cares do not disturb the serenity of her soul. And Archie, through all these later years, has been a pride and comfort to Richard. He possesses a little of Robert's elegance and winsome manner, but nothing of his disposition. At New York they consider him one of the most promising of the " Seminary boys." He is looking forward to the time when he shall take Holy Orders, and go to Rothelan a young deacon, as Philip once planned under this very tree.

For Philip is rector at Rothelan. The reaping and gathering angel of the Lord has taken Mr. Chaloner home in the ripe harvest time, after a long and useful life. Philip is greatly beloved, as Mabel once wished, " for his own sake." Rothelan has enlarged her borders on every side. At the river side in beautiful Gothic and Italian villas, down by the Station, in simple cottages, a mill or two, and many new inhabitants. Archie has been planning a chapel for this spot. Philip has some trials, but many joys, and the warmest sympathy of his parishioners in every good word and work. Foremost among his vestrymen, faithful, efficient, ready for any labor of love, stands Wilfred Joslyn. His sisters are married and gone from home. He and his mother are alone, will always be, save when the daughters come home, bringing their children. It will be a pleasant place for them, and in any want or distress an abiding shelter. He is a great favorite. His horses and carriage, and himself, are at the service of the ladies, and those a little *passée*, or not abounding in this world's goods, welcome his coming with a frank smile. They can depend on his kind heart for many attentions. But no one counts on marrying him. He shows so plainly in every act, every word, that he has settled himself in the groove where he is to bide all the days of his mortal life. No one fancies that he has been disappointed. But the sun rose over him once. He is content with that morning, though glowing midnoon and ripe fragrant evening must come to him only in dreams. But he does not go at once to the night and darkness.

He knows Mrs. Auchester has come home, richer by two children than when she went away. When she visits Rothelan, he will take his mother over in a quiet, old-fashioned way, to call upon her; — his mother was always fond of Lily Bertrand. If, somewhere in a quiet nook, he should come across her children, straying off with the free daring of babyhood, he may, unperceived, give them the kiss he dared not give their mother, for the sake of the dreamland children who are never to grow up around his fireside. He does not blame Lily. He would much rather have her memory to halo his path, than any other woman's love. Of the many things she has said and done, he recalls one poem she repeated in the shady woods — something about sweet white brow, lips of geranium red, and the hair's young gold. Two lines are all he can remember consecutively : —

> "But one thing, one, in my soul's full scope,
> Either I missed, or itself missed me."

God will forgive him. HE was there, you know, in the hour of the man's bitter agony, when he went down, as many of us have gone, during these eighteen hundred years, into a garden of Gethsemane, and prayed first, " Father, remove this cup," but afterward, " Thy will be done." Among the souls of heroes you shall not find a nobler one than that of this man, who understands the word only in its commonest acceptation. He is content.

And on the lowest terrace, crowned with the setting sun, stands Lily Auchester, her husband's arm thrown carelessly around her waist. The same handsome, refined, and stately man, with gracious dignity of carriage, and unstained loftiness of soul shining out of his deep eyes.

But this woman! A little more than five years ago the
girl went away. You have all many times in your lives
realized the simile of the bud and the rose. It is trite, but
fragrant, and perfect in the way of comparison. For this
Lily Auchester is regal. She has been glorified by wife-
hood, and glorified again by motherhood. There is something
almost sacred about her beauty ; it awes you, hushes you
into that strange quietude, in which you almost forget to
breathe. Tall, rounded with the perfection of symmetry
which sculptors adore ; tinted with the coloring painters try
for, but rarely succeed in prisoning on the canvas. The
expression of the face bewilders you. You feel that she
could be haughty, icily cold, hold herself far above the
common forms of womanhood, if she chose. But in her
own life she had dignified and exalted them. She has
lived as if in a happy dream, —

" Ransacked the ages, spoiled the climes," —

lingered over the marvels of the old world, with that best of
all guides — a man who loved them first for their own sake,
and again because they were so precious to the woman he
loved best. What days they have had ! — so full, so perfect.
Love with them is of perpetual growth. He rejoices in her
beauty, she has a more than wifely pride in his genius. But
above all, shining with pure and steady light, stands affection.

She smiles a little over admiration now. At St. Peters-
burg she had her fill, at Paris a surfeit of it. The emperor
remarked the wondrous perfection of that rarest of all types,
her pure blonde beauty. In her world there is but one king.
O loving and loyal subject, " the heart of thy husband doth
safely trust in thee ! "

A rosy-cheeked German girl, whose imperturbable good-
nature shines out in every feature, walks up and down with
a twenty months' baby in her arms, and a little four years'
old at her side. He kicks the gravelly sand with the toe of
his pretty slipper, and nurse admonishes him with a gentle

shake. It answers for a moment; then another shower of sand flies before the little feet, and another shake is given. But Master Richard is a sturdy little rebel, and contests a point persistently. Nurse hints something about "papa," and he looks shyly out of his great dark eyes at the tall figure, seeming now the perfect embodiment of ease and indulgence. But he has already learned, in his childish fashion, that disputing papa leads to an encounter in which he comes off not second best, or best in any degree — so he desists. And yet the child gives his father a most earnest and passionate affection, too profound for his years. Both boys have inherited their father's rather than their mother's beauty. That may be a girl's dower.

On a rustic seat sits Tessy, and lounging over the back, twining flowers in her hair, is a familiar figure, distinct from the rest, and yet who may one day be numbered among the household. Tessy has Lily's shining hair, but in less wealth of abundance, but not her wondrous beauty, nor even Mabel's classic sweetness. She has an individual sweetness of her own, however, that one instinctively trusts, and is very dear to Daisy. She is a plant of slower growth than the others, but unfolds in daily fragrance.

Leonard Auchester has hardly reached his full stature — not alone as to height and breadth of muscular development, though that is growing more compact and symmetrical. But the man's soul is coming up into something grand, that will presently ring out with electric force, and go vibrating down along the years. Wise and powerful statesmen are made of this *matériel*. He has a good face. The boyish crudenesses have been replaced by manhood's firmness and dignity. It does not remind you of Fred's dangerous beauty, that sensuous Grecian elegance that carries about with it a strand of the old-world heathenism — Fred, who is still winning and breaking hearts, and laughing daintily.

Every summer Leonard comes to while away a few pleasant weeks in Tessy's vicinity. Nothing has been said, but they can all see the end from the beginning. No one cares to disturb this first bloom of love's young dream. It is too sacred to be rudely broken in upon.

So they all talk in the desultory fashion of old friends met together. Many blessed associations cluster about this place. Here they learned their first lessons of joy and grief. Here they have laughed and wept. Up stairs, in a drawer, there is a box of shining rings of hair that Richard will keep for a memento, long after Tessy is gladdening another home. Here they saw the first steps of a ladder, not less glorious than that of Bethel remembrance, reaching up to heaven. Some have traversed it already, softly saying, "Thy rod and thy staff, they comfort me." The rest wait in summer plenitude and hope.

Philip leans over his wife. "Bel," he begins, in a low tone, "do you remember the time we sat under this tree appointing a wedding day? I said then that Richard, above all other men, was the one to cherish a loving wife, and have babies prattling at his knee. Look now — the picture is filled perfectly."

She looks. Richard is sitting on a little elevation in grave and tender manliness; Daisy leaning over his shoulder — Daisy in that glory of girlhood, that came, as all her best things did, in later life. It is such an earnest, entreating face, so full of humility, so abundant in sweetness and truth. Aubrey has possession of one of papa's hands, lapping the fingers one over the other, until he gets them into a proper position, when he utters a magical "Jack, fly away," at which they all disperse, and resolve into fingers again, to his great amusement. The other arm is around baby Lily. She steadies herself a moment, gives a little gurgling sound of admiration very satisfactory to herself — although her lingual acquirements are rather limited — and perfectly intelligible to papa, who smiles as the little soft chin goes down upon his knee, and the dear eyes look up for a commendation that babyhood's unreasoning faith rests in securely.

And then, by a sort of electrical intuition, Lily turns her eyes upon them. Daisy has a consciousness that they are all thinking of her, and the old, shy, dainty blush — another thing she will never outgrow — crimsons her face. She leans it down on Richard's shoulder, where it is hidden by his beard as he turns from baby to wife. His lips meet hers. He kisses in the midst of a smile, and feels rather than sees the sunshine; he also kisses in the midst of tears. They never bring any idea of sorrow to him now. Daisy would be a little less than Daisy without them.

"Richard," the sweet mouth murmurs.

"My darling!"

He remembers what his father said so long ago. Did the dying eyes, so soon to open on the glory of God, see more clearly? "A Benjamin's portion."

It is his.